DEVELOPMENTAL PSYCHOLOGY
The adolescent and young adult

The Dorsey Series in Psychology
Advisory Editors
Wendell E. Jeffrey
University of California, Los Angeles

Salvatore R. Maddi
The University of Chicago

John Paul McKinney
Hiram E. Fitzgerald
Ellen A. Strommen
all of the
Department of Psychology
Michigan State University

DEVELOPMENTAL PSYCHOLOGY

The adolescent and young adult

1982   Revised edition

THE DORSEY PRESS Homewood, Illinois   60430

ISBN 0-256-02407-3
Library of Congress Catalog Card No. 81–70439

Printed in the United States of America

1 2 3 4 5 6 7 8 9 0 ML 9 8 7 6 5 4 3 2

PREFACE

In the preface to the first edition of this text, I wrote: "Adolescence is a time of transition, a period in the growth cycle which marks the end of childhood and the promise of adulthood. For many youngsters it is a period of uncertainty and even despair; for others, it is a time of close friendships, of loosening the ties to parents, and of dreaming of the future."

None of that has changed. What has changed, and will continue to change, is the environment in which youngsters grow up and their unique response to their own development in a changing world. Writers have often been tempted to characterize this age with glowing generalizations or conversely with denunciation, only to find on inspection of the data that the generalizations do not fit. If we can say one thing for sure it is that there is as much variability, if not more, within this age group as within any other.

No easy categories will define all adolescents nor will ad hoc explanations of their behavior help us to understand them. For the person who wants to understand adolescent behavior, there is no substitute for close attention to carefully conducted research. Much of this research has been guided by promising theories, but theory alone without evidence is useless.

The important role of theory is in guiding the researcher in asking the appropriate questions. The reciprocal interplay of theory and research is at the core of the scientific endeavor.

We have tried in this brief volume to introduce some of the most fruitful theoretical conceptions about adolescence as well as some of the most careful research. We hope you share some of the excitement we experienced in writing this work. Once again, I have the pleasure of recalling the many personal associations that have contributed to my understanding of adolescence. I owe a continuing debt to my former teachers, especially to Professors George Thompson and John Horrocks, as well as to the late Professor Ray Kuhlen.

Many former students in the Seminar on Adolescence have read and commented on the first edition of this text. Their criticism, enthusiasm, and encouragement have been rewarding. Several should be mentioned by name for their help with this new edition: Stephen Truhon, Bill Bukowski, Mary Reinhart, Carrie Saetermoe, and Jeff Bucek. Several people reviewed the first edition and made suggestions for this revision: Anne Petersen of the University of Chicago, Anthony B. Olejnik and David E. Mismer of George Williams College, Margaret C. Waimon of Illinois State University, Daphne J. Timmons of the Department for Juvenile Placement and Aftercare, Columbia, South Carolina, and the consulting editor at Dorsey, Wendell E. Jeffrey of the University of California–Los Angeles.

A personal note. Since the publication of the first edition of this book, I've watched at close range as our own four children have been running into and through adolescence at different speeds. The run's been fun. So Peter, Martin, Maureen, and Libby, it's to you that this book is especially dedicated. I've learned more from you and your friends than can be written in books. *En jij ook, lieverd*. Thank you.

John Paul McKinney

CONTENTS

DEVELOPMENTAL PSYCHOLOGY
The adolescent and young adult

BOX 1–1
Study questions

Why is adolescence such a difficult period to define?

What changes mark the onset and termination of adolescence?

How does dispersal in other animals relate to the concept of adolescence in humans?

Compare G. Stanley Hall's view of adolescence with that of Albert Bandura.

How does the concept of identity help to clarify the study of adolescence?

What factors contribute to the lack of information concerning adolescent development?

How has the concept of adolescence evolved?

Compare the advantages and disadvantages of the longitudinal and cross-sectional approaches in the study of adolescence.

CHAPTER 1

ADOLESCENCE: AN INTRODUCTION

Halfway up the stairs isn't up, it isn't down.
It isn't in the nursery, it isn't in the town.
And all sorts of funny thoughts run 'round my
*   head:*
"It isn't really anywhere! It's somewhere else
*   instead!"*

A. A. Milne

ADOLESCENCE DEFINED

A transition stage

Though adolescence is not the subject of Milne's poem, the lines above accurately describe the plight of the individual halfway between the security of childhood and the yet unknown world of the adult. In a sense, adolescence has become a stage of human development in its own right, a transition between childhood and adulthood. Defined by the termination of childhood at one end and the beginning of adulthood at the other, the concept of adolescence lacks precision for the student of adolescence and for the adolescent himself.

A chronological definition of adolescence

The term *adolescent* is generally used to refer to a person in the teenage years between childhood and adulthood. The onset of adolescence is generally regarded as puberty, which includes a relatively rapid growth of the body including all the organs and systems as well as maturation of primary sex characteristics and development of secondary sex characteristics.

During adolescence a number of psychosocial forces are at play which separate the individual from childhood and move him or her toward adulthood. The developmental tasks of this stage include the gradual separation from family, the choosing of one's own friends, and the consideration of a career choice.

While the onset of adolescence is marked by physiological changes in puberty, termination of adolescence occurs with the sociological achievement of

3

full adult status. As with all stages of development, movement from one stage to the next is marked by several changes that are likely to occur over a period of time. The physiology of puberty, for example, is a complex set of phenomena (Shock, 1946), including rapid body growth, bone ossification, hormonal changes, and the sudden development of primary and secondary sex characteristics, as well as psychological reactions to these changes (Frazier & Lisonbee, 1950; Jones & Bayley, 1950). Not all of these physiological changes are highly correlated, nor are the psychological reactions to them identical or equally intense for all individuals.

The termination of adolescence is equally difficult to define. Persons are generally considered adults when the adult community expects them to accept the responsibilities of community membership and allows them the resulting privileges. But this definition is also ambiguous. For instance, most legal contracts in the United States recognize the adult status of an individual who is over 18 years of age; yet other laws vary with respect to the age at which an individual begins to be treated as an adult. Each of the following, for example, has its own specific age requirement: drivers' licenses, marriage licenses, freedom to buy and consume alcoholic beverages, voting rights, and the right to work. In many cases the minimum age also varies from state to state.

Psychoanalytic writers defining the termination of adolescence stress the importance of mature relationships with other persons, called object relations, and the ability to make work commitments.

Some societies clarify the transition from childhood to adulthood by means of initiations and puberty rites (Brown, 1963). Such dramatic debuts have the effect of clarifying the discontinuity in the developmental cycle. In some cultures there is less discontinuity in cultural conditioning than in others, but among the cultures in which such discontinuity exists there is a great deal of variation in how adequately the change in status is clarified. "Rites of passage" (Van Gennep, 1960) clarify the change in many societies, but the American counterparts of these rites—for example, such secular ceremonies as graduations and debuts and such religious observances as confirmations and bar mitzvahs—are not universal enough to provide this clarification of status.

For many reasons, then, the period of adolescence evades exact definition. Inasmuch as it is a transitional stage between childhood and the full maturity of adulthood, it relies on the definition of those periods for its own clarification. And in this very difficulty with definition we encounter one of the main characteristics of adolescence, namely, the lack of clarification of the adolescent's position within the community. Kurt Lewin (1939) has made this point very nicely in a paper on the development of adolescence, wherein he refers to the adolescent as a marginal man. The term *marginal man* comes from sociology, where it is used to refer to a person whose membership in a group is no longer firm and clear. A member of a minority group, for example, who shares the values and goals of the majority and obtains some social reinforcement therefrom, becomes a marginal person in his or her own minority group. Immigrants with two languages and two cultures, and often two conflicting sets of values, frequently gain acceptance into the culture of their immigration only at the risk of becoming marginal to the culture of their birth. In effect, they never belong to either group completely but to both groups incompletely and in a way that lacks clarity. Adolescents are marginal in the sense that their rights and responsibilities are not so clear-cut as those of children or adults. Adolescents are partly responsible for their own welfare but are still subject to adult authority. Whereas children can be totally dependent upon adults, and adults must assume total responsibility for their children, adolescents function in a less well-defined area of responsibility.

A uniquely human phenomenon

We are told that "adolescence is a developmental phenomenon unique to man." In explaining this statement, the Group for the Advancement of Psychiatry (1968) has observed that human infants are in a relatively more immature state at birth than are the newborn of other primates. In fact, it isn't until puberty that some of the hormonal and central nervous system development is complete in the human. In lower animals this development can occur within months or even weeks. Similarly these animals also develop procreative and adaptive capacities relatively much earlier than in the human. "Consequently, human offspring have a protracted period of dependency upon the mother or parents, whereas the period of dependency of other animals, by comparison, is relatively short." (Group for the Advancement of Psychiatry, 1968, p. 19.)

Although these facts explain the longer childhood of human beings compared to other animals, they do not explain the uniqueness of adolescence as such, unless one were to think of adolescence as simply the last stage of childhood. As we shall see, this hardly seems to be the case. Adolescence in the human appears to be a distinct phase of development, albeit a transitional one, with its own biological, social, and intellectual hallmarks. But is there a distinction between the development of humans and the development of other animals that may give us a clue to the nature of this "phenomenon unique to man"?

Dispersal in animals

One result of the shortened period of development in other animals is that dispersal—leaving the family of one's infancy—generally coincides with sexual maturity. This is not the case with man. On the average, boys and girls become sexually mature sometime between their 13th and 15th year. Seldom, however, do children leave their homes and begin their own families at this early age. Certainly in Western culture, the main focus of our concern in this text, children remain dependent upon their parents for several years after puberty or sexual maturity. It is in this discontinuity between puberty and social independence that we find the basis for the fascinating, somewhat mysterious, and often puzzling phenomenon of adolescence.

Part of the solution to this puzzle lies in an understanding of puberty, which defines the onset of adolescence. The solution would be complete if we understood fully the termination of adolescence, namely, social independence. Unfortunately, even for animals our understanding of the phenomenon of dispersal is limited. One view is given by Harper (1970): "Frequently the young (particu-

FIGURE 1–1   Adolescence has been considered a uniquely human phenomenon.

Photo courtesy of J. P. McKinney

larly males) are driven from the parental homesite as they reach reproductive maturity. . . . Aside from its effects on regulating population density and the impetus it provides for expansion of the species' territory, this enforced dispersal has often been interpreted as an aspect of the parental educative process'' (p. 79). What we do know about animal dispersal behavior could be relevant to our understanding of dispersal in human adolescents.

Let us take a brief look at dispersal from the family group in other species. Shorten (1954), a British student of animal behavior, has written a fascinating account of the development of squirrels. She says that ''After weaning has been completed, the mother may become pregnant again and leave her brood; or she may remain with them if she is not breeding" (p. 139). At this age young squirrels are already molting (losing baby fur and acquiring adult fur) for the first time. Some engage in simulated sexual activity in play. Occasionally a female will be found living with several fully grown young squirrels until they become sexually mature. During that time she may reject male suitors. At other times half-grown squirrels can be found in a nest separate from but very near to the nest of the mother with a new litter.

In other words, the dispersal of squirrels appears to be generally contiguous to the site of their own weaning and to be related to the ongoing sexual activity of the mother, who leaves them if she is about to have another litter.

The dispersal of rabbits is somewhat similar. According to Rue (1965) "Nestlings start a process of self-weaning as soon as they leave the nest . . ." (p. 31). Cottontails are known to remain in the area of the nest for almost three weeks when they are fully weaned and then leave. By that time the mother may well be about to have another litter, and since she is preparing the nest for the new birthing, she is too busy to have anything more to do with the nestlings. At that age the young rabbits are fully weaned, and if they have not already been killed by predators, they scatter.

Once again, we see that the dispersal of the young is related to the sexual activity of the mother. The female cottontail experiences estrus and may become pregnant again immediately after the birth of her young. The gestation period in the cottontail is 28 days. This is roughly the period of time that is required for weaning. Therefore, the weaning of one litter may be completed at about the same time as the new litter arrives.

The same association between the dispersal of the young and the sexual activities and reproductive cycle of the parents has been found to occur in several other species of animals. A rather fascinating account of this "difficult age" in the bear is given in a popular form in *The Mountain Visitor* (August 29, 1971). The author states that in June or July of the young bear's second summer "the mother's instinctive drive to start a new family takes the place of affection for her cubs. In time, the mother's indifference and the hostility of her new mate toward the cubs force the 'teenagers' to move on" (p. 1).

These same two factors, the sexual activity of the mother and the growing hostility between the young and their parents, appear to contribute to the phenomenon of dispersal in other animals as well. Ratner and Denny (1964) cite the case of weasels: "Weaning of the young from the parent involves physiological changes associated with the reproductive cycle of the parent plus the changing appearance of the developing young." In addition, the authors note that the adultlike behaviors of the young contribute to a breakup of the family group: "When the movements and appearance of the young resemble those of mature members of the species, this elicits fighting with the parents which in turn elicits escape from the parents" (p. 227).

An even more drastic example of this parent-young conflict at adolescence is given by Anthony (1969). In discussing a stereotype of the human adolescent as "victimizer," Anthony notes that throughout history each period has had its own way of dealing with the "dangerousness" of this transition stage. After referring to the Darwinian and the later Freudian speculations about a "primal horde" in which the father was eventually killed, he makes the following comparative observation: "In this context, it is interesting to note that adolescent male monkeys when caged with a typical monkey family—father, three or four wives, and one or two adolescent females helping to care for a few infants—are often slain by the father at the onset of puberty" (p. 56). It is important to remember that Anthony is referring to captive animals. Captivity could conceivably introduce a whole new set of motivational variables which would make animals' behavior at puberty different from that of animals in the wild.

In any event, there is an interesting counterpart to this behavior in human development, namely, the so-called second period of negativism, the first negativistic period having occurred when the child was just a toddler. The conflict with parents during this postpubescent period is well known, and a variety of psycholanalytic explanations have been given to account for the phenomenon (Freud, S., 1925, 1953; Freud, A., 1948). Perhaps the ethological literature provides a more parsimonious explanation. Just as the young animal comes into conflict with its parents at the time its appearance and movements resemble those of an adult, perhaps a similar "territorial" conflict is elicited when the human youngster begins to look like an adult, or begins to assert himself or herself by demanding privileges usually reserved for adults, such as use of the family car, the right to come home at any hour, the right to vote, and so on.

It appears, then, that adolescence may be a peculiarly human phenomenon because in other species dispersal is associated with the continuing sexual activity of the adults and the display of mature behavior on the part of the young. Although it is difficult, and at times even dangerous, to make comparisons across species, especially on topics as complex as this, we consider it important to examine the issue of dispersal in a comparative context. Although many patterns of behavior are species-specific, the process by which animals separate from their early caregivers may shed light on similar developments among humans. It is true that the concept of territoriality has a highly specific meaning to the student of animal behavior. Still, something analogous to that concept may be a useful theoretical tool; it may help us to understand children's strivings for independence when they seem physically mature despite adults' reluctance to grant them that independence before they reach a certain chronological age. In humans, the period between puberty, or sexual maturity, and the establishment of full adult independence and responsibility is referred to as adolescence.

THEORETICAL APPROACHES TO ADOLESCENCE

Contrasting views of the adolescent period

One of the first students of the adolescent period of development was the psychologist G. Stanley Hall, who described the sexual, social, intellectual, and emotional development of adolescents in a two-volume work. It was Hall's view that adolescence is characterized mainly by stress and trial. He likened this stage of development to the *Sturm und Drang*—storm and stress—which abounded in German literature of the 18th century. This view has continued to have its proponents, particularly among psychologists and sociologists of a psycholanalytic orientation. There are those, for example, who feel that the main function of the adolescent period is conflict itself. One sociologist (Friedenberg, 1959) has suggested that individual identity develops from the conflict adolescents experience with their parents and other authority figures. In other words, adolescents can clarify the uniqueness of their own experience only by contrasting it with the experience of those who have gone before them. They can assert the uniqueness of their own individuality and independence only by coming into conflict with those who would keep them submissive.

This view has its adversaries as well as its advocates. For example, Albert Bandura (1964) has argued that the notion that adolescence is necessarily a stormy period is a myth. He says that adults have paid too much attention to some of the superficial signs of nonconformity in the young—that adults have paid more attention to the fads of the young than to their conformity, to their rebellion than to their obedience. He argues that the mass media have sensationalized this view of adolescence and that adolescents themselves may be conforming to a view which has been perpetrated by an adult society.

It would appear that neither Hall's nor Bandura's view is entirely correct. Surely, for most American children the second decade of life is characterized by a continuing search for the role that they will play in society. The search extends to defining appropriate sex roles, satisfying vocational choices, and identifying compatible marriage partners.

In an important longitudinal study of teenagers, Offer and Offer (1975) concluded that stress was not a necessary nor healthy concomitant of adolescent development. The variety of coping styles identified by the Offers clustered around three modes which they labeled: *continous growth group, surgent growth group,* and *tumultuous growth group.* Once again, as with any age group, adolescents distribute themselves along a normal curve on these characteristics.

In other words, although adolescence may not be a period of stress and trial for every individual, it is surely a time when the individual is establishing his or her own identity. For some adolescents this is done through conflict, and some authors have chosen to stress this aspect of youth. One psychoanalyst (Gustin, 1961, p. 82), for example, has stated the case rather strongly: "Buffeted from within by powerful impulses and pushed from without by a strange unfriendly world, the adolescent must find some new ways to make his life tolerable." But not all adolescents seem to go through such a stormy period. The data from a study in which large numbers of adolescents were interviewed suggested that conformity is more characteristic of the adolescent stage than is rebellion (Douvan & Adelson, 1966).

Identity: A unifying construct

If neither rebellion nor conformity, anguish nor indifference, can be said to be universal at the adolescent stage, is there some term or psychological construct which can account for the presence of each of these characteristics in different adolescents at different times? The answer would appear to lie in the notion of identity. In the development of his theory of psychosocial stages, the well-known psychoanalyst Erik Erikson (1959) has suggested that the period of adolescence is one in which the individual struggles between identity and identity diffusion. Since he first outlined this notion, Erikson (1950) has returned repeatedly in his writings to this powerful explanatory concept (for example, Erikson, 1958, 1959, 1964b, 1965, 1968, 1969). Others have also used the concept, until by now, unfortunately in some respects, *identity crisis* has become almost a household word. In our estimation, however, this popular use of the concept has not weakened its explanatory value but has simply demonstrated its validity.

As used by Erikson, the term *identity* refers to "the accrued confidence that the inner sameness and continuity prepared in the past are matched by the sameness and continuity of one's meaning for others" (Erikson, 1950). The search for identity is part of the human experience at every age, although it is during the time of rapid growth and physiological changes of adolescence that identity assumes a major role in development. The question for the growing adolescent is how to preserve continuity within the person who was once immature, asexual, and nonresponsible and is now mature, sexual, and responsible. The question "Who am I?" becomes poignant in the face of rapid change. The struggle to "find oneself" may take a variety of forms—the search for a vocation or career, the elaboration of one's sexual role, singular accomplishments, and identification with others. Thus, rebellion from the established group as well as conformity can be a sign of the search for identity. A person could establish his or her identity by conformity with the prevailing modes and values or, in a negative way, by rebellion and delinquency. In his book *Growing Up Absurd,* Paul Goodman (1956) has taken just this view of the adolescent's situation. Goodman feels that the basis of conformity and the basis of rebellion and delinquency are one and the same, namely, the need to establish an independent identity.

Identity formation, then, will be the theme of the present book. After examining physical and cognitive development in the next two chapters, we will consider Erikson's theory more fully in a chapter on social and emotional development. In each of the following chapters we shall refer to the theorist whose work seems to describe best the behaviors discussed in the chapter. Other theorists may have concerned themselves with those behaviors, but we will exemplify a given position by the one whose work seems, in our view, to be expressed most clearly or most forcefully on the given topic. Each theorist mentioned in association with one given topic may have views on the other topics as well. However, what we hope to do is to familiarize the student with various theorists in the context of the area of adolescent development about which they wrote most compellingly.

The status of adolescent psychology

The reader will note that the present volume, unlike many texts on infancy and middle childhood, will deal at length with theory and will have less empirical data to support the generalizations that many developmental theorists have made about youth. If increasing importance has been attached to the period of adolescence during the past 50 years (see Adelson, 1980), the stature of this field of study is still relatively insignificant compared to that of its rival sibling, child psychology, and especially infancy. In reviewing the 1972 edition of Carmichael's *Manual of Child Psychology,* one of us (McKinney, 1972) has noted that research on adolescent psychological development is still scarce. One researcher (L'Abate, 1971) made a careful assessment of the status accorded adolescence during the preceding several years and found that only a small fraction of the psychological research reported in the literature had been devoted primarily to the adolescent age group. Moreover, very few training programs in major university departments of psychology have specialized in adolescent development. Furthermore, fewer faculty members appear to be interested in this area of research as compared to research in the other developmental stages.

Only recently has a major handbook been devoted exclusively to the field of adolescence (Adelson, 1980). In contrast, there has been a good deal of theorizing about adolescent development. An excellent source for the study of contemporary theories is Muuss's (1975) book *Theories of Adolescence.*

Perhaps there is a certain reluctance to study those "intimate" aspects of development which are crucial to adolescence, such as sex, drugs, and self-esteem. Our culture doesn't deal easily with such topics.

The reluctance to deal with adolescence is not confined to research but extends to therapy as well (Anthony, 1969). One may well wonder about the basis for this relative paucity of hard information on an important developmental stage. The need for more and better information is certainly evident. Many of the social and personal problems of development center on adolescence. The difficulties surrounding the establishment of independence, separation from family, and the choice of a vocation are all typical adolescent problems. In addition, the socially pressing problems of delinquency, drug abuse, unmarried parenthood, academic discipline, exploitation of youth, and the political franchise for young people all demand a clearer picture of normal adolescent development.

If psychologists have been reluctant to approach these questions with solid research techniques, there has been no dearth of lay analyses of our growing "youth culture." The news media have been filled with such analyses. As a number of social scientists have mentioned, it is difficult to remain dispassionate about young people, who can themselves be characterized by a certain devotion to passion. Some observers, both lay and professional, have seen only good in the behavior of youth, whereas others have viewed all adolescent behavior as negative. Such overgeneralizations make for poor science, of course.

Anthony (1969) attributes the paucity of scientific research on adolescents to the fact that "in the past . . . the developmental phase was poorly described and lacked guiding constructs [theoretical concepts] that would help to raise meaningful questions" (pp. 74–75). But in a sense such an explanation only begs the question, "Why the lack of guiding constructs?" Some would argue that adolescents are simply disliked or feared by adults, and it would be possible to construct an argument, albeit a rather weak one, that the reluctance to study adolescents stems from such a dislike or fear. Friedenberg (1959, 1965), for example, holds the opinion that an ambivalence toward adolescents is rather general and is prompted by adults' waning authority over them. An alternative psychodynamic interpretation stresses adults' need for defenses against their own forbidden impulses, which adolescents may rekindle.

Stereotypes of adolescence

Anthony (1969) also suggests that the reactions of adults to adolescents and adolescent behavior can be characterized as stereotypes. He postualtes a number of these stereotypes: the adolescent as a dangerous and endangered object, the adolescent as a sexual object, the adolescent as a maladjusted individual, the adolescent as an object of envy, the adolescent as a lost object, and finally the "good" reaction to adolescence in which stereotyping is at a minimum and adolescents are dealt with as individuals. In addition, Anthony believes that the stereotypes operate like self-fulfilling prophecies: "To compound the mischief even further, the stereotypes have also functioned as mirrors held up to the adolescent by society reflecting an image of himself that the adolescent gradually comes to regard as authentic and according to which he shapes his behavior" (p. 54). In summary, however, Anthony's stereotypes boil down to two: the adolescent as victim and the adolescent as victimizer. Neither of these is very flattering, and again one wonders, why the negative stereotypes of this age group?

But perhaps even the notion that most adults maintain stereotypes of adolescents is itself a caricature. It would seem intuitively reasonable that adults respond to the seemingly extreme attitudes and behavior of youth in like fashion, that is, with an extreme stereotypic reaction, either positive or negative, good or bad. However, though adolescents do seem to take extreme positions, and a number of theories postulate reasons for this supposition (including such constructs as clarification of one's life space, identity formation, and the reaction of a marginal man), little evidence has been adduced to show either that youth behave in an all-or-none fashion or that adults respond to them in this way. As a matter of fact, it has been demonstrated that extreme response set—that is, a bias in using the end points of rating scales, personality questionnaires, and so on—declines with age. Thus, younger children are more likely than adolescents to respond by marking the extreme end points on such scales (Light, Zax, & Gardiner, 1965).

Another source of evidence also runs counter to the "adults have negative stereotypes of adolescents" theory. In one study (Hess & Goldblatt, 1957) a group of adolescents and their parents were asked to rate the typical teenager. The investigators found that both the adolescents and their parents rated teenagers rather favorably. When the youngsters were then asked how they supposed their parents had rated them, they predicted that the adults would be much less favorable in their ratings than in fact they were. What all this suggests is that the problem is not one of an unfavorable attitude but rather a failure of communication of adults' real attitudes toward adolescents. Whether the failure originates with the holders of the attitudes and the senders of the communications (here, adults) or the recipients of the information (here, adolescents), or a combination of the two, remains a question. It would be as easy to assume that adults fail in communicating their real appreciation of youth as to assume that teenagers distort the message that their parents attempt to convey.

If the negative stereotype view lacks supporting data, perhaps there is something in the nature of adolescence that makes it a difficult or discouraging area of study for some. One difficulty, of course, is that many of the important developmental changes at this period deal with private matters, or with matters about which the individual is already self-conscious, for example, one's changing body, interest in sex, developing sexual drive, concern about one's vocation and the impression one makes on others. Such areas are by nature less amenable to empirical investigation than, say, language development in the two-year-old or academic achievement in the middle childhood years. Indeed, questions of such a personal nature may make the investigators themselves uncomfortable. In addition, it may be that stereotypes tend to persist in the very areas where a lack of contact exists across generations. For example, drug use and sex life are intimate matters, which, even if one could find the words, one is reluctant to approach with a person from another generation.

Second, part of the nature of adolescence is change itself. Just when one thinks he has a concept which will help him to understand adolescent behavior, the behavior seems to change under his examining eyes. It would appear that one characteristic of adolescence is the tendency to escape external definition, to seek one's own clarification, on one's own terms, and to be free, that is, not determined by external constraints. A few years ago when one of us was studying the vocational values of high school youth in Holland, a very articulate 16-year-old Dutch boy provided a beautiful example of this drive to keep one's options open. When asked to visualize his future life and his lifework, he replied, "It would be easier for me to tell you what my life will not be like. I will not be living in that house (pointing across the street), and going to the same job day in and day out at the same time every morning and returning at the same time every evening always to do the same thing in the evening at home. I want to travel to other countries and perhaps do what I can to make life better for others" (McKinney, 1970, p. 392).

The history of the concept of "adolescence" as a developmental stage

Though the scientific study of adolescence is recent, attitudes toward this age group extend back to antiquity. Plato, for example, was concerned with the proper education of youth and noted the modifiability of their attitudes (Plato, 1953). Aristotle wrote about the "passionate, irascible" character of adolescents and commented on their tendency to go to extremes and to assert opinions with unmitigated assurance (Aristotle, 1941).

However, it should be noted that adolescence as a distinct period of human development has had a relatively short history. In studying the history of the family, a number of cultural historians (Aries, 1962; Huizinga, 1950) have noted that the concept of the child has changed from one cultural period to another. Müller (1969) attributes these changes to the changing demographic structure over historical periods. He suggests, for example, that in the period before 1750, when birth control was not practiced and medicine was not very effective, many children were conceived, but the infant mortality rate was high. "The consequences of such a demographic structure for the individual were harsh; he [the child] was fragile, easily replaceable, and so of little importance" (p. 8).

Compared to this view of children as replaceable, the demographic revolution which occurred around 1750 ushered in a more benign attitude toward children. Advances in medical science were undoubtedly responsible for a decrease in the death rate. Correspondingly, the desire to hasten the maturation of children declined. A second demographic revolution occurred when the birthrate dropped. Müller pinpoints the beginning of a corresponding new attitude toward children at around 1880, as the proportion of children to adults decreased. "We tend to imagine that a profound change of attitude took place; people with children knew that they had to provide for their education, and they had to do so for a period which was becoming progressively longer with the introduction of compulsory education" (p. 13). Families had gradually become more limited units, no longer responsible for the variety of economic roles they had played before. Parents more often lived in towns with their children rather than in the country with the extended families that had characterized earlier generations.

Müller postulated that the beginning of a fourth phase in the developing concept of childhood took place around 1930. He believes that in our own day the child has become "the little prince around whom everything evolves." It would be interesting to speculate on the effects that the recent concern with overpopulation and the current liberalization of women's roles will have on future attitudes toward children and on our conception of their roles in the family and society.

Although children were once treated like "miniature adults," it is now generally accepted that the period of childhood has its own rights, privileges, and obligations. For example, in November 1959 the United Nations General Assembly saw fit to publish a Declaration of the Rights of the Child, a far cry from the 18th century concept of the "replaceable" child.

Just as the child's role has changed over the years, it has also become more differentiated; the infant, the toddler, the schoolchild, and the adolescent have emerged as distinguishable periods of development. Adolescence appears to be one of the more recently articulated periods, probably beginning with the landmark publication of Hall's work on the subject in 1904. Thus, the scientific study of that stage between childhood and adulthood is relatively recent.

In a similar way, another, even newer, age-defined social group is emerging, namely, postadolescence. Because of the commonality of experience and the developmental tasks of individuals between the high school years of adolescence and the adult years of occupational stability, homemaking, child rearing, and so on, a number of psychologists have focused their attention on this age group as belonging to a special developmental stage. One sociologist (Keniston, 1968) has called this period "youth," and a recent yearbook of the National Society for the Study of Education (Havighurst, 1975) was devoted to this topic, including the theory and research of several contributors. It should be obvious to the reader, however, that the term *youth* has been used in a variety of ways. G. Stanley Hall (1904) used the term to refer to the prepubertal stage which we now call middle childhood. Much more recently, Arnold Gesell and his co-workers (1956) wrote a book entitled *Youth: The Years from Ten to Sixteen,* in which they described the stage we are here calling adolescence. Keniston is using the term in a new way to refer to a yet older age group. Whatever the terminology, it seems clear to many observers that stages of life, although not discrete, do help us to deal with the commonality of experience and behavior which is more characteristic of one age period than another. It goes without saying that this "stage" position is not used here as an explanation for behavior but merely as a convenient descriptive device. Those who explain behavior by an appeal to a period of life ("Oh, that's just the stage she's in") have explained nothing.

The concern of psychologists, sociologists, and physicians interested in young people has shifted from the more purely biological concerns of puberty and early adolescence, to the interpersonal and cultural determinants of development during the period of youth, roughly the years from 15 to 25. It has become clear that identity isn't solidified during the high school years but continues as a task into early adulthood, with the separation from parents, the choice of a mate, a vocation, and a community in which to live and raise one's own children.

In summarizing the society's objectives for its youth, Havighurst, (1975) paraphrased the goals as stated by the Panel on Youth of the President's Science Advisory Committee: "The central objective of society for its youth is that they should achieve a sense of identity and self-esteem . . . they need skills and knowledge and experience which fall into two broad classes—those involving self-development and those involving other people." (Havighurst, 1975, p. 87). As objectives of the first category, Havighurst includes:

1. "Cognitive and noncognitive skills necessary for economic independence and for occupational competence . . .
2. Capability for effective management of one's own affairs . . .
3. Capability to engage in intense concentrated involvement in an activity . . .
4. Capabilities as a consumer, not only of goods, but more significantly of the cutural riches of civilization," (Havighurst, 1975, p. 88)

The objectives involving other people are stated as:

5. "Experience with persons differing in social class, subculture, and in age . . .
6. Experience of having others dependent on one's actions . . .
7. Experience of interdependent activities directed toward collective goals." (Havighurst, 1975, p. 88).

It would appear, then, that the status of research in adolescent psychology is related to the historical recency of this period and to the very nature of the period itself—that is, as one of change and of emerging attitudes and behaviors which are intrinsically difficult to study empirically. Let us next examine the techniques which psychologists are using and which suggest themselves as suited to the study of this age group.

METHODS IN THE STUDY OF ADOLESCENCE

Research techniques

Descriptive measures: The normative approach   The most basic technique for studying adolescent growth and behavior is simply direct measurement of the variables under consideration. Both physical and psychological information have been collected in this way. The data might be collected from one individual, as in a case study, or from a group of persons, as in survey research. Gordon Allport (1942), who used both approaches extensively in the study of personality, termed the former approach *ideographic* and the latter *nomothetic*. Although such techniques allow the investigator to ascertain the presence of a variable and/or its extent, they offer no information about cause-effect relations, or about the genesis of the variable under investigation, or about any of its correlates.

Among the variables that have been studied by direct measurement are the average age at menarche, the reading and television viewing interests of adolescents, and concerns with physical development. An important variation on this technique involves the addition of the variable of time in a sequence of measurements on the same subject or subjects (the longitudinal approach) or testing subjects of differing ages simultaneously (the cross-sectional approach).

The advantages of the longitudinal approach derive from the fact that since the same subjects are used at each age, the subjects are their own controls. Age differences cannot be confounded by extraneous subject variables. Secondly, all subjects have the same cohort. Thus, age differences cannot be confounded by the sociohistorical era during which the subjects grew up.

These same facts, however, lead to certain disadvantages of the longitudinal approach compared with the cross-sectional. Since only one cohort is used, generational differences can't be studied. All the subjects are influenced by the same historical background. In the cross-sectional method, however, such influences are confounded by the age of the subjects. If I test 4- , 10- , and 16-year-old children today (1981), I am testing individuals born in 1965, 1971, and 1976. Will the differences be age differences? Or differences in the era during which the subjects lived?

There are some rather practical advantages to cross-sectional research. Because it can be done all at once, one has less concern with attrition than with longitudinal research. Also, the same staff can assuredly test all subjects. Long term funding is often difficult to arrange, making longitudinal work prohibitive at times. Finally, the same measures can be given to all subjects. Sometimes measures become obsolete. After several years new measures must be found.

A serious problem for the developmental researcher is that of attrition (Schaie, 1973). A *representative sample* of 50-year-olds is not as representative of the population of its cohort (people born at the same time) as a sample of 30-year-olds would be representative of its cohort. More of the 50-year-olds have died, leaving a more biased pool from which to draw a sample. The same problem can plague the researcher of adolescence, especially if samples are drawn from the school population. Although attrition due to death may be minimal, attrition due to failure and dropping out of school can have a similar effect.

Schaie argues that cross-sectional studies do not provide information about age differences but rather about intergenerational differences. He further demonstrates the serious problems inherent in a longitudinal approach: attrition due to death, change of residence, loss of interest, and so on, as well as such effects of repeated measures as the tendency for high and low scores to change more on a second testing than do average scores.

In sum, Schaie observes that there are three components of developmental change: age, environmental impact over time, and generational differences. The longitudinal method confounds the first two, while the cross-sectional method confounds the first and the third. Schaie argues convincingly for consideration of "sequential" designs which can allow the researcher to assess independently the effects of two of these components of change rather than just one.

Consider the case of a hypothetical researcher who wanted to compare the anxiety of 13-year-olds to that of 18-year-olds in the United States in 1980. If the researcher finds a significant difference, it might indeed be attributable to the age of the subjects (perhaps 18-year-olds are more anxious than 13-year-olds). However, someone may argue that it is only true of these particular 18-year-olds who were born in the early 1960s and who therefore have a particular social history. This effect is the *cohort,* or age-mate, effect. Still another person may argue that this difference wouldn't occur were it not for the fact that the subjects are being tested in 1980 when the U.S. government decided to reinstitute registration for the draft. Thus, the 18-year-olds are more anxious because of the particular *time of measurement.*

It is possible to disentangle these effects. By combining the cross-sectional and longitudinal methods, one can arrive at one of three sequential designs: (a) a cross-sequential design which controls for the cohort and the time of measurement but leaves age confounded, (b) a time sequential design which controls for the age of the subject and time of measurement but leaves cohort confounded, and (c) a cohort sequential design which controls for cohort and age but leaves time of measurement confounded. An excellent example of the use of a cross-sequential strategy is given in a study of adolescent personality changes between 1970 and 1972 (Nesselroade & Baltes, 1974). An examination of one of the tables (see Table 1–1) from that study may help clarify how it is possible to examine both time of testing and cohort simultaneously.

TABLE 1–1
Short-term longitudinal sequences for the study of adolescent development: Data collection and design*

Cohort	Sex	Age					
		13	14	15	16	17	18
1959	M F	1972					
1958	M F	1971	1972				
1957	M F	1970	1971	1972			
1956	M F		1970	1971	1972		
1955	M F			1970	1971	1972	
1954	M F				1970	1971	1972
1953	M F					1970	1971
1952	M F						1970

Note: Entries represent times of observation (repeated measurement). Mean testing time (range ± 2 months) is January 1 of the year listed. The broken parallelogram indicates the data matrix used for main analyses reported.
* To estimate instrumentation and testing effects (internal validity), a set of randomly selected groups of cohorts 1954–58 were observed for the first and only time in 1972. In addition, to estimate selective dropout effects (external validity), the core longitudinal sample was contrasted with the dropout sample at the first time of measurement (1970).
Source: J. R. Nesselroade and P. B. Baltes, Adolescent personality development and historical change: 1970–1972, *Monographs of the Society for Research in Child Development*, 1974, 39, 1–79. With permission of the Society for Research in Child Development.

Some idiographic techniques

One interesting application of the idiographic approach, namely, the use of personal documents, was suggested by Allport (1942). Allport suggested that this might be especially appropriate to the study of the adolescent age group. In addition to the historical diagnoses of disturbed adolescents, Allport referred to such things as letters, diaries, autobiographies, and artistic and projective documents. Although such documents may be especially illuminating in individual case studies, Allport warned against overinterpretation and cited a number of dangers inherent in their use: the potential unrepresentativeness of the sample, the fascination which the writer may have with style over and above objective reporting, the blindness of the writer to his or her own motives, the effect of temporary moods, and errors of memory when the documents are retrospective. Despite these objections, Allport felt that the careful use of such materials had not been exploited nearly enough in the study of adolescents, who as a group are prone to writing personal documents, such as diaries and daily records. A good example of this approach is the collection of personal documents of famous historical figures compiled by Kiell (1964) in *The Universal Experience of Adolescence*. Included in the collection are the documents of writers, teachers, statesmen, and artists. Two other books of first-person accounts are the collections compiled from the writing of their students by Golburgh (1965) and Goethals and Klos (1970). Since both of these collections contain the writing of college students, they are particularly applicable to the study of late adolescence, or the period which Keniston has called youth. The use of such documents is, of course, subject to all of Allport's warnings concerning fascination with style, insincerity, and so on, and all the more so since the writers were themselves students of psychology and could very conceivably have distorted their accounts of their experiences in the direction of the currently prevailing theories.

In connection with the idiographic approach, it is important to note that there are excellent examples of case studies in the psychoanalytic literature of adolescence. Notable among these is Erikson's (1958) psychohistorical study of Martin Luther, *Young Man Luther*.

Some have suggested that literary fiction about adolescents can be used to advantage when the literary documents of adolescents themselves are unavailable. In using such sources, however, Allport's cautions are doubly important. For example, one might wonder to what extent the authors of such works are describing actual adolescence or an overly psychologized view of adolescence gleaned from reading the latest psychoanalytic treatment of the subject. The study of personality through literature is not new. For the student interested in a cautious assessment of the validity of this approach, Kiell (1959) is an excellent reference. Two other collections of fiction about the adolescent are *The Rite of Becoming* (Waldhorn & Waldhorn, 1966) and *The Adolescent through Fiction* (Kiell, 1959).

Correlational procedures

Once two or more pieces of data about a number of subjects can be gathered, their covariation can be explored. Such variables are generally called "subject" variables to distinguish them from environmental variables, which can be manipulated in an experiment. What correlation does is to refine one's description of data. It does not give evidence of causal relationships, but it does allow the experimenter to make predictions about the likelihood of an event, given information about a second event and the correlation between the two. Correlational procedures, then, are simply statistical ways of handling observational data. In addition, they allow us to use higher-order constructs in making predictions. For example, once we know that there are high correlations between, say, age at menarche, the adolescent growth spurt, and the development of secondary sex characteristics, we can speak of *maturation rate* in a more global way and know that the term has meaning to the extent that the correlations are significant. The important point is to be clear about the operational definitions of constructs. One might, for example, want to use any one of the three measures indicated above as an index of maturation rate; or one might want to use a composite of all three if the composite made sense. If the correlations among the measures are high enough, one can assume that the construct is a meaningful global concept.

Correlations can be positive and run from 0 to 1.0 or they can be negative and run from −1.0 to 0. Thus a correlation of .80 (positive) would mean that two variables are quite strongly correlated with one another. As one variable increases (e.g., height) so does the other (e.g., weight). A correlation of −.80 would mean that the two variables are negatively correlated. As one goes up, the other goes down. For example, the likelihood of dropping out of school is negatively correlated with the amount of support and encouragement one receives at home.

Experimental procedures

An unquestionably more precise and controlled way to obtain scientific information about adolescent development is through experimentation.

Basically the experiment differs from simple observation in two ways: the control of potential stimulus variables and the experimental manipulation of one independent variable. The experimenter is then able to assess the effect of this manipulation on a dependent variable, that is, the subject's specified behavior.

Very often, the experimental approach is used in conjunction with a subject variable design by selecting groups known to differ on some *within* variable and exposing them to an identical experimental treatment. A study of conformity by Costanzo and Shaw (1966) is an excellent example of this procedure. In their study, subjects of four different age groups (subject variable) were exposed to a series of cards similar to those used by Asch (1958) to measure conformity. Each card contained three comparison lines and a standard line. The experimenter manipulated the information given to the subject, namely, erroneous responses supposedly given by three other subjects who were being tested simultaneously. The response measure of conformity was the number of trials on which the subject agreed with these erroneous responses. Costanzo and Shaw found that conformity increased from childhood (7 to 9 years old) to early adolescence (11 to 13 years old) and then declined among older subjects (15 to 17 and 19 to 21 years old).

The beauty of the experimental approach lies in the control the experimenter has over the independent variable, which enables him to specify the necessary antecedent condition of the subject's response. In the above example, erroneous information "caused" subjects to give more conforming responses in one age group than in younger or older age groups.

It is not clear why the experimental approach has been so little exploited in the adolescent area of developmental psychology. Perhaps it is because the major questions of physical development and sexual maturation have lent them-selves to simple statistical approaches. Perhaps it is because an understanding of the psychological correlates of these changes involved little beyond correla-tional analyses. Finally, it is possible that the relevant variables of psychological functioning in the adolescent have simply not been specified precisely enough to permit optimal use of experimental techniques.

Statistical significance

The significance of statistical analyses is usually indicated with a probability statement. The likelihood of getting the same result (or greater) if the experiment were run 100 times is given as a p value. For example, $p < .05$ (the .05 level) means that the probability is less than 5 out of 100 that the result could occur by chance. $p < .01$ means the probability of one's result being a chance occur-rence is less than one in a hundred. These two levels, the .05 and the .01, are the most usually used indicators of significant findings.

While such a level of significance may seem impressive indeed and although essential in interpreting scientific findings, statistical significance by itself tells us nothing of the *psychological importance* of the result. Consider, for example, the following fictitious finding. High school boys and girls from state A have been found to be taller than their age mates in state B. In fact, the difference is significant beyond the .001 level. There is only one chance in a thousand that such a result could be mere chance. We are that sure of the difference in height. But what is this difference? Let's say it was found to be 2 millimeters. Of what practical significance would that be? Surely tailors or the designers of school desks would not have to take that difference into account, however statistically significant. Meaningfulness, either in the sense of contributing to a theory or having practical relevance, is not automatically assured by statistical significance.

Ethical considerations in research with adolescents

It may be appropriate here to consider some of the ethical implications of doing research with adolescents. Recently the American Psychological Associa-tion (1973) has seen fit, after much discussion, to establish a revised code of ethics to guide researchers and clinical practitioners.

The code makes each investigator responsible for seeing that the subjects are treated humanely. If unusual procedures seem to involve deviations, it is the investigator's obligation to seek ethical advice. Subjects must be informed of any conditions which might influence their willingness to participate. When decep-tion or concealment are necessary to the execution of an experiment, ex-perimenters are obligated to inform subjects concerning the reason for this. Subjects' rights to decline to participate must be respected, and no subject should be coerced to participate (for example, through any position of power which the investigator may exercise). Communications between subject and ex-perimenter must make clear their corresponding obligations to each other. No procedure is tolerated which would harm or distress the subject unless the subject's prior permission is obtained. Afterward, the experimenter is obligated to explain the reasons for all procedures to the subjects. If unforeseen, undesirable consequences should occur, it is incumbent upon the researcher to correct such aftereffects. Finally, the confidentiality of the subjects must be protected.

How specifically do the principles of the American Psychological Association's ethical code guide the investigator doing research with adolescents? Does the age of the subjects impose special considerations? Most assuredly, in our view. First of all, it is important to define *informed consent* in such a way that young subjects will have an unambiguous understanding of what they are being required to do. In the case of young subjects (some would say of all minors), parents or those responsible for the children must consent to their participation before an investigator may proceed. This implies that the nature of the procedures must be explained as fully as possible to the youngsters and those responsible for them.

Because of the age difference between the experimenter and young subjects, it is especially important to protect the latter's right to refuse to participate without experiencing guilt or discomfort. In all cases material should be kept confidential, and wherever possible it should be anonymous. That is, data should be so coded that, though analyses of individuals are possible, the identification of a particular individual's responses would be impossible. The relationship of trust between an experimenter and his young subjects should be continually protected.

The foregoing ethical considerations provide only a brief summary for the student interested in psychological research with children and adolescents. A fuller account can be found in the previously mentioned *Ethical Principles* subscribed to by members of the American Psychological Association (1973) and in a much lengthier working draft of those principles (American Psychological Association, 1972). An excellent consideration of the whole question of ethical practices in research with children can be found in a chapter written by Radke-Yarrow (1960) in the *Handbook of Research Methods in Child Development*. Finally, that volume is itself an excellent source for the student interested in research methodology with children.

SUMMARY AND CONCLUSIONS

We have seen in this chapter that adolescence is a difficult period of development to define. In fact, the very experience of adolescence involves a certain lack of clarity and definition. Generally the term adolescence is used to refer to the period between the onset of puberty and the achievement of full adult status in the community.

Adolescence has been considered a uniquely human phenomenon. This is probably because in most other animals dispersal from the family group occurs before or around the time of sexual maturity. In humans this is rarely the case.

Attitudes and stereotypes about adolescents have been almost as varied and extreme as the behavior of adolescents themselves. An early student of this age group, G. Stanley Hall, considered adolescents to be experiencing a period of storm and stress, and this view is maintained today in much of the psycholana-lytic writing about adolescents. Others, however, have found adolescents to be passive and conforming. We have suggested that the notion of identity as a unifying construct may help to explain these various views of particular seg-ments of the adolescent experience. In other words, it may be that some adoles-cents conform for the same reason that other adolescents (or, at other times, the conforming adolescents themselves) are rebellious—that is, both conformity and rebelliousness may be expressions of a search for identity, the former via identification with others, the latter via assertion of one's uniqueness.

The concern of professionals working with young people has shifted from the more purely biological concerns of puberty and early adolescence to the inter-personal needs of those in this period of youth. These needs are intimately tied to the task of solidifying one's identity while facing separation from parents, the choice of a mate, and the establishment of a meaningful vocation.

Research on adolescent development is scarce. Only recently has a major handbook (Adelson, 1980) been devoted exclusively to the field of adolescence. This reluctance to study those aspects of development that are crucial to adoles-cence may stem from the taboo our culture has placed on such intimate topics as sex, drugs, and self-esteem.

Several techniques have been used in the study of adolescent growth and behavior. Manipulation of the variable of time brings with it certain advantages and disadvantages. The longitudinal approach cannot be confounded by age differences or cohort differences among subjects. However, the cross-sectional approach appears to be more practical in light of the difficulties of obtaining long-term funding for research.

A precise and controlled way to obtain scientific information about adoles-cent development is through experimentation. Basically the experiment differs from simple observation in two ways: the control of potential stimulus variables and the experimental manipulation of one independent variable. The beauty of the experimental approach lies in the control the experimenter has over this independent variable, which enables him or her to specify the necessary an-tecedent condition of the subject's response.

We have suggested that the theme of identity, which has achieved promi-nence in the writings of the psychoanalyst Erik Erikson, is central to adolescence and that it will therefore be a guiding theme in this text. Succeeding chapters, however, will also stress in detail the work of other theorists. The main areas that will be covered are physical and sexual development (Chapters 2 and 3); cogni-tive development and the emotional and social development, including social relations in the culture, family, and peers (Chapters 4, 5, 6, 7, and 8), and finally, values and adolescent psychopathology (Chapters 9 and 10).

SUGGESTED ADDITIONAL READING

Erikson, E. H. Identity and the life cycle. *Psychological Issues,* 1959, 9(1), whole issue.

Grinder, R. E. *A history of genetic psychology.* New York: John Wiley & Sons, 1967.

Muuss, R. E. *Theories of adolescence.* 3d ed. New York: Random House, 1975.

How is the period of adolescence explained in Hall's theory of recapitulation?

Name some of the characteristics of the adolescent period that Hall views as storm and stress.

What are the differences in the occurrence of the growth spurt in males and females?

What physical and psychological factors appear to be involved in the secular trend?

How has the secular trend been explained?

What is the importance of the pituitary gland to adolescent development?

What differences and similarities are there in the body concerns of adolescent males and females?

Outline the development of primary and secondary sex characteristics in males and females.

How do late and early maturation affect self-regard in adolescence?

How is culture a determinant of the concern that adolescents may have with their body image?

CHAPTER 2

PHYSICAL DEVELOPMENT DURING ADOLESCENCE

One of the main defining events of adolescence is its onset, namely, the physiological changes that occur at puberty. This chapter will be devoted to those changes and to their psychological significance. The chapter will begin, however, with a discussion of an early theorist of adolescence, G. Stanley Hall. This is because Hall was one of the first people to emphasize the importance of the adolescent period in psychological development. His theory was based largely on the importance he attached to the physical changes which occur at this time. Since Hall's theory is really a biogenetic view of adolescence, it is appropriate that our discussion of the physical characteristics of adolescence begin with a brief review of his position. Following this theoretical introduction, we will consider some of the main physical and physiological changes of adolescence, including its endocrinology, physical growth changes, and changes in the primary and secondary sex characteristics. Finally, we will discuss the psychological importance of these changes.

A BIOGENETIC VIEW OF ADOLESCENCE

Hall the psychologist

Granville Stanley Hall (1844–1924), one of America's most illustrious psychologists, was also an organizer and administrator. He was named the first president of Clark University in 1888, and there he established one of the first genetic psychology laboratories in the country. (*Genetic psychology* is simply the old term for *developmental psychology*.) Hall was the founder of the *Ameri-*

G. Stanley Hall

can *Journal of Psychology,* and some scholars believe that this event in 1887 marked, if not the birth of psychology, at least its adolescence, or departure from its philosophical parents.

Hall's theory of adolescence

Despite the impressive evidence of Hall's importance to the maturation of American psychology, his main claim on our attention lies not so much in his organizational skill as in the fact that he was among the pioneer genetic psychologists in this country. Moreover, as mentioned, he was one of the first to recognize the importance of adolescence in psychological development. In 1904, he published the two-volume work *Adolescence: Its Psychology and Its Relations to Physiology, Anthropology, Sociology, Sex, Crime, Religion, and Education.* Hall was fascinated with genetics, and especially with Darwin's theory of evolution. He saw an analogy between the development of the species through evolution and the development of the individual from the time of conception through adolescence and into adulthood. This "recapitulation" theory holds that the development of the individual repeats in many respects the development of the species, that ontogeny recapitulates phylogeny. Just as Darwin had observed in the palmar grasp of the newborn baby something reminiscent of the prehensile activity of its simian ancestors, so Hall saw the period of adolescence as somehow recapitulating that period in humanity's evolutionary history when, through a turbulent revolution, human beings were able to shed a more savage past for the beginnings of civilization. Let us look briefly at Hall's description of this period:

> Adolescence is a new birth, for the higher and more completely human traits are now born. The qualities of body and soul that now emerge are far newer. The child comes from and harks back to a remoter past; the adolescent is neo-atavistic, and in

> him the later acquisitions of the race slowly become prepotent. Development is less
> gradual and more saltatory, suggestive of some ancient period of storm and stress
> when old moorings were broken and a higher level attained (1904, vol. 1, xiii).

In his book *Theories of Adolescence,* Muuss (1975) compares this description
of storm and stress to the period of *Sturm und Drang* in German literature, which
was characterized by commitment to an ideal and by upheaval and passion. The
analogy is clear. As Muuss points out, Hall saw a similarity between the characteristics of adolescence and those of the late 18th century period of German
literature, particularly the writings of Schiller and Goethe. The characteristics of
both periods include: commitment to an ideal, strong feelings, highly personalized expression, and suffering. Although Hall saw commitment to an ideal
as a characteristic of this period, he also noted that the seemingly committed
adolescent appeared to vacillate from one sort of commitment to another. In the
second volume of his work on adolescence he devoted a chapter to "Evolution
and the feelings and instincts characteristic of normal adolescence." Here he
discussed the alterations in mood "between inertness and excitement, pleasure
and pain, self-confidence and humility, selfishness and altruism, society and
solitude, sensitiveness and dullness, knowing and doing, conservatism and
iconoclasm, sense and intellect" (Hall, 1904, vol. 2, p. 40).

When discussing the psychic changes that occur during adolescence, Hall
was not on as sure ground as he was when he was dealing with the purely
physical and physiological changes of puberty. He was aware of the fact that, as
he said,

> we here face problems both more complex and more inaccessible than those con-
> nected with the somatic changes. The most important and basal of these are con-
> nected with the fact that powers and faculties essentially nonexistent before, are now
> born, and of all the older impulses and instincts some are reinforced and greatly
> developed while others are subordinated so that new relations are established and
> the ego finds a new center. (Hall, 1905, vol. 2, p. 70)

One reason why Hall found it more difficult to make assertions about
psychological development as compared to physical development was that the
available methodology was not nearly so good then as it is now. In Hall's day
measuring instruments for collecting psychological data about an individual
were all but nonexistent. Hall had always been vitally interested in the development of such instruments. For example, he was the first to use the questionnaire technique for securing psychological data about children. Although
today this may not seem to be an overly sophisticated technique, it should be
remembered that just 70 years ago it was a new and singular method for obtaining important psychological information.

Hall's main thesis, then, was that early adolescence in an individual was
somehow reminiscent of earlier stages in the development of the human race.
Hall perceived the psychic changes of adolescence as a natural consequence of
basic physical and physiological changes. He therefore considered adolescence
to be a universal phenomenon and assumed that the storm and stress which
adolescents were supposedly suffering was a universal experience. As we shall
see, his theory has not really stood the test of time. Later research and the field
observations of cultural anthropologists dispelled his notions of a universal

Sturm und Drang (Mead, 1949, 1953) and emphasized instead the plasticity of the developing human organism and its susceptibility to cultural influences during adolescence.

In any event, the relative sophistication of today's measuring techniques enables us to assess the kinds of physical changes Hall considered when he stressed the importance of somatic development.

PHYSICAL GROWTH IN ADOLESCENTS

Change in stature

One of the major physical changes that occur in early adolescence is a rapid increase in stature which has come to be known as the adolescent growth spurt. As documented by Tanner (1962), this phenomenon is universal, though it is known to be influenced to some extent by genetics, nutrition, and season, and to a much lesser extent by climate and race. One reason for the lesser known influence of these last two variables may lie in the difficulty involved in separating the antecedent conditions of race and climate from such other potentially crucial factors as socioeconomic condition and nutrition.

The timing of the adolescent growth spurt appears to vary considerably between boys and girls as well as within each sex. For boys, the spurt occurs sometime between 12½ and 15 years on the average, while for girls it occurs about two years earlier. Figure 2–1, taken from Tanner, indicates that the peak velocity in growth occurs at about 12 years for girls and at about 14 years for boys. Although the peak velocity for girls comes earlier, it does not, on the

FIGURE 2–1   Adolescent growth spurt in height for boys and girls.

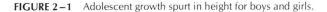

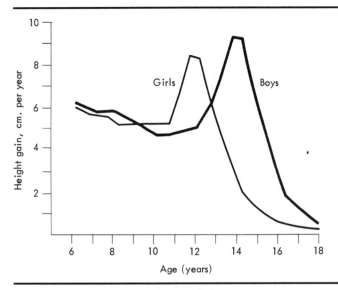

Source: J. M. Tanner, *Growth at adolescence* (Oxford: Blackwell Scientific Publications, 1962). With permission of Blackwell Scientific Publications, Ltd.

FIGURE 2–2   Growth curves of height by age for boys with average, accelerated, and retarded rates of maturation.

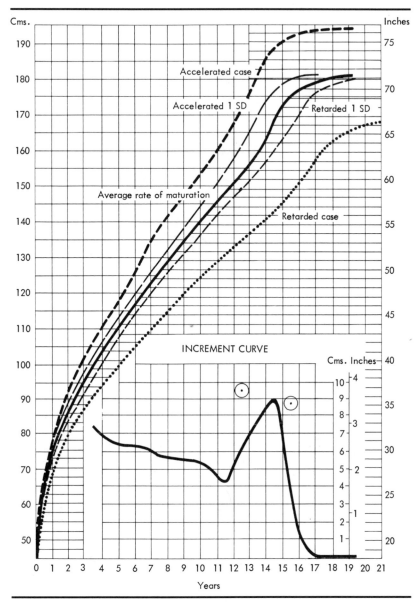

Source: N. Bayley, "Growth curves of height and weight for boys and girls scaled according to physical maturity," *Journal of Pediatrics,* 1956, *43,* 187–194. By permission.

average, reach the same intensity for girls as it does for boys. Thus, adult males tend to be somewhat taller than adult females, although there are a few years in adolescence during which females tend to be taller than their male age-mates. A similar spurt in growth at adolescence can be shown for weight, muscle size, head and face growth, and especially for the reproductive organs. In fact, ac-

FIGURE 2–3 Growth curves of height by age for girls with average, accelerated, and retarded rates of maturation.

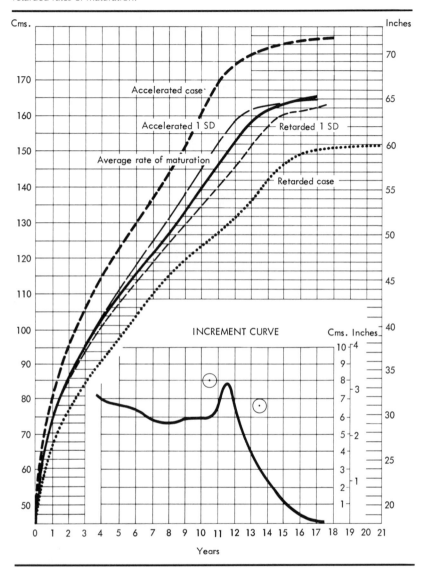

Source: N. Bayley, "Growth curves of height and weight for boys and girls scaled according to physical maturity," *Journal of Pediatrics*, 1956, *43*, 187–194. By permission.

cording to Tanner (1962), "every muscular and skeletal dimension of the body seems to take part in the adolescent's spurt" (p. 10).

Within each sex there are also wide variations in the onset of the adolescent growth spurt. Some early-maturing girls and boys experience the peak velocity of their growth spurt far earlier than the 12- and 14-year averages, and some girls and boys mature far later. The growth curves of such early- and late-maturing boys and girls are given in Figures 2–2 and 2–3. The reader should keep in mind that these figures represent the actual height of individuals at each age, unlike the curves of velocity (e.g., Figure 2–1) which indicate the amount of growth increase at each year.

Early-maturing persons tend to have a more intense adolescent growth spurt than do late-maturing persons (see Figure 2–4). Tanner suggests that "in early maturers, the whole process goes more quickly, and also more intensely, so that a greater total result is achieved despite the smaller amount of time taken" (p. 94).

FIGURE 2–4 Average yearly increments of growth in standing height for early- and late-maturing boys and girls (early and late categories determined by age at maximum growth).

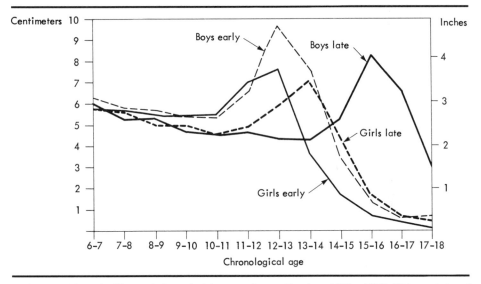

Source: J. Horrocks, The psychology of adolescence (Boston: Houghton Mifflin, 1962). With permission of author and the Society for Research in Child Development. Adapted from F. K. Shuttleworth, The physical and mental growth of girls and boys age six through nineteen in relation to age of maximum growth. Monographs of the Society for Research in Child Development, 1939, 4, 245–247.

An interesting corollary of this persistence of growth, however, is that, for both sexes, the differences between early and late maturers are more apparent in the adult weight than in the adult height, so that by adulthood early maturers tend to have more weight for height than do late maturers. It has also been found that individuals with a mesomorphic (average, well-muscled) body build tend to mature earlier than to those with an endomorphic (heavy) build.

A number of studies have indicated that the various measures of adolescent growth are fairly highly correlated. In boys, for example, the peak velocity in height is highly correlated with the maturation of the sex organs. Tanner has combined the results of several studies to show that similarly high correlations among the various indices of sexual and physical growth exist for girls. It goes without saying that such correlations, when considered in light of the wide variations in the onset of puberty, have an important psychosocial impact. Later in this chapter we shall deal in some detail with the psychological importance of these physical changes and their timing. Suffice it to say here that in a culture which places a high premium on physical appearance and sexual development, it would be a mistake to discount the early appearance of these characteristics in some adolescents or their late appearance in others. As Tanner notes, "Some girls have completely finished their adolescence and are menstruating regularly before others begin any development whatever" (p. 38). Similarly, some boys are completely undeveloped as adult males while some of their age-mates have all the primary and secondary sexual characteristics of fully grown men.

The secular trend

One fascinating aspect of the adolescent growth spurt is that for at least the past 100 years the total growth process seems to have been occurring earlier and earlier; that is, children today tend to be growing faster and to be reaching full adult stature at an earlier age than were children 100 or even 50 years ago. This tendency toward earlier maturation has been called the secular trend. Figure 2–5, taken from Meredith (1963), indicates the extent of this change in North American white males between 1880 and 1960. Not only are boys and girls maturing more quickly, but the full adult stature is also somewhat greater in 1960 than it was in 1880. This secular trend extends not only to the variable of stature, but also to the development of other organs and characteristics. For example, Figure 2–6, taken from Tanner, shows the change in the age at menarche, or first menstruation, between 1830 and 1960 in a number of countries. In all of these countries there has been a steady decrease in the age at menarche, so that, for example, the average menarcheal age for Norwegian girls declined from over 17 in 1830 to under 14 in 1960.

Body proportions have also changed over the past 100 years (Himes, 1979), although these changes have been variable in different parts of the world and for different social classes. There have also been secular increases in strength which may be attributable to concomitant changes in stature and weight since strength is significantly correlated with these other factors.

What is the basis for this acceleration in development, and when will it end? A number of factors have been said to account for the secular trend. The most common explanations have been diet, health, climate, and hybrid vigor. Boys and girls are certainly better nourished today—ingest more vitamins and have access to a more balanced diet—than were boys and girls in earlier years, and some writers assume that this nutritional difference explains the secular trend. However, this may be changing. In a major monograph on the secular trend, Roche (1979) observed that the increased incidence of obesity and increased use of refined sugar both suggest some dietary deterioration over the last several years.

It may be that the secular trend is largely attributable to improved health status as demonstrated in lower infant mortality and morbidity over the last

FIGURE 2–5 Schematic curves of mean stature for 1880 and 1960. Inset shows differences between the curves at selected ages.

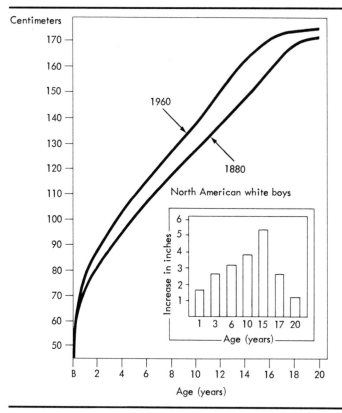

Source: H. V. Meredith, "Change in the stature and body weight of North American boys during the last 80 years," in L. P. Lipsitt and C. C. Spiker (Eds.), *Advances in child development and behavior*, vol. 1 (New York: Academic Press, 1963). With permission of the author and Academic Press.

hundred years. Many infectious diseases are now less common thanks to better medicine and health care, and yet some diseases, such as juvenile diabetes, may be more prevalent. Overall, however, children today experience much better health than in the past, and some researchers (see Malina, 1979) consider this the most important cause of the secular trend in stature and maturation.

The hybrid vigor hypothesis is quite different. Muuss (1970a) points to such inventions as the bicycle and the steam engine as contributing to the development of a hybrid vigor. He argues that with increased mobility individuals were able to select mates from more distant communities. The hybrid vigor hypothesis has been advanced by Jensen (1969), who supports this assertion with evidence from outbreeding experiments with animals.

Some researchers (for example, Muuss, 1970a) have suggested that the secular trend extends to sociological and psychological phenomena as well as to the

FIGURE 2–6   Secular trend in age at menarche, 1830–1960.

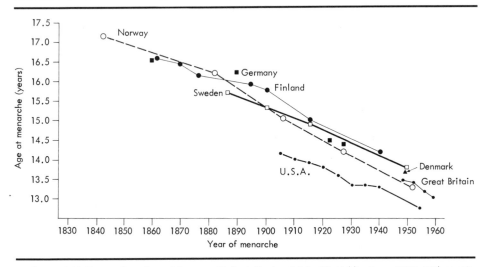

Source: J. M. Tanner, *Growth at adolescence* (Oxford: Blackwell Scientific Publications, 1962). With permission of Blackwell Scientific Publications.

physical characteristics already mentioned. For example, they note that boys and girls seem to be interested in dating and other heterosexual activities at an earlier age. It should be pointed out, however, that the historical span covered by such studies is not nearly so great as the span of time which is generally cited in support of the secular trend. For example, Kuhlen and Houlihan (1965) found that the heterosexual interest of adolescents was greater and arose earlier in 1963 than in 1942. This 21-year span, however, is hardly comparable to the time span of the secular trend in physical development. It is possible that social and psychological changes occurring in such a short period of time may be temporary, socially induced fluctuations rather than continuations of a long-term historical trend.

PHYSIOLOGICAL DEVELOPMENT IN ADOLESCENCE

The endocrinology of puberty

The reader is undoubtedly familiar with the basic glands of the endocrine system. Some of these glands, along with their location in the body, are identified in Figure 2–7. Many endocrine glands participate in the general rapid growth of adolescents; that is, they also undergo a growth spurt. The main endocrine glands of interest to the developmental psychologist studying puberty are the pituitary gland and the sex glands, or gonads. The reason for this is that, though important morphological changes occur in practically all the endocrine glands, the changes in the secretion of the anterior pituitary and the gonads are of special interest because of their effect on the psychosexual development of the child and because of the variety of bodily changes that occur at puberty.

FIGURE 2–7   Locations and functions of the major endocrine glands.

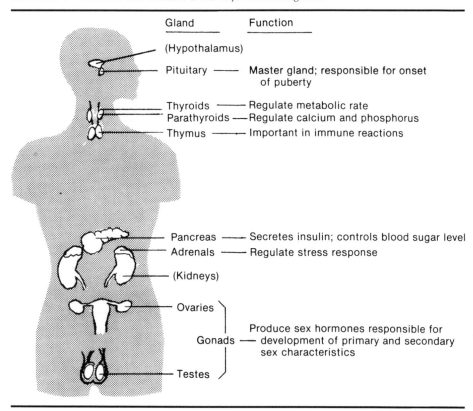

Diagram courtesy of Christi Rager.

The pituitary gland, or hypophysis, is seated at the base of the brain. It is perhaps the most important of the endocrine glands. It has been called the master gland because its secretions stimulate or inhibit the activity of a number of other glands. The pituitary is divided into three segments, the posterior, intermediate, and anterior lobes. The anterior lobe, which has the largest claim on our attention here, secretes no less than six hormones, three of which are called *gonadotropic* hormones because they stimulate the activity of the gonads. Another very important hormone secreted by the anterior pituitary is the adrenocorticotropic hormone (ACTH), which stimulates the adrenal cortex. The suffix *tropic* is used to indicate that a hormone has as its target another endocrine gland. The anterior pituitary secretes these important tropic hormones at puberty because of stimulation from the hypothalamus. Why this stimulation occurs at this particular period in the child's life is unclear. This hypothalamic-pituitary-gonadal relationship is functional long before puberty (Katchadourian, 1977). Apparently puberty begins when this system is further activated not when it is first awakened. As mentioned, the cause of this activation isn't clear. In any event it does occur, and as a result the secretion of the hormones of the anterior pituitary initiates what is known physiologically as puberty. The gonadotropic hormones secreted by the anterior pituitary include: (a) the follicle-stimulating hormone (FSH); (b) the luteinizing hormone (LH) in females or its counterpart in males, the interstitial cell-stimulating hormone (ICSH); and (c) the luteotropic hormone (LTH).

Once stimulated by gonadotropic hormones, the sex glands, or gonads, begin to secrete their own hormones. Androgen, the male sex hormone, is responsible for the development of the penis, the prostrate gland, and the seminal vesicles as well as secondary sex characteristics. The important female gonadal hormones are the estrogen group. These hormones are responsible for the development of the uterus, the vagina, the Fallopian tubes, the breasts, and secondary female sex characteristics. The estrogens influence the menstrual cycle and a variety of functions, such as normal uterine contractions, and control the growth of breast duct tissue (though they have nothing to do with the production of milk). McCary's (1967) book *Human Sexuality* contains an excellent account of the importance and the functioning of the estrogens.

The small Graafian follicles in the ova are stimulated by FSH from the anterior pituitary. In ovulation when an egg is then discharged from a follicle, the remaining cells with the follicle multiply quickly and fill the gap left by the ruptured follicle. This new growth in the old follicle is the corpus luteum, so called because of its yellow color. The new corpus luteum cells produce progesterone. The production of progesterone is stimulated by a pituitary secretion, the luteinizing hormone. The production of progesterone is a reason for the well-known cyclic variations in emotional satisfaction which correspond to the monthly menstrual cycle in many women. Progesterone is important because it prepares the uterus for pregnancy. If implantation does not occur, that is, if the female does not become pregnant, the lining of the uterus, which progesterone had built up, breaks down, since progesterone is no longer being produced; this degeneration of uterine tissue triggers the onset of menstruation, the blood flow. The corpus luteum itself then begins to degenerate, loses its yellow color, and shrinks. Finally the low progesterone level and the decrease of estrogen cause new production of the pituitary gonadotropic hormones, and the cycle begins again.

Sexual development

One main effect of the production of gonadal hormones is the development of primary and secondary sexual characteristics in boys and girls at the time of puberty.

The development of the primary sexual characteristics is well known. The male sex organs enlarge out of proportion to the general body growth; that is, the penis and the associated vas deferens, prostate gland, and urethra, as well as the testes and the scrotum, are all considerably enlarged at puberty. A number of studies have described the maturational pattern. Reynolds and Wines (1951) suggest the following five stages of genital maturity: "(1) infantile; (2) enlargement of scrotum, first reddening and texture change, 11.5 years; (3) first 'sculpturing' and enlargement of penis, 12.7 years; (4) pronounced 'sculpturing' and darkening of penis, 13.4 years; and (5) essentially adult, reddish brown, loose penile skin, and loss of sharp 'sculpturing,' 17.3 years" (pp. 529–530). Along with the development of the penis itself come nocturnal emissions, emissions of semen, including sperm cells, during sleep. Such secretions may also occur through masturbation or coitus.

The development of the primary sex characteristics in the female also occurs as an effect of the production of gonadal hormones. That is, the female reproductive apparatus, consisting of the two ovaries, the Fallopian tubes, the vagina, and the uterus, develops and gains in weight and size following gonadotropic stimulation. At about 13 years of age menarche, the first menstrual cycle, occurs. There is some evidence that immediately following menarche most girls are sterile, that it is some months after menarche before most girls experience regular periods and that it may be some months after that before they are fertile.

The development of the secondary sex characteristics is also stimulated by the secretions of the gonads. Among girls, these characteristics include pubic and underarm hair, breasts and the fatty tissue around the hips, the characteristic female bone structure of the hips, and a broadening in the shoulders.

The chronological order of appearance of the secondary female sex characteristics is given by Greulich (1944): "During normal puberty, the development of the breasts is among the earliest external manifestations of beginning sexual maturation, and the breast changes are usually well under way before the pubic hair appears in any considerable quantity. The growth of axillary hair usually begins after the pubic hair is fairly well-developed and is ordinarily preceded by the menarche, the first menstruation" (pp. 17–18). The development of the breast has been described as occurring in five stages (Reynolds & Wines, 1948): (1) infantile form; (2) bud stage (10.8 years); (3) intermediate stage (11.4 years); (4) primary mamma stage (12.2 years); (4) mature stage (13.7 years).

Reynolds and Wines developed a similar five-point scale for the development of pubic hair. Although there is a wide variation among girls as to the onset of secondary sex characteristics, the correlations between their beginnings are fairly high. For example, in Reynolds and Wine's sample the age at menarche correlated .86 with the appearance of breast buds and .70 with the appearance of pubic hair. The appearance of breast buds correlated .66 with the appearance of pubic hair.

In boys, the most important secondary sex characteristics seem to be the development of pubic and axillary hair, the development of facial hair, and the lowering of the voice.

PSYCHOLOGICAL EFFECTS OF ADOLESCENT PHYSICAL DEVELOPMENT

Implications of the physical changes

The physical changes of adolescence are important for a number of reasons. First, they confront the child with a number of discontinuities with his or her previous physical experience. The sudden increase in height and weight and the onset of sexual development and the accompanying sexual drives are dramatic changes from the growth pattern of middle childhood. In addition, these changes may or may not take place at the same time and rate that they are taking place among one's friends. Again, it is at the time of these physical changes that the different rates of maturation of boys and girls are seen most clearly. The onset of puberty begins at least two years earlier in girls than in boys. Never before and never again is the difference in the maturation rate so large. Finally, some of these changes are important simply because they involve the extent to which a person is perceived or perceives himself or herself as masculine or feminine. For example, a girl who develops very late may question when she will develop female characteristics. A short and somewhat underdeveloped late-maturing boy may experience concern about his sexual identity. In other words, the process of becoming a man not only means no longer being a boy but also assuring himself that he is a normal male.

The physical changes of adolescence can cause a boy or a girl to question his or her normality in many ways. The fact that these experiences are discontinuous with what occurred in childhood gives rise to natural doubts about the future: "What will become of me? Will I always have acne? Am I normal? Will others like me?" With changes in logical thinking which allow adolescents to consider themselves more from the point of view of others, they can see themselves as objects, whether reflected in the mirror or in the eyes of the contemporaries who are their new reference group. In an attempt to make themselves normal or acceptable, some adolescents seem to go to ridiculous extremes from the point of view of adult observers. Hair curling, cosmetics, supports, flatteners, hairpieces, shoe lifts, and depimpling devices of all sorts get sold over the counter and through mail-order advertising in teenage magazines. Anyone who has worked with adolescents knows the anguish on which such marketing depends. Recently, one of us talked to a girl who slouched for fear of exposing her developing breasts; a boy afraid to shower with his classmates for fear his lack of circumcision made him abnormal; a boy who felt that he was a "freak" because at 14 he was almost 6 feet tall; and many adolescents who felt that some aspect of their body was unattractive because it was different and therefore unacceptable. These are not esoteric clinical problems—they are daily occurrences.

Concern about one's physical attractiveness is obviously not limited to early adolescence. However it is only then that this issue begins to take on importance. In a study of college students, Lerner and Karabenick (1974) found high correlations between the subjects' estimation of the physical attractiveness of various parts of their bodies and their overall self-esteem. This held especially true for the female subjects. One suspects that the self-esteem of boys may be more related to estimations of physical fitness and strength.

In another study (Faust, 1960), girls in junior high school who were more physically mature (determined by menarcheal age) were also found to have a higher prestige rating among their peers. Indeed, menarche seems to have a crucial impact on the way in which a girl perceives herself and in which she presumes others to perceive her. When pre- and postmenarcheal girls were asked to do human figure drawings (Koff, Rierdan, & Silverstone, 1978), those who had already experienced menarche drew more sexually differentiated figures and were more likely to draw their own sex first when instructed simply to draw a person. After they had drawn a female, the subjects were given a test asking them to imagine their drawn person as a character in a story. They were asked how they thought this girl would feel about herself, and about her various body parts. Postmenarcheal girls were more likely to attribute satisfaction to their characters' consideration of their "feminine" body parts (i.e., bust, hips, and waist) compared with premenarcheal subjects. These data suggest an important projection of the adolescent girls' attitudes toward her own body.

Despite the importance of menarche as a determinant of prestige and body satisfaction, menstruation itself is still considered in mostly negative terms by both adolescent boys and girls (Clarke & Ruble, 1978). Foremost in their description of this event were such things as physical discomfort, disruption of normal activities, and heightened emotionality. In a study of pre- and postmenarcheal girls, Koff, Rierdan and Jacobson (1981) found that, while some girls saw menarche as a positive sign of maturity, "this positive aspect is overshadowed by a negative interpersonal significance as girls become increasingly self-conscious, embarrassed, and secretive." (p. 148).

For teachers and parents, the most important aspects of the data on physical development may not be the average sizes, ages, and so on, but the range, which bespeaks tremendous variability in sexual and physical development. What is "normal" need not be the statistical mean. Normality can include an aesthetic of human features based on individual differences rather than on a norm contrived by fashion designers and cosmetic advertisers.

Some of the specific concerns which adolescents have with their physical development have been studied in an interesting way by Frazier and Lisonbee (1950), who asked 580 10th-grade boys and girls about their physical self-perceptions and concerns. The replies showed that there was far more concern among the boys about being thin and among the girls about being either thin or heavy. There was more concern among the boys who considered themselves short, while there was more concern among the girls about being either tall or short. Although both the boys and the girls were concerned about slow development, the girls were far more concerned than the boys about early development. It appears from these data that the ideal for masculinity is more unidirectional than the ideal for femininity. That is, boys prefer to develop early and to be tall and on the heavy side, whereas the ideal for girls appears to be somewhere in the middle. Thus, though girls prefer not to be heavy, many girls are concerned about being too thin. Girls generally prefer not to be tall, yet a large percentage are concerned about being short. Most girls do not want to develop too slowly, yet many are concerned that they are developing too early. We will return to this notion of ideal masculine and ideal feminine maturation rates when we look at the maturation data of the California growth studies.

Frazier and Lisonbee found some other physical concerns among these 10th-grade boys and girls. Over half the boys and the girls described themselves as having blackheads or pimples. However, of these subjects 51 percent of the boys and 82 percent of the girls expressed concern about this. In general, girls expressed more concern about a greater variety of physical symptoms than did

FIGURE 2–8. Physical development during adolescence takes on psychological importance.

Photo courtesy of J. P. McKinney

boys. This fits with the predominant stereotype of the importance of physical looks for women in our culture.

A number of studies have suggested a link between hormonal functioning and certain cognitive abilities. For example, Petersen (1976) found cognitive differences between boys and girls who developed physically in a very sex-stereotypic way and those who were more androgynous, or less typical of their own sex. For example, although all boys will develop pubic hair, acquire lower voices, and develop mature genitals, there are wide variations among fully mature individuals in terms of how characteristically masculine, these traits will be. There are tenors as well as basses, small penises as well as large. Analogous variations are also obvious among women. Fully mature women vary tremendously in terms of breast size and hip width. The exciting thing about Petersen's data is that these physical manifestations of "masculinity" or "femininity" which are directly influenced by hormones are also significantly related to two aspects of cognitive functioning: namely, spatial ability and verbal fluency. Petersen used muscle development, genital or breast size, and overall body shape as physical indicators of hormonal masculinity or femininity versus androgyny. She then found that adolescent boys who were more masculine had poorer spatial ability and more fluent production compared with more androgynous males. In females, fluent production was unrelated to these physical manifestations of sex-stereotypy, but girls who were less feminine (more androgynous) had better spatial ability.

Maturation rate has also been related to cognitive functioning (Waber, 1976). Boys and girls who are late developers do better on tests of spatial ability than on tests of verbal skill. The reverse is true for early developers (Waber, 1976).

The timing of puberty

The timing of the physical changes of puberty may also exert psychological effects. That timing, or maturation rate, has been studied extensively in both boys (Mussen & Jones, 1957) and girls (Jones & Mussen, 1958). In general, the studies indicate that early-maturing boys have a psychological advantage over their late-maturing peers in both adolescence (Mussen & Jones, 1957) and adulthood (M. C. Jones, 1957). Early reports had suggested the converse for girls. It was predicted that the early-maturing girl, being developmentally ahead of her female peers and greatly ahead of her male age-mates, would be at a social disadvantage (H. E. Jones, 1949). Jones and Mussen (1958), however, discovered that, if anything, late-maturing girls present a more negative picture. They have lower scores on self-regard and a higher need for recognition. Among boys, the early maturer has a distinct heterosexual advantage over his peers since he is developmentally closer to girls his age. M. C. Jones has shown that the early-maturing boy has a significantly higher self-regard than the late maturer. It is not unlikely that this greater self-esteem is largely influenced by the early maturer's awareness of his success in an area that is highly valued by his peers.

SUMMARY AND CONCLUSIONS

From the foregoing, some of the psychological implications of adolescent physical development are quite clear. In summarizing the main aspects of growth and physical development during adolescence, we can cite the following: (1) The annual increment in height and weight accelerates rather dramatically during the prepubescent and pubescent years. (2) The primary sex characteristics develop during puberty, and associated with that development are the onset of menstruation in girls and the production of semen in boys. (3) The secondary sex characteristics also develop during this period.

Many endocrine glands participate in the growth spurt of adolescents. The changes in the secretion of the anterior pituitary and the gonads are of special interest to the developmental psychologist because of their effect on the psychosexual development of the child. The results of these rather dramatic changes relative to the comparative quiescence of the childhood years are apparent. The research of Frazier and Lisonbee (1950) indicated that a large percentage of boys and girls who perceive themselves as having physical deviations during the adolescent period show concern about those deviations. The work of Mussen and Jones (1957, 1958), Jones and Mussen (1958) on the psychological correlates of maturation rate indicates that the early maturer, at least among boys, is more highly regarded and possesses a greater degree of self-esteem than the late maturer.

However, the teacher, clinician, teenager, or parent need not conclude that adolescence is universally a period of storm and stress, as was the view of G.

Stanley Hall, nor even that the physical changes of adolescence are necessarily associated with deep trauma. Rather, they should recognize that changes in body image are almost certain to occur as bodily changes occur. The direction these body image changes take will undoubtedly be influenced as much by the attitudes of those around the adolescent (his or her peers and society in general) as by the physical changes themselves. In a culture which often values the size of a woman's breasts as an indication of her femininity and ultimately of her worth, it is not surprising that young girls show some concern because their breasts are not developing on time. Similarly, in a culture which places a high premium on athletic skills in males, one should not be surprised that a youngster who is slow in developing physically is also likely to be low in self-regard. Perhaps the future will see a change in such sexist attitudes as those described here. Surely the current focus on women's issues has been a force for such change.

A number of factors have been said to account for the secular trend. The most common explanations have been diet, health, climate, and hybrid vigor. Some researchers have suggested that the secular trend extends to sociological and psychological phenomena as well. It should be noted, however, that these social and psychological changes occurring may be temporary, socially induced fluctuations rather than continuations of a long-term historical trend.

SUGGESTED ADDITIONAL READING

Katchadourian, H. *The biology of adolescence.* San Francisco: W. H. Freeman, 1977.

McCary, J. *Human sexuality.* Princeton, N.J.: Van Nostrand, 1967.

Tanner, J. M. *Growth at adolescence.* Oxford: Blackwell Scientific Publications, 1962.

BOX 3–1
Study questions

In gathering or analyzing data on sexual attitudes and behavior, why must a distinction be made between behavior and motivation?

What assumption does Freud make about the basis for a child's internalization of parental values?

What developments characterize the genital stage (adolescence) in Freud's scheme of development?

According to Anna Freud, how do the ego defenses of asceticism and intellectualization help the adolescent to manage internal conflict?

What evidence supports or refutes the concept of a sexual revolution among today's young people?

What personality measures have shown important differences between virgins and nonvirgins especially at the high school level?

How does sex role stereotyping affect the perceptions of adolescents?

Why do Ford and Beach classify the United States as a sexually restrictive society?

What difference did Offer find in the attitudes toward sexuality of early and late adolescents?

Discuss briefly Reiss's four standards of premarital sexuality and their consequences.

According to Vincent and McCary, why is the adolescent of today in strong need of sexual education?

CHAPTER 3

ADOLESCENT SEXUALITY: DEVELOPMENT, ATTITUDES, AND BEHAVIOR

In the last chapter we dealt with the physical and physiological changes of puberty. In this chapter we will focus our attention on the biological and social changes involved in sexual development, and discuss the changes in attitudes toward sexuality and in sexual behavior that occur during adolescence. Whereas the data on physical development are fairly straightforward, one has to be careful in interpreting the data about sexual attitudes and behavior. First, a distinction must be made between sexual behavior and sexual motivation. An adolescent may indulge in heterosexual fantasies or behavior for a variety of reasons. Simply knowing that a person's fantasies or behavior are overtly sexual tells us nothing about the motivational bases for these phenomena. Thus one person may engage in premarital intercourse for purely physical enjoyment, whereas for others premarital intercourse may be an expression of love. Still others may see this behavior as a way of maintaining a friendship (a need for affiliation), of helping a friend in need (nurturance), of proving independence from parents (autonomy), of controlling one's partner (dominance), and so on.

Second, because of the intimate nature of sexuality, many adolescents are naturally reluctant to participate in research which deals with their attitudes or examines their behaviors in this sensitive area. Despite the methodological difficulties, a good deal of research has been done on adolescent sexuality. On the side of theory, much of our interest in this subject owes a debt to Freud, who emphasized its psychological importance. In addition, Freud was one of the first to examine normal and abnormal sexual behavior and motivation in detail despite the Victorian prudery of his day, or perhaps because of it. Freud noticed that when certain ideas were unacceptable to an individual, these ideas were often kept out of consciousness, although they were not entirely forgotten by the individual. He called this method of keeping unacceptable ideas hidden from oneself *repression*. Sexual thoughts and feelings were often among the repressed material. According to the Victorian attitudes of Freud's day, the discussion of such thoughts and feelings was considered inappropriate. Although some argue that he overemphasized this aspect of human development, it is important to keep in mind that he had to overcome a good deal of resistance, bred of Victorian prudery, which is largely nonexistent today.

A PSYCHOSEXUAL THEORY OF ADOLESCENCE

Organization of personality

Freud believed that every individual went through a series of psychosexual stages and that excitations arising from various regions of the body were especially characteristic of each of these stages. Freud called the psychological component of these excitations *libido*. In Freud's theory libido, which resides in the *id,* is a general psychic energy and not specifically and exclusively genital sexuality. Its use here to introduce the topic of adolescent sexuality should not mislead the reader into thinking that Freud's libido refers merely to overt sexual expression. In adolescence, however, genital sexuality is one expression of libidinal urges. It is then the job of the *ego,* which develops gradually in the individual, to contend with excitations whose indulgence would bring pleasure and whose denial would bring pain. The *ego* is Freud's term for the aspect of the personality that originates in sense perception and is the agent of memory, judging, willing, and so on—in other words, the executive branch of the personality. Largely

Sigmund Freud

National Library of Medicine

conscious, the ego is the intermediary between id impulses and the external environment, and it tests the environment for the consequences of intended behavior. The third component of the personality, which Freud called the *superego*, develops as the child grows older. The superego requires the ego to keep a check on id impulses whose gratification would be at variance with the commonly accepted moral practices of the child's socializing community.

Freud considered the main socializing agents of the child to be the parents. For him, the internalization of the values of the parents amounted to the development of the superego (Freud, 1960). Specifically, the child develops both an ego ideal, the psychological component of which is pride, and a conscience, the psychological component of which is guilt. The superego, Freud's representation of moral character, was an internalization of parental values. Freud assumed that the basis for this internalization was the child's identification with its parents.

Freud's concept of identification is based on the notion of an Oedipus complex. Briefly, Freud concluded that the young boy falls in love with his mother and identifies with his father. The basis for the identification is presumably the fear that the father will emasculate the son if the father becomes aware of the son's incestuous attachment to the mother. The designation comes from the Greek myth of Oedipus who killed his father and married his mother. If Freud's theory of identification were based only on the notion of castration anxiety, it would, of course, be inadequate to explain the identification of females. For that reason Freud developed an homologous notion, namely, penis envy. In Freudian theory, penis envy assumes the same function in the development of identification in the female as does castration anxiety in the male. The notion is that in the process of falling in love with her father a girl recognizes the biological differences between herself and her father and becomes envious of the male characteristics. She then identifies with her mother, who also lacks external genitalia, and in so doing she incorporates the values of her mother. To many, the notion of penis envy seems to be a less powerful construct in Freud's theory because it suggests that socialization should take place more fully in the male. Since there is no evidence for this, this aspect of Freudian theory seems somewhat weak.

Stages of development

Freud emphasized the three psychosexual stages which occur early in life—the oral stage, the anal stage, and the phallic stage. Each of these stages is characterized by a particular body zone whose excitation is responsible for the psychosexual energy that is being generated. For example, during the oral stage the child is stimulated mainly by feeding at its mother's breast, whereas during the anal stage psychosexual stimulation centers on retaining and expelling feces, and during the phallic stage the genitals are the source of psychosexual excitation. Here again, one sees the masculine orientation of Freud's theory in his reference to the genital stage by a term derived from *phallus,* a word for the male sex organ.

Freud concluded that the most important part of psychological development occurred during these early stages. Following these stages, he postulated a period of psychosexual latency, that is, a period of quiescence during which the superego was able to keep aggressive and sexual impulses in check. Hall (1954) in his *Primer of Freudian Psychology* says that the latency period lasts for a number of years, generally from the age of 5 to about the age of 12. The onset is related to the repression of the Oedipus complex through castration anxiety. The end of the latency period is identified in Freudian theory by the great increase in the sexual instinct attributable to physiological changes associated with puberty. According to Freudian theory the so-called *Sturm und Drang* of adolescence is occasioned by the revival of these impulses.

It can be seen that during the early stages of psychosexual development, gratifications, which Freud called cathexes, are mainly self-indulgent, or in Freudian terms, *narcissistic*. One of the main psychosexual changes of the adolescent period is a decrease in narcissism and an increase in cathexes to external persons and objects. That is, the adolescent may love others for altruistic rather than selfish reasons. Freud calls the adolescent stage of devleopment the genital period. This period does not completely replace the earlier psychosexual periods but rather becomes integrated with them. Freud, for example, would see a fusion of the narcissism of pregenital stages with the altruism of the genital stage in such activities as kissing, petting, and lovemaking in general.

In addition, during adolescence the earlier incestuous attachments to one's parents are replaced by a love object, which in early adolescence is generally an older woman for the boy and a more mature man for the girl. Freud assumed that one of the main tasks of the adolescent period was for the child to overcome dependency on the parents and to attach himself or herself to a love object of the opposite sex of his or her own age. With reference to this period of psychosexual development, Hall and Lindzey (1978) state that this is a time in which "sexual attraction, socialization, group activities, vocational planning, and preparations for marrying and raising a family begin to manifest themselves" (p. 58). By the time the period of adolescence ends, the individual has become socialized as an adult; pleasure-seeking narcissism has given way to reality orientation.

Anna Freud's contribution

As significant as Freud's contributions are to the study of personality, no less important are those of his daughter, Anna Freud. Even more than her father, she has written specifically about the adolescent (1958, 1966). Anna Freud's description of adolescence is remarkably similar to G. Stanley Hall's view that this period is marked by extremes.

Anna Freud viewed adolescence as marked by the resurgence of sexual conflicts which had erupted in infancy and early childhood and then lay dormant during the period of latency or middle childhood. The conflict between the ego and the instinctual impulses of the id, called libido, is reawakened. However, this resurgence, unlike the earlier struggle, is complicated by the fact that the ego also has to deal with a superego, or the internalization of parental values, a process which has gone on during the latency years. The ego, torn between the demands of the id and the inhibitions of the superego, needs defenses. Anna Freud mentions two which she believes are particularly characteristic of adolescence: asceticism and intellectualization. Asceticism refers to the rejection of all sorts of pleasures and an amost religious pursuit of self-denial. When adolescents find the libidinous urges of the id to be overwhelming, they begin to be suspicious of every kind of pleasure and attempt to overcome these impulses by ascetism, or a denial of pleasure.

Similarly, an increased interest in abstract intellectual concerns is another way of defending against newly awakened sexual urges. Whatever defenses are used, it should be remembered that Freudian theory emphasizes that the main component of the developmental task of adolescence is sexual. With this in mind, let us examine the sexual attitudes and behavior of adolescents and ask whether these have changed significantly since Freud's day.[1]

SEXUAL DEVELOPMENT: ATTITUDES, VALUES, AND BEHAVIOR

Evidence for a sexual revolution: Pro and con

There is a widespread believe that today's youth are in the midst of a sexual revolution which, depending on one's point of view, is seen as a sign either of liberation or of decadence. Cited as examples of this revolution are: the increased availability of hard-core pornography in most large cities, the showing of XXX-rated movies even in formerly conservative areas, the ready access to contraceptive information and devices among the unmarried young, the Supreme Court ruling permitting abortion, the teaching of sexual matters in the public school, and the increased frequency of premarital pregnancies. In terms of personal sexual behavior, however, the empirical evidence for a sexual revolution is not so clearcut.

If one uses an increase in premarital intercourse as the index of a sexual revolution, one might argue that although there may have been nothing revolutionary about men's sexual conduct during the past 25 years, the story is different for women. After citing the reviews of 28 studies of premarital sex behavior since 1953, Dreyer (1975) concluded that the incidence of such behavior had not increased significantly among men, but that "the number of white women aged 15 to 25 having premarital sexual intercourse has risen dramatically until today there is virtually no difference between the proportions of young men and women who engage in such behavior" (p. 197).

In reviewing studies between 1960 and 1980 dealing with adolescent sexual

---

[1] For a more complete discussion of the early stages of psychosexual development, the student is referred to the earlier volumes of this series. For the student interested in primary sources, there are a number of excellent collections, including *The basic writings of Sigmund Freud,* edited by A. A. Brill (1938), and the five-volume *Collected papers of Sigmund Freud,* which were edited by Ernest Jones (1959). In addition, there is available a brief but excellent secondary source, *A primer of freudian psychology,* Calvin Hall (1954), as well as excellent discussions of Freudian theory in Hall and Lindzey (1978), *Theories of personality,* and in S. Maddi (1976), *Personality theories: A comparative analysis.*

behavior, Kallen (1980) found important changes both in behavior and in the standards governing sexual behavior. He cited the following major changes:

1. Proportions of adolescents reporting coitus. The data clearly indicate an increase reported by high school and college students.
2. Proportions of males versus females reporting coitus. A greater increase among females has resulted in an almost equal proportion of males and females reporting coitus, whereas formerly the percentage was far higher for males than females.
3. Age at first coitus. Coitus is being reported at an earlier age. For example, Zelnik and Kantner (1977) report that between 1971 and 1976 the age at first intercourse for females in the U.S. dropped by four tenths of a year.
4. Number of partners. Kallen observed a growing tendency among adolescents to limit their sexual behavior to one partner within a given time period.
5. Type of relationship. In addition, sexual behavior is increasingly being practiced primarily within a relationship which includes love and affection. While this has traditionally been true for females, it is becoming more common among males as well.

Still, the main "revolution" seems to deal with attitudes and values. One investigator (Bell, 1966) minimizes the increase in premarital petting or coitus but supports the widely held view that values about sexual matters have changed significantly in the past several decades. He notes that parents have become more deliberate in their transmission of sexual values and that both the parental views of sex as well as the peer values held by adolescents have changed significantly. As examples, he cites changes in the attitude toward premarital sex and virginity in girls and the decreased fear of pregnancy as a major deterrent for most girls.

Some have described these changes in attitude as a "sexual renaissance" (Reiss, 1966). Others have challenged this designation and have insisted that what we are experiencing among the young is indeed a revolution. Broderick (1966), for example, argued that insofar as the notion of a sexual renaissance implied a rebirth of openness and understanding toward sexuality, it was a misnomer. Rather than viewing the current openness as a revisitation of an earlier form of such understanding (the two periods separated by a period of Victorian prudery) Broderick insists that at least with respect to childhood sexuality and our attitudes toward it, we are confronted with a real revolution—something completely new in the history of humanity.

This position is also supported by recent data (Jessor & Jessor, 1975). In a carefully designed project involving two separate longitudinal studies, one of high school students and one of college students, Jessor and Jessor examined personality, perceived environment, and behavioral factors associated with the transition from virginity to nonvirginity. The data indicate a much higher incidence of nonvirginity among high school students (33 percent) and college students (84 percent) than had been found in earlier studies. Moreover, contrary to earlier research, the incidence of nonvirginity among females was equal to or higher than that among males. However, as the authors carefully indicate, the results are based on the questionnaire data of only 52 percent of the random sample selected. In addition, all subjects were from a homogeneous middle-class sample living in a college community. One important methodological consideration in comparing groups from one generation to the next is that the samples be drawn from similar populations and that the data be gathered in a similar fashion. For example, it may be easier to refuse to answer a questionnaire than questions in an interview in which the interviewer has a better chance to assure the subjects of confidentiality, to dispel their doubts, and so on. Moreover, it is conceivable that those not answering may represent a group who hold more conservative views about sexuality.

Aside from these methodological considerations which make it difficult to use Jessor and Jessor's data as evidence of a sexual revolution, the study's main thrust reveals important differences between virgins and nonvirgins, especially at the high school level. The nonvirgins, especially females, show a greater proneness to transition than do the virgins. They value independence more and affection (females) less, and show a more positive attitude toward deviance. In keeping with that attitude, their behavior tends to be less conforming, as measured by such items as marijuana smoking, political activism, and problem drinking. The authors' prediction that these differences could be detected before the transition to nonvirginity was supported by their data. In addition, the authors predicted that these differences between virgins and nonvirgins would be greater in high school students "since the applicability of problem behavior theory to adolescent development should be greater at relatively earlier developmental stages" (Jessor and Jessor, 1975, p. 475). Again, their hypothesis was confirmed, pointing to the importance of distinguishing among levels of development within the adolescent period. The early, middle, and later adolescent stages are marked by some quite different behaviors and by some behaviors which appear similar but have different antecedents, correlates, and meanings.

Sex role identification and stereotyping

One aspect of adolescent sexuality which sometimes gets ignored, since it doesn't deal with sexual behavior directly, is the area of sex role identification and stereotyping. The first term, *identification*, refers to the way a boy or girl perceives him or herself as a sexual being, that is, as male or female. It is usually measured with a projective technique, such as the Thematic Apperception Test, which requires the respondent to tell a story about an ambiguous picture. In the process, the respondent is assumed to identify with the main character in the story and with the sex assigned to the character. After several such stories, it is apparent if the person's sex identification is appropriate, that is, consonant with one's own biological sex. One might be concerned that with the changing roles of males and especially females in our society, the role models may become sexually ambiguous and lead to less appropriate sex identification. There is no evidence to support such concern, however. Pasquali and Callegari (1978) assessed the sex-role identification of 104 female adolescents in Brazil. Half of the girls had mothers who worked outside of the home, while half did not. Both groups of mothers responded to a measure of job satisfaction. The researchers found that there was no difference between the sex identification of those youngsters whose mothers worked at home versus outside. There was, however, a significant difference between the daughters of satisfied and dissatisfied women, the satisfied women having daughters with enhanced sex identification.

Sex-role stereotyping refers to the expectancy that certain behaviors and traits are appropriate only for women and others only for men. Using an objective check list, Urberg (1979) found that both males and females stereotype. Their subjects were 7th and 12th graders and two groups of adults, one young (25 to 40) and one older (50 to 65). The greatest stereotyping occurred among the 12th graders. In addition, there were sex differences in the stereotyping. When asked to provide *self* descriptions, there was almost no difference between the males and females. When asked, however, to describe the *ideal* female, "The 7th- and 12th-grade males and females differed on submission, dependence, and hetero-sexuality, with males seeing the female ideal as higher on these variables than did females" (Urberg, 1979, p. 91). Furthermore, the 12th grade females saw the ideal male as higher on affiliation, personal effectiveness, and heterosexuality than did the male respondents. In each case the students perceived the opposite-sex ideal in more stereotypic terms than the same-sex ideal.

Boys and girls differ also in their expectancies for success and failure. Frieze (1975) found that boys expect to do better than girls at a whole variety of tasks and attribute their success to ability and their failures to luck or lack of effort. Girls, however, are less apt to attribute their own success (e.g., academic) to ability but rather to external factors.

Crandall (1978) found that such differences in expectancy don't start in adolescence but are evident even in preschool, where both boys and girls expect boys to do better. Furthermore, Crandall found that those girls who stereotype most (i.e., believe that traits, such as competence, independence, and competitiveness, belong only to men, while gentleness and sensitivity are true only of women), have the lowest achievement expectancies for intellectual skills.

Sexual attitudes of adolescents

Since one's views about the prevalence of a sexual revolution or renaissance will depend upon whether one is talking about attitudes or behavior, it is important to make a distinction between these two aspects of sexuality. By sexuality we usually mean a good deal more than simply a sex act. Sexuality is intimately bound up with a culture's moral and religious beliefs, its legal system, and its child-rearing practices, as well as with the attitudes that people have toward one another and, ultimately, toward themselves.

It is not surprising, therefore, that there are wide variations in the sexual attitudes and practices of various cultural groups. In their book *Patterns of Sexual Behavior*, Ford and Beach (1951) cite examples of sexually restrictive societies (they include the United States in this group), sexually semirestrictive societies, and sexually permissive societies. In the restrictive group are the Ashanti of Africa, who forbid their children from a very young age to masturbate, as well as the Kwona of New Guinea, who constantly warn their children not to play with their genitals. In fact, Ford and Beach state that "if a [Kwona] woman sees a boy with an erection she will beat his penis with a stick, and boys soon learn to refrain from touching their genitals even while urinating" (p. 180). Ford and Beach point out that in such restrictive societies the adults not only prohibit sexual activities among the children, but also do their best to keep the children from acquiring sexual knowledge. The children are kept ignorant of sexual matters and are kept from accidentally observing sexual behavior. Although such attitudes among the adults may prevent the children from practicing sexual behavior in front of their elders, it is doubtful whether they are entirely effective in preventing children's sexual behavior in private. Ford and Beach note that there is evidence of sexual behavior among the young in these restrictive cultures despite the sanctions against such behavior. They contend that the resulting conflict between attitudes and behaviors generates a good deal of guilt in the youngsters involved. They cite the Manus as an example, noting that Manu children masturbate only in private and with a sense of guilt.

At the other extreme, Ford and Beach describe societies which are characterized by permissiveness with respect to sexual expression in childhood. In such societies, children are allowed to engage in a certain amount of sex play even in public. Thus, the fingering of their own genitals or the genitals of others of both the same and the opposite sex is quite permissible among, for example, the Kazak, the Alorese, and the Pukapukans of Polynesia. In the Trobriand Islands children also engage in a variety of other sexual behaviors, including simulated coitus. Generally, in societies where children are allowed freedom of sexual expression, they are also allowed to observe adult sexual behavior and have access to sexual information. Just as restrictive societies have reasons for their sanctions against early sexual expression, strong beliefs also underlie the sexual attitudes of more permissive societies. For example, the Chewa of Africa believe that children's indulgence in early sexual behavior is important for the later begetting of offspring. The Lepcha of India believe that sexual intercourse among girls is an aid to their maturation. By the time children reach adolescence among the Lepcha, sexual life has already begun. Most Lepcha boys and girls engage regularly in intercourse by the time they are 11 or 12 years old. The Ila-speaking people of Africa regard childhood "as a time of preparation for adult life and mature sexual functions" (Ford & Beach, 1951, p. 191). Thus, at harvest time boys and girls are allowed to play house at one of the homes in the area, and there they often engage in sexual intercourse. Ford and Beach report that by the age of 10, most children have engaged in this practice.

Ford and Beach see American society as sexually restrictive. They state: "The social code pertaining to sexual behavior of children and unmarried adolescents in the United States is clearly a restrictive one." (p. 185) That is, sexual behavior is sanctioned only within the legalized confines of marriage. Thus, much pressure frequently exists, and in the United States (as well as in other countries) a so-called double standard often characterizes premarital sexual mores.

Although it may be true that, compared to the Alorese or the Pukapukans, the United States is a restrictive society with respect to its attitudes toward childhood and adolescent sexual practices, it is also true that these attitudes have changed dramatically in the last 50 to 60 years. If the sexual revolution means anything, it means that sexual attitudes have become far less restrictive and that the double standard has become far less prevalent.

A major work by Reiss (1960), *Premarital Sexual Standards in America,* argues that the major changes in sexual customs in the United States took place in the "iconoclastic environment of the 1920's." Reiss contends that the people born between 1900 and 1910 are the ones who really revolutionized our sexual customs. He uses data from Kinsey's studies which support this conclusion for both petting to orgasm and premarital intercourse.

In a later book which Reiss edited, *The Sexual Renaissance in America,* he states that "there is a widespread belief that much has changed in terms of premarital sexual behavior in the last 20 to 25 years. However, the evidence from all available major studies is in strong agreement that although *attitudes* have changed considerably during this period, many areas of sexual *behavior,* such as premarital coital rates, have not" (Reiss, 1966, pp. 125–126). In support, Reiss cites the work of Ehrmann, Freeman, and Kinsey. Reiss believes that a revolution in behavior took place during the 1920s which has since been followed by gradual changes and a consolidation of attitudes. These changes provide an interesting example of the principle of cognitive dissonance; that is, when individuals have changed important behavior, such as premarital sexual behavior, then their attitudes also change to conform to their actual behavior. In this way the dissonance generated by a discrepancy between beliefs and behavior is reduced. As Reiss points out, although it is generally thought that behavior follows attitudes, here attitudes have changed as a function of changed behavior.

A more recent study dealing with teenagers' attitudes toward sexuality has been reported by Offer (1972). Between the years 1962 and 1970 Offer interviewed 1,500 middle-class teenagers who were either 13 to 14 years old or 16 to 18 years old. As part of a broader longitudinal study dealing with development in adolescents, Offer was concerned with sexual attitudes. He used a self-image questionnaire which consisted of 11 scales, including a sexual attitude scale. Among the 10 items on the scale were such things as "Having a girl (boy) friend is important to me," "Sexual experiences give me pleasure," and "Sexually I am way behind." For all but two of the items, Offer found that there were significant differences between the young and the old teenagers. "The younger teenager thinks that the opposite sex finds him a bore, finds it harder to know how to handle sex, thinks that dirty jokes are not so much fun, does not attend sexy shows, finds sex more frightening, believes it is important to have a girlfriend, and claims that he does not think often about sex" (pp. 83–84).

Although Offer found that there were significant differences between younger and older teenagers, he found little evidence of change in sexual attitudes over the years studied, that is, between 1962 and 1970. The differences in the attitudes of the younger adolescents as compared to the older adolescents are themselves interesting and suggest that older teenagers experience less inhibition and show a greater willingness to admit the pleasure that they derive from sex. The lack of evidence of attitudinal change between 1962 and 1970 may simply indicate that by the 1960s the sexual attitudes which began to change in the 1920s had consolidated on the sorts of items that Offer used to measure attitudes.

One difficulty with studies of this sort is that the items they use are necessarily limited and may not be representative of the wide variety of attitudes which might be expressed about sexuality. For example, attitudes toward premarital sex may become quite liberal, whereas attitudes toward telling dirty jokes in public may not become liberal. It is impossible to assume a general liberalization of sexual attitudes. One has to look at attitudes toward specific events or behaviors. Additional problems with studies like Offer's are, of course, the availablity of subjects, the openness and frankness of subjects in dealing with what some still consider a delicate matter, and the motivations behind the answers that the subjects give. For example, Offer mentions that in a 1968 study by Simon et al. it was shown that among a group of college students who were asked about their current love affairs, 25 percent of the females and 35 percent of the males responded that they were sexually more active than they wanted to be. Such data could be interpreted to mean that the attitudes of these students are actually more conservative than their behaviors. The data could also indicate a certain amount of guilt for the behaviors which college students have engaged in. And finally, in studies of this sort there is always the possibility of the social desirability response set; that is, respondents may be influenced to answer in the way in which they think the examiner would like them to respond.

Not only do some college students report that they are more active sexually than they want to be, but on the average their expectations of their peers' norms are more permissive than is their own behavior (Collins, 1974). Both male and female students in an Australian university assumed that the typical sexual behavior of their peers was less restricted than their own. The question remains whether behavior, under such circumstances, changes over time in the direction of the expected norm (see Table 3–1).

Sexual standards in America

Reiss (1960) postulates that there are essentially four standards of premarital sexuality in the United States:

1. *Abstinence*—Premarital intercourse is wrong for both men and women, regardless of circumstances.
2. *Permissiveness with affection*—Premarital intercourse is right for both men and women under certain conditions when a stable relationship with engagement, love, or strong affection is present.
3. *Permissiveness without affection*—Premarital intercourse is right for both men and women regardless of the amount of affection or stability present, providing there is physical attraction.
4. *Double standard*—Premarital intercourse is acceptable for men, but it is wrong and unacceptable for women. (pp. 83–84)

TABLE 3–1
Number and percentage of respondents indicating their behavior and peer expectations by intimacy level, sex, and courtship stages

| | Behavior | | | | Peer expectations | | | |
| | Males | | Females | | Males | | Females | |
Level of intimacy	Number	Percent	Number	Percent	Number	Percent	Number	Percent
On first date:								
Kissing	79	71.8	155	74.9	91	82.7	176	85.0
Necking	58	52.7	82	39.6	56	50.9	104	50.2
Light petting	43	39.1	48	23.2	32	29.1	54	26.1
Heavy petting	22	20.0	13	6.3	4	3.6	10	4.8
Petting to orgasm	10	9.1	7	3.4	1	0.9	2	1.0
Intercourse	11	10.0	4	1.9	2	1.8	1	0.5
After several dates:								
Kissing	98	89.1	181	87.4	104	94.5	189	91.3
Necking	89	80.9	145	70.0	103	93.6	184	88.9
Light petting	79	71.8	114	55.1	94	85.5	177	85.5
Heavy petting	46	41.8	57	27.5	62	56.4	106	51.2
Petting to orgasm	28	25.5	22	10.6	39	35.5	48	23.2
Intercourse	18	16.4	17	8.2	27	24.5	30	14.5
When going steady:								
Kissing	100	90.9	187	90.3	105	95.5	194	93.7
Necking	96	87.3	180	87.0	105	95.5	194	93.7
Light petting	92	83.6	174	84.1	104	94.5	194	93.7
Heavy petting	71	64.5	144	69.0	99	90.0	183	88.4
Petting to orgasm	58	52.7	102	49.3	93	84.5	153	73.9
Intercourse	47	42.7	58	28.0	84	76.4	126	66.0
When marriage is considered:								
Kissing	100	90.9	188	90.8	105	95.5	200	96.6
Necking	96	87.3	182	87.9	105	95.5	200	96.6
Light petting	92	83.6	176	85.0	104	94.5	200	96.6
Heavy petting	72	65.4	151	72.9	103	93.6	197	95.2
Petting to orgasm	60	54.5	114	55.0	100	90.9	189	91.3
Intercourse	49	44.5	71	34.3	100	90.9	172	83.1

Source: J. K. Collins, Adolescent dating intimacy: Norms and peer expectations. *Journal of Youth and Adolescence*, 1974, 3, 317–328. With permission of Plenum Publishing Corp.

It is not our purpose to say which of these standards is the "correct" one since such a decision would obviously depend on the complex value system of the individual making it. However, it is possible, as Reiss has demonstrated, to examine the historical antecedents of these differing social standards and their social consequences.

The notion of a double standard is seen in a variety·of human activities, not just sexual behavior. Differential salary scales and a variety of social customs, educational opportunities, and even roles within religious groups, all attest to the fact that a person's sex has had a decided effect on his or her status in the community. Reiss traces the double standard in sexual behavior to ancient cultures in which inheritance laws ruled in favor of the male heirs. The paradoxical thing about the double standard is that if unmarried women are expected to remain virginal and married women are expected to remain faithful, it would be difficult for unmarried men not to be virginal (at least, heterosexually). The resolution of this dilemma has generally been the designation of a class of unmarried women (prostitutes) whose role is to satisfy male desires while all other unmarried women are expected to maintain virginity. An example of this distinction between "nice girls" and "lays" is given by Whyte (1943) in his description of adolescent sexuality in the slum district of "Eastern City."

Some of the social consequences of the double standard are almost too obvious to belabor: the perpetuation of a notion of male dominance, the casting of women into stereotypic roles with moralistic connotations, the placing of sexual behavior on a bartering basis, and the separation of sexual behavior from affection. Although the double standard is an ancient position, it is gradually giving way to other standards in both sexual behavior and interpersonal relations in general.

The standard of permissiveness without affection, like the double standard, separates sexual behavior from emotional involvement. This standard has never enjoyed widespread acceptance, probably because the idea that both men and women have equal drives and should have equal access to sexual enjoyment without regard to the consequences has violated our stricter religious traditions.

The permissiveness with affection standard differs from the above in placing importance on the more mature and relatively stable emotional attachment which both partners are expected to be enjoying. It also attaches importance to the balance of consequences to both partners. Such things as potential conception, the possibility of contracting veneral disease, the possible guilt feelings of one partner, and so on, would naturally be taken into consideration by those for whom affection for the partner is a prerequisite to sexual intercourse.

Perhaps the standard that gets the most formal support from our cuture is the standard of abstinence. Adolescents following this standard hold that sexual behavior is too serious, too sacred, or too intimate to be exercised outside marriage and are willing to wait until then for sexual expression which includes intercourse. Within this group are various subgroups of individuals who accept or reject kissing and/or petting with and without affection. Thus, although the group of youngsters who believe in abstinence agree on the importance of waiting until marriage to have intercourse, they differ in terms of their practice of a variety of other behaviors, some of which may make abstinence from intercourse decidedly more difficult.

Although each of these standards varies as a function of social and educational class, it is possible to discern changes in their general acceptance and, as Reiss does, to predict future trends. Reiss contends that among unmarried adolescents the permissiveness standards, especially permissiveness with affection, are gaining in acceptance while the other standards are declining. Surely the recent revolution for equality between the sexes has made the ancient double standard less tolerable for many. The same would often apply to permissiveness without affection, where the "without affection" was a male attitude. The abstinence standard appears to be losing adherents as the fear of pregnancy has been reduced through readily obtainable contraceptives, a reduction in guilt feelings in a more permissive society, reduced fear of veneral disease, and so on.

Given these standards as guides, it may be useful to examine the data that are available on the actual incidence of sexual behavior among adolescents.

Sexual behavior in adolescence

A study by Kinsey, Pomeroy, and Martin (1953) was one of the early comprehensive studies on the difficult topic of sexual behavior. The Kinsey study was based on the case histories of 5,940 white females.[2] The study found that the number of individuals reporting premarital coitus differed as a function of sex, religiosity, socioeconomic status, and age. In general, the following data taken from Kinsey, Pomeroy, and Martin (1953, p. 330) summarize the active incidence of premarital intercourse as reported to the Kinsey group:

Age	Female	Male
Adolescence–15	3%	40%
16–20	20	71
21–25	35	68

In a recent study examining the coital experiences of college students, Simon, Berger, and Gagnon (1972) obtained much the same results that Kinsey had obtained two decades earlier. The study documented rates of premarital coitus. The data were collected from a sample of college students in 1967 and a sample of 14- to 18-year-olds in 1972. The results indicated a slight increase in the incidence of premarital intercourse but not nearly as dramatic a rise as Kinsey had reported took place at the turn of the century. Table 3–2, taken from Simon, Berger, and Gagnon, shows the data for each of the four years in college. The first coital experience of a large number of the respondents took place during their college years. Although in this study the level of social class did not bear a significant relation to the likelihood of experiencing premarital intercourse, it was found that when frequency of attendance at religious services and degree of intimacy with parents were considered, respondents who were high on both measures were significantly less likely to be sexually experienced by age 18 than were respondents who were low on both measures.

TABLE 3–2
Gender, year in school, and sexual status and age at initial coital experience

Years in college	Sexual status (percent nonvirgin)		Age at first intercourse (percent 17 or less)	
	Male	Female	Male	Female
Freshman	36% (151)	19% (138)	22% (151)	9% (138)
Sophomore	63 (145)	30 (151)	28 (145)	7 (151)
Junior	60 (150)	37 (147)	23 (150)	5 (147)
Senior	68 (147)	44 (148)	29 (147)	7 (148)
Total	56 (593)	32 (584)	25 (593)	7 (584)

Source: W. Simon, A. S. Berger, and J. H. Gagnon, "Beyond anxiety and fantasy: The coital experience of college youth." *Journal of Youth and Adolescence*, 1972, *1*, pp. 208–217. With permission of the author and Plenum Publishing Corp.

[2] Kinsey and his colleagues had done an earlier similar study (Kinsey, Pomeroy, & Martin, 1948) on the sexual behavior of the human male to which these data on females can be compared.

Not surprisingly, the authors also found a relationship between early coital experience and frequency of dating. The males and females who dated most frequently were six times as likely to have coital experience as the less frequent daters.

The authors report an interesting sex difference in the meaning of the relationship for those who are experiencing intercourse. In describing their initial coital experiences, 60 percent of the females reported that they were in love and planning to marry the person with whom they first had intercourse, whereas only 14 percent of the males reported this. These differences in the assumed degree of intimacy are given in Table 3–3.

TABLE 3–3
Gender, age at first coitus, and relationship to first coital partner (percentage distribution)

Gender	Age at first inter- course	Relationship with initial partner						
		Pickup or casual date	Dated often, no emotional attachment	Emotional attachment, not love	In love, no mar- riage plans	Plan to marry	Prosti- tute	N
Male	10–17	34%	17%	23%	12%	9%	4%	150
	18	18	13	27	17	17	8	89
	19	26	15	21	23	15	0	53
	20	15	17	23	26	18	3	34
	21	—	—	—	—	—	—	6
	Total	26	16	23	17	14	4	332
	χ^2 significance level=0.264							
Female	10–17	1%	0%	22%	20%	50%		40
	18	1	2	17	23	56		57
	19	7	2	2	31	58		45
	20	0	0	17	17	65		29
	21	0	0	13	0	87		15
	Total	4	1	14	22	59		186
	χ^2 significance level=0.015							

Source: W. Simon, A. S. Berger, and J. H. Gagnon, "Beyond anxiety and fantasy: The coital experiences of college youth." *Journal of Youth and Adolescence*, 1972, *1*, pp. 208–217. With permission of the author and Plenum Publishing Corp.

The argument has often been made that nontraditional sexual behavior is the result of frustration caused by an inability to have sexual relations via a more approved route. The incidence of deviant sexuality in penal institutions (Sykes, 1958) and in places where normal heterosexuality is denied for other reasons (Cohen, 1961) has tended to bolster the view that individuals resort to such behavior out of frustration arising from lack of access to more normal avenues of sexual expression. This position has not been supported, however, with respect to sexual aggression (Kanin, 1967). In fact, Kanin demonstrated that among college students the sexually aggressive males (that is, those who admitted to having used physical force in an attempt to gain coital entry) were significantly more active sexually than their nonaggressive counterparts. One might argue that the groups differed only in the techniques of coercion used. Perhaps the nonaggressive were weaker males and used less physically threatening maneuvers, such as attempting to get the girl intoxicated, falsely promising marriage, falsely professing love, or threatening to terminate the relationship. Not so! The researcher found that these techniques were also reported significantly more often by the sexually aggressive males. In other words, the aggressive maneuver has nothing to do with sexual deprivation or the lack of other exploitative approaches. Quite the contrary. The sexually aggressive male is sexually more active and uses a greater variety of other techniques. This is not to say that sexually aggressive males are not frustrated. In fact, Kanin found that they reported less satisfaction in their sexual activity. They were doing it more but enjoying it less. In short, Kanin found some support for the notion that sexually aggressive males report more dissatisfaction but no support for the idea that their frustration is based on deprivation.

Noncoital sexual behavior

Adolescents' sexual experiences include a variety of behaviors other than intercourse. Tables 3–4 and 3–5 report cross-national data on the reported inci-

TABLE 3–4
Sexual behaviors experienced by an international sample of males

Type of sexual behavior	United States	Canada	England	Germany	Norway
Light embracing or fond holding of hands	98.6%	98.9%	93.5%	93.8%	93.7%
Casual goodnight kissing	96.7	97.7	93.5	78.6	86.1
Deep kissing	96.0	97.7	91.9	91.1	96.2
Horizontal embrace with some petting but not undressed	89.9	92.0	85.4	68.8	93.6
Petting of woman's breast area from outside her clothing	89.9	93.2	87.0	80.4	83.5
Petting of woman's breast area without clothes intervening	83.4	92.0	82.8	69.6	83.5
Petting below the waist of the woman under her clothing	81.1	85.2	84.6	70.5	83.5
Petting below the waist of both man and woman, under clothing	62.9	64.8	68.3	52.7	55.1
Nude embrace	65.6	69.3	70.5	50.0	69.6
Coitus	58.2	56.8	74.8	54.5	66.7
One-night affair involving coitus; didn't date woman again	29.9	21.6	43.1	17.0	32.9
Whipping or spanking before petting or other intimacy	8.2	5.7	17.1	.9	5.1
Sex on pay-as-you-go basis	4.2	4.5	13.8	9.8	2.5
(N)	(644)	(88)	(123)	(112)	(79)

Source: E. Luckey and G. A. Nass, "A comparison of sexual attitudes and behavior in an international sample," *Journal of Marriage and the Family*, 1969, 31, 364–379. Copyright 1969 by National Council on Family Relations. Reprinted by permission.

TABLE 3–5
Sexual behaviors experienced by an international sample of females

Type of sexual behavior	United States	Canada	England	Germany	Norway
Light embracing or fond holding of hands	97.5%	96.5%	91.9%	94.8%	89.3%
Casual goodnight kissing	96.8	91.8	93.0	74.0	75.0
Deep kissing	96.5	91.8	93.0	90.6	89.3
Horizontal embrace with some petting but not undressed	83.3	81.2	79.1	77.1	75.0
Petting of woman's breast area from outside her clothing	78.3	78.8	82.6	76.0	64.3
Petting of woman's breast area without clothes intervening	67.8	64.7	70.9	66.7	58.9
Petting below the waist of the woman under her clothes	61.2	64.7	70.9	63.5	53.6
Petting below the waist of both man and woman, under clothing	57.8	50.6	61.6	56.3	42.9
Nude embrace	49.6	47.6	64.0	62.1	51.8
Coitus	43.2	35.3	62.8	59.4	53.6
One-night affair involving coitus; didn't date man again	7.2	5.9	33.7	4.2	12.5
Whipping or spanking before petting or other intimacy	4.2	5.9	17.4	1.0	7.1
(N)	(688)	(85)	(86)	(56)	(56)

Source: E. Luckey and G. A. Nass, "A comparison of sexual attitudes and behavior in an international sample," *Journal of Marriage and the Family*, 1969, *31*, 364–379. Copyright 1969 by National Council on Family Relations. Reprinted by permission.

dence of some of these behaviors for males and females. In comparing these data to the Kinsey data reported earlier, note that besides the increase in frequency (of coitus, for example) there is a smaller discrepancy between male and female data, suggesting a change from the traditional "double standard."

The data in Tables 3–4 and 3–5 are in keeping with more recent data on 411 American adolescents compiled by Sorenson (1973). In a major survey of a national sample, Sorenson found that by age 15 over 50 percent of his subjects had experienced extensive petting. It is important to remember, however, that Sorenson's data reflect cumulative incidence (that is, whether the subject had ever experienced the behavior up until that age).

Masturbation

Autoerotic stimulation provides a sexual outlet for many adolescents. While Kinsey's interview data revealed that almost all the males in his sample (92 percent), as well as over 30 percent of his female sample, had experienced masturbation by age 20, Sorenson's questionnaire data on the same topic suggest a much lower incidence for boys (58 percent) and roughly the same frequency (39 percent) which Kinsey (and many others) had found among girls. The reason for the discrepancy between the Kinsey and Sorenson data for males is not clear. Both involved national samples, selected according to appropriate demographic guidelines. Much of Kinsey's data was retrospective, while all of Sorenson's was current, and parents had to agree to allow their teenagers to participate in Sorenson's study. However, it is not immediately clear that such a restriction would bias his sample in terms of responses to such questions. Sorenson's own interpretation is that his subjects were not being completely candid on this issue. He feels that there is no area which his respondents considered more private or about which they felt more guilty. Surely a long tradition in both religion and medicine had reinforced such feelings. More than 20 years earlier Kinsey could find no grounds for concern over the physical or psychological effects of masturbation except the guilt, disgust, and loss of self-esteem generated by a view of masturbation as unnatural or sinful. Although some counselors today might caution against the narcissistic and compulsive aspects of frequent masturbation, most would also view it as a rather normal component of adolescent development.

Some social consequences of sexual behavior among adolescents

Unmarried parenthood   A large percentage of those between the ages of 13 and 19 who are having intercourse fail to take adequate contraceptive precaution (Sorenson, 1973). Twenty five percent of Sorenson's male subjects responded "Always" to the statement "I just trust to luck that the girl won't become pregnant." Thirteen percent of the male sample reported that they had indeed gotten a girl pregnant, while 23 percent of the females reported that they had been pregnant. Of the total sample, 30 percent of the boys and 18 percent of the girls reported that if the girl were to become pregnant they would prefer an abortion. Twenty four percent of the boys and 38 percent of the girls favored getting married, while 30 percent of the boys and 36 percent of the girls favored having the baby without getting married. In that event, a majority of the girls reported that they would bring up the child without help from the father, while a majority of the boys said that they would prefer to help the mother. Other options included adoption, letting their parents decide, and so on.

The availability of contraceptive information and techniques, though essential, is not sufficient to insure a meaningful reduction in the frequency of unwanted pregnancies. A majority of the females interviewed on one university campus (Koenig & Falkenstein, 1972) were in favor of having the university health center distribute birth control pills to any students who requested them. When the question was expanded to include "the pill and/or other devices," over 79 percent were in favor of making these available to anyone on campus. These data are not surprising. What is surprising is the number of single adolescents whose sexual behavior leads to an unintended pregnancy despite their knowledge of available birth control techniques.

With abortions more easily available, information can now be gathered from patients about their motivation for pregnancy, their information about birth control, and so on. From such data Cobliner (1974) found that most pregnant adolescents seeking abortion never intended to become pregnant. The small percentage intending to become pregnant did so mainly in anticipation of a hoped-for marriage. Cobliner also found that of those who had hoped to avoid pregnancy almost all had some understanding of birth control, although fewer than half of them had specific information about any one technique, and only 10 percent made any attempt to use some contraceptive.

In an effort to understand the lack of planning in the risk-taking group, Cobliner provides an important insight into their cognitive functioning. Although most previous work had dealt with motivational variables involved in teenage pregnancies, Cobliner uses the cognitive concepts of Jean Piaget to explain a potentially important difference in thinking between those who take risks and those who anticipate the possibility of conception. He argues that those who do not plan are using figurative thinking, which requires sensory input for comprehension of a situation. Those who anticipate are thinking on an operative level which allows them, by constructing potential models of action, to anticipate contingencies and to plan for possible future outcomes. As we shall see in Chapter 4, this sort of thinking characterizes those who have attained the level of logic more typical of later adolescence and adulthood. If this cognitive theoretical explanation holds true, one would expect to find important differences between younger and older adolescents in their psychological antecedents to illegitimate pregnancy. Recent interview data on a small group of pregnant women aged 15 to 26 (Hatcher, 1973) tend to support this conclusion.

Cobliner found that social factors were also associated with unintended teenage pregnancies. For example, few of the girls who do not intend to get pregnant share a close emotional intimacy with their sex partner. On the other hand, there is no suggestion of widespread promiscuity among them. Generally, their interviews reveal a lack of companionship at home or school and an attempt to fill the void of loneliness.

Regardless of the maturational level of the unwed mother, the problem of illegitimacy is real. It is estimated that in 1969 there were 310,000 unwed mothers in the United States, of whom 135,000 were under 20 years of age (Pannor, Massarik, & Evans, 1971). The options open to the teenage unmarried parent are few and cruel: placing the child up for adoption, entering into a precipitate marriage, or trying to bring up the child as a single parent. Nor do the choices open to the pregnant girl before the birth of her child look any less grim. To the above list could be added abortion which, though legal, many still consider an undesirable if not unethical alternative.

Educational implications: The need for sex education   One thing is clear from these data, namely, the need for more and better training of the young with respect to their own sexuality. It is a truism to say that if one waits until a youngster is in high school, it is already too late. An obvious indicator of this need is the rise in illegitimate births. Table 3–6 compares the figures for 1938 with those for 1957 and 1963.

TABLE 3–6
Number, ratio, and rate of illegitimate births in 1938, 1957, and 1963, by age of mother*

Year		Number of illegitimate births					
	Under 15	15–19	20–24	25–29	30–34	35–39	40 and over
1938	2,000	40,400	26,400	10,000	5,000	3,100	1,000
1957	4,600	76,400	60,500	29,800	18,000	9,400	2,800
1963	5,400	101,800	82,600	35,400	19,300	10,900	3,500
Change from:							
1938 to 1957	+130%	+39%	+129%	+298%	+260%	+204%	+180%
1957 to 1963	+ 13%	+33%	+ 37%	+ 19%	+ 10%	+ 16%	+ 25%
Illegitimacy ratio (illicit births per 1,000 live births):							
1933	608.5	135.5	36.6	16.4	13.2	15.3	14.2
1957	660.9	138.9	44.4	26.1	24.9	25.7	20.1
1963	711.9	173.6	56.8	34.6	32.4	33.8	37.3
Change from:							
1938 to 1957	+9%	+ 3%	+21%	+59%	+89%	+68%	+200%
1957 to 1963	+8%	+25%	+28%	+33%	+36%	+32%	+ 28%
Rate of illegitimacy (illicit births per 1,000 unmarried females):							
1938	0.3	7.5	9.2	6.8	4.8	3.4	1.1
1957	0.6	15.6	36.5	37.6	26.1	12.7	3.3
1963	0.6	15.3	39.9	49.4	33.7	16.1	4.3
Change from:							
1938 to 1957	+100%	+108%	+297%	+453%	+444%	+274%	+200%
1957 to 1963	0	− 2%	+ 9%	+ 31%	+ 29%	+ 27%	+ 30%

* Adapted from the following sources: J. Schacter and M. McCarthy, "Illegitimate births: United States, 1938–1957," *Vital Statistics—Special Reports, Selected Studies*, vol. 47, no. 8 (Washington, D.C.: U.S. Government Printing Office, 1960): and *Vital Statistics of the United States, 1963*, tables 1–26, 1–27, 1–28, and 1–29 of vol. 1: *Natality* (Washington, D.C.: U.S. Department of Health, Education, and Welfare, 1964).

Source: C. E. Vincent, "Teenage unwed mothers in American society," In I. L. Reiss (Ed.), "The sexual renaissance in America," *Journal of Social Issues*, 1966 22(2), whole issue, p. 26. By permission of the author and the Society for the Psychological Study of Social Issues.

The case for sex education is made very well by Vincent and McCary in a collection of papers on sexuality (Grummon & Barclay, 1971). The thrust of Vincent's argument is that youngsters, inundated with sexual stimuli, are in strong need of techniques to deal with this material and the feelings it generates. It is unlikely that the media, designers, and so on will be pressured to block out all sexual references from the view of children and teenagers. Barring that unlikely event, we do an injustice to the high percentage of youngsters in need of education to deal with such stimuli if we do not provide early, effective information in a manner which encourages these youngsters to receive it.

While 7 out of 10 never-married U.S. women between the ages of 15 and 19 report they have had some course in sex education, (Zelnik, 1979), only a third of those who claim they have had such a course can correctly identify the time of the month when they are most likely to conceive. These findings, based on 1976 data from the National Survey of Young Women, suggest the need for the teaching of specific practical information. For example, of those who said they had had a sex education course, over 90 percent reported that it included information about venereal disease, and yet only 73 percent said it included contraceptive information. These figures represent 64 and 51 percent of the *total* number of respondents, however, since many didn't have such a course.

As communicators of information about sex, parents are not a main source. After reviewing the data from 15 studies dealing with sources of sex information, Fox (1979) concluded that parents play a rather minor role in this aspect of education. In only one study, for example, did parents emerge as the predominant source as reported by the adolescents. Girls most often cite their mother as the parent who provides information, while boys occasionally cite their father (his role in this regard appears to be almost nonexistent).

Only three studies have been found (Fox, 1979) to deal with the way in which sexual information is communicated in the mother-daughter relationship. Generally the results indicate limited information. Bloch (1972), for example, found that in a sample of 124 mothers of seventh grade girls in California 50 percent had not mentioned the father's role in reproduction and 68 percent had not discussed contraception.

Although parents are not the main source of verbal information about sexual matters, they are surely important as role models. Kallen (1980) mentions that sexually active adolescents spend less time with their parents. Chilman (1978) cites a number of studies which report that premarital intercourse is higher among those adolescents who are unhappy at home or perceive themselves to be in poor communication with their parents. Unfortunately, fewer studies deal with the motivation behind premarital intercourse. It would appear from these results that a need for affection and communication should be examined. While one cannot infer the direction of causality from correlational studies (e.g., maybe parent-child communication breaks down because the child indulges in proscribed behavior), future research will undoubtedly examine this issue.

SUMMARY AND CONCLUSIONS

The importance of sexuality in human development was most strongly stated in the theory of Sigmund Freud. Although Freud's notion of libido does not refer exclusively to genital sexuality, he and his psychoanalytic followers have done the most to move this area out of Victorian prudery and into the light of scientific research. For Freud, psychosexual development included the oral, anal, phallic, and genital stages, the last two being separated by the important latency years, the period of middle childhood.

Since Freud's day a revolution in sexual behavior and attitudes has occurred, with many observers indicating that the behavioral changes occurred before the more recent changes in sexual attitudes. Recent evidence suggests that among adolescents the transition from virginity to nonvirginity is accompanied, and can be predicted by, a host of personality and attitudinal variables.

It has been argued that, compared to other cultures, American society has had a restricted view of sexuality and that older adolescents have much more liberal views on sexuality than do younger adolescents.

We have been careful throughout this chapter to indicate some of the important precautions that must be taken in conducting research in this important but sensitive area. Comparability of the samples used, comparability of methods, and adequacy of the items used to measure sexual attitudes are among the principles most commonly violated. Moreover, we believe it important to specify not only the population but also the specific age group for which one's data can be considered valid. Early, middle, and late adolescents have different sets of expectations, attitudes, and behaviors regarding sexuality.

Data presented in this chapter demonstrate that the existence and frequency of premarital sexual intercourse vary as a function of social and psychological variables, including socioeconomic status, religiosity, tolerance of deviance, age, values for independence, and affection. Aggressive sexuality has been found to be related to dissatisfaction but not to a lack of sexual outlets. Masturbation is seen as a normal component of adolescent development without deleterious consequences aside from those contingent on one's view of this activity as debasing, sinful, or abnormal.

One important social consequence of premarital sexual behavior is the increase in unwanted pregnancies. Adolescents are often not educationally prepared for the consequences of their sexual activity, and even when knowledge and contraceptives are available, many "trust to luck." Data presented here support the argument that those who fail to anticipate the consequences of intercourse are functioning on the cognitive level of figurative thinking, whereas those who plan ahead are operative thinkers. Sex education for adolescents should take such cognitive differences into account. The need for such sex education is clear and pressing.

SUGGESTED ADDITIONAL READING

Grummon, D. L. & Barclay, A. M. *Sexuality: A search for perspective.* New York: Van Nostrand Reinhold, 1971.

Sorenson, R. C. *Adolescent sexuality in contemporary America.* New York: World Publishing, 1973.

Vincent, C. E. Teenage unwed mothers in American society. *Journal of Social Issues,* 1966, *22,* 22–23.

BOX 4–1
Study questions

What are the basic concepts in Piaget's theory of cognitive development?

To what biological phenomena does Piaget compare the growth of intelligence?

To what extent do adolescents rely on formal reasoning?

What are some personality correlates of the development of formal operational logic?

What dimensions of cognitive style correlate with the use of formal reasoning?

What sex differences in cognitive and verbal skills emerge during adolescence?

Name the two aspects of Elkind's egocentrism. Give examples of both.

The idealism often seen in adolescents is based on an ability to perform at which stage of Piagetian development?

In what important ways might teachers' and parents' awareness of the distinction between creativity and intelligence benefit adolescents?

CHAPTER 4

THE DEVELOPMENT OF COGNITION IN ADOLESCENTS

The term *cognition* refers to the psychology of thinking or knowing. This chapter, then, will deal with the ways in which adolescents have come to know the world about them. It will deal both with the ways in which adolescents learn to perceive and construe their environment and with the ways in which they act upon their environment. As we shall see, cognition has to do with both of these processes.

A COGNITIVE THEORY OF DEVELOPMENT

As the student is by now aware, the man who is considered to be the main developmental theorist of cognition is the Swiss psychologist Jean Piaget.[1] Since Piaget's developmental theory has been outlined at some length in an earlier volume of this series, we will review briefly the terms of his theory and then go on to detail his position with respect to adolescent thinking.

Piaget the theorist

Piaget, who was born in 1896, was for a number of years the director of studies of the Institut Jean Jacques Rousseau in Geneva. Although his training had been in the biological sciences, he soon became interested in the philosophical and psychological issues of epistemology—the philosophy of knowing. Piaget's psychological methods are quite different from the usual experimental and statistical procedures employed by American psychologists. Rather, by

---

[1] While this edition was being written, Jean Piaget died on September 16, 1980.

Jean Piaget

Courtesy of the World Health Organization

careful observation of a relatively small number of individual children, Piaget attempts to understand the development of the processes of thinking.

Basic concepts of Piaget's theory

Not surprisingly, the main concepts in Piaget's cognitive theory come from biology. It is important to remember, however, that he is not interested in a physiological interpretation of behavior, but that he uses biological concepts to explain human reasoning. (In much the same way, Lewin adapted terms from physics and chemistry to the phenomenological theory of personality known as *field theory*—that term itself coming from physics.) For example, Piaget (1963) refers to intellectual functioning as adaptation, an analogy to the evolutionary development of biological structures and functions that enable organisms to adapt to their environment. One might ask what structure in the behavioral realm is analogous to the biological structure that enables an organism to adapt. Piaget's term for the analogous structure is *schema*, which he considers the most basic element in the psychology of thinking (Piaget, 1967). In its most primitive form, a schema would be a simple reflex, for example, the sucking reflex, the grasping reflex, or any other such stereotypic and stimulus-specific response. More often, however, and in actual practice, a schema is far more complicated and elaborate. The sucking reflex quickly becomes elaborated into a whole alimentary response, including orienting, opening the mouth, sucking, swallowing food, digestion, and so forth. In addition, the basic schema may be extended to include not only sucking at the breast, but also sucking on toys, dolls, silverware, and so on.

In the foregoing example of biological adaptation, that is, digestion, two complementary processes are involved. One is accommodation, and the other is assimilation. First, the child needs to accommodate its own mouthing and sucking behaviors to the size and shape of the object with which it is presented. In other words, the child accommodates its own behavior to the environmental situation. The complementary process of assimilation, however, is equally important to the total adaptation process. That is, the child transforms the material with which it is presented and incorporates that material into structures that are already present. A similar process is involved in behavioral assimilation. For example, just as the child can assimilate food, it may, having learned a new word, assimilate that word into its vocabulary and use the word in a variety of ways.

Stages of cognitive development

The stages of cognitive development, according to Piaget, are stages of increasing internalization of action. Although the schemata that we have described so far have had to do with specific behaviors, the same concept is employed by Piaget to refer to the mental representation of behaviors. For Piaget, the process of internalization is at the root of cognitive growth. This has already been seen, for example, in the development of object constancy in the infant, in the learning of language to represent objects, and in the acquiring of concrete operations. In concrete operations, it is necessary for the child to be able to represent one dimension of the environment and to hold that dimension constant while mentally varying some other dimension of the environment.

In each of these stages of cognitive growth, some invariant principles have been observed. One of the most important of these is Piaget's notion of decentration. By the term *decentration,* Piaget refers to the child's ability to abstract from the concrete objective characteristics of a situation and to deal with those characteristics in terms of their mental representations. This was seen, for example, during middle childhood, when the development of concrete operations was observed. The child was able to master the conservation of volume or of weight, for example, by decentering. That is, the child was capable of mentally holding one dimension constant while another dimension varied. In addition, the child could take into account the reversibility of these mental operations.

There are four main stages in Piaget's theory of cognitive development. First, there is the sensorimotor stage, which lasts from birth to about age two (Piaget, 1954). This is the period of infancy during which the child is acquiring skills and adapting to the environment in a direct behavioral way. In the sensorimotor stage, unlike the preoperational stage which follows it, these adaptations are usually not accompanied by mental representations of the environment. The preoperational stage, which lasts from age two to age seven, is the stage during which the child develops a language but is not yet able to perform the concrete operations which, as we have already seen, define the third major stage. The fourth major stage of development, and the one we are most interested in here, is the stage of formal operational logic. It is during this stage that the individual learns to formulate hypotheses, becomes capable of deductive reasoning, and can engage in causal thinking and provide scientific explanations for events.

Concrete versus formal operational logic

A principal way in which the logic of the adolescent in the formal operational stage differs from that of the previous stage of concrete operations, is that the adolescent pays attention to the *form* as well as the content of an argument, an experiment, a syllogism, or a proposition. The reasoning of the preadolescent is still determined by the specific content of a given argument or problem, whereas the adolescent can deal with its structural aspects. The adolescent, in other words, can reason about his or her own reasoning. This implies a new subject-object separation.

The decentering involved in this procedure is a gradual development which has gone on since infancy. Whereas the infant exhibited little differentiation of subject from object (for example, of its own sucking movements from the sight of the bottle), the preoperational child was able to symbolize the bottle with a verbal label and could imagine it even in its physical absence. The child could not, however, attend to two dimensions of the same object simultaneously, such that one might vary while the other remained constant. This sort of decentering is characteristic of children in the stage of concrete operations. Because children in the concrete-operational stage can recognize that operations are reversible and that changing the shape of a form does not necessarily change its mass, they can master, for example, problems involving the conservation of matter. In the stage of formal operations, adolescents can decenter still further and can deduce laws from operations which need not be concrete. For example, they can imagine logical extensions of the data with which they are presented.

An example of this development is given by Inhelder and Piaget (1958). They cite an experiment involving Archimedes' law of floating bodies. The experiment consists of giving the subject a variety of objects and several containers of water. The subject is then asked to classify the objects in terms of whether or not they float. After having made this classification, the subject is asked to arrive at a law which would explain the classification. The preoperational child, who cannot conserve weight while shape changes, cannot deal with this problem except on a magical or inconsistent basis. The concrete-operational child generally uses weight as the basis of classification and may continue to be disturbed by what appear to be inconsistencies in reasoning when this explanation is invoked. When faced with these inconsistencies, the child may come up with a two-way classification of the objects, namely, those which are big and light versus those which are big and heavy as contrasted with those which are small and light versus those which are small and heavy.

The adolescent possessing formal operations, however, answers the problem by extension of all the possibilities not just the examples before him. In addition, he can manipulate logically the dimensions of interest here, that is weight and volume, thus arriving at a notion of density. This relationship of relationships is the new observation of the formal operational adolescent which gives him the power to form hypotheses and to test them. Moreover, the adolescent may then spontaneously test his hypotheses with several additional objects, whereas the concrete-operational child seldom sees the need for such a "proof."

This demonstration points up a second quality in the logical thinking of adolescents, namely, their consideration of the unreal as well as the real. Formal operational logic allows adolescents to consider what will not work as well as what will work, that is, to hypothesize in an "I wonder what would happen if . . ." way. In other words not only is possibility now an extension of reality, but "it is *reality* that is now secondary to *possibility*" (Conger, 1973, p. 159).

An excellent example of this ability of adolescents to propose and test hypotheses is given in a study by Elkind (1966). Elkind presented a group of children (8 to 9 years old) and a group of adolescents (13 to 14 years old) with the following task. Each subject was given pairs of cards on which were drawn familiar objects, namely, tools and vehicles. One of the objects in each pair had wheels, whereas the other object did not. The instructions were to choose between the two cards. When the subject chose the "correct" card, a light went on. Only about 50 percent of the children in the younger age group were able to make the correct choice. Moreover, those children who made the correct choice arrived at it only after having been given many or all of the 72 pairs. The adolescents, on the other hand, were all able to solve the problem, and many were doing so by the 10th presentation.

Elkind notes the difference in thinking between the adolescents and the younger children by citing the reasons given by the adolescents for the choices they made. The adolescent subjects would typically form hypotheses, such as "Maybe it's transportation." After testing these guesses on several trials, these subjects were willing to modify their hypotheses. In other words, they would test their hypotheses against the reality of whether or not the light would go on and would change their hypotheses in the face of negative data. On the other hand, once the younger children had formed a hypothesis they tended to stick with it. In the face of negative data they were unwilling to alter their original guesses. On occasion they would even distort the reality of the pair presented to them rather than change a hypothesis. For the younger children, hypothesis and reality were less distinguishable from each other than was the case for the adolescents, who were readily able to change their prediction in the face of new data.

Age of onset of formal operational logic

The change from concrete-operational logic to formal operational logic differs from the earlier logical transitions in one important way: in contrast with the earlier transitions, there is little consistency in the age at which formal logic begins. Indeed, it seems that some adults never do acquire formal operational logic. It is important to remember that formal operations can refer both to a stage of reasoning (that is, a developmental stage) and to a style of reasoning. As a reasoning style, formal operations refer to an optimum approach. On any specific occasion, a particular adolescent may or may not have recourse to formal logic. Such things as the amount of that adolescent's previous experience with a given problem, the sort of problem with which the adolescent is being confronted, his or her state of alertness or fatigue, and his or her general intellectual capabilities would be important variables in determining whether or not the adolescent would use formal logic.

For example, Keating (1975) demonstrated with a group of fifth and seventh graders that the brightest children, on standard psychometric tests, were also the ones who used formal operations most frequently on a set of Piagetian tasks. Earlier work (e.g., DeVries, 1973, 1974) had suggested that there were two sorts of intelligence, one defined psychometrically and the other represented by Piaget's cognitive stages. Keating, however, argues that "brightness psychometrically defined implies cognitive developmental precocity within the stage theory of Piaget" (1975, p. 276). In another study, again after finding ability differences correlating with the acquisition of formal operational reasoning, Keating and Schaefer (1975) concluded: "It seems more plausible that the Piagetian tasks tap a smaller range or subset of the domain of abstract reasoning that could be and has been assessed in many ways" (p. 532).

Stages in the development of formal operations

Some aspects of formal thinking are acquired before others. Roberge (1976) discovered significant differences according to grade level but no correlation between scores on tasks presumed to measure two components of formal operations: combinatorial thinking and conditional reasoning. Lawson (1977), on the other hand, found high correlations between three tasks used to assess formal reasoning. The difference between these results may lie in a difference between the experimenters' methods of selecting subjects. Roberge's subjects (fifth-, sixth-, seventh-, and eighth-graders) were probably intellectually more homogeneous. He describes them as ". . . above average (IQ > 110) . . ." Lawson's subjects (seventh graders), "ranged widely in mathematical ability," and so could be presumed to vary widely on Piagetian tasks. Controlling for grade level differences, Roberge's subjects may not have been different enough from one another for correlations among tasks to show up. One needs to be careful, also, not to assume that nonsignificant correlations *demonstrate,* or prove, no relationship. They merely do not provide evidence that there is a relationship.

It would appear, however, that the acquisition of formal thought is not an all-or-none affair but occurs in stages. Moshman (1977) demonstrated that the formal reasoning entailed in two examples of formal operational thought occurs in four phases. These phases, predicted as characteristic of cognitive development by Flavell and Wohlwill (1969), are based largely on the distinction between *competence* at a task (i.e., underlying ability) and *performance,* or the application of one's ability to a particular task. In the first phase of a new cognitive structure, there is no competence and no performance. In phase two, an incomplete competence allows for some performance depending on the task. By phase three competence is complete, but performance still depends to some extent on the nature of the task. By phase four both competence and performance are complete. While in this study and in later work Moshman (1979) has demonstrated the sequential manner in which formal logic develops, he observes that in one of his studies "formal operational performance was far from universal, even in college students" (p. 104). Similarly, when Martorano (1977) gave 10 Piaget tasks to 6th-, 8th-, 10th-, and 12th-grade females, "not even the oldest age group consistently evidenced formal operations performance across all tasks" (p. 666). It would appear, in other words, that not all adolescents rely on formal reasoning, and probably no adolescent relies on it completely. But remember that we are talking here about performance. While this observation may appear to be contradicted by some research (e.g., Danner & Day, 1977) which shows that nearly all adolescents can use formal operations on some tasks, keep in mind the nature of the task as well as the mode of presentation. In the Danner and Day (1977) study, for example, in which "nearly all of the adolescents however, performed at a formal operational level without prompts on the third task" (p. 1600), subjects were given prompts on the first two tasks and, in effect, "taught" how to use formal operations. While they might not have used formal operations initially, they were able to use them once prompted. To use Moshman's (1977) terms, it would seem that these adolescents might be at phase two or three of their development of formal reasoning—that is, with some level of formal competence even though they don't use that competence in their performance.

"After prompts on two tasks, 85 percent of the 13-year-olds and 95 percent of the 17-year-olds used the formal operational strategy of systematically separating and testing variables on a third task" (Danner & Day, 1977, p. 1604). These data, the authors argue, provide evidence that most adolescents, even young adolescents, have a sort of "latent" ability to do formal reasoning, which can be elicited if proper attempts are made.

Similarly, Stone and Day (1978) found different *levels of availability* of formal strategies among students aged 9, 11, and 13 years. By administering the same task twice in succession with intervention, they were able to classify the subjects into three groups: Nonformal (didn't use formal reasoning on either presentation), "latent" (used formal reasoning on the second, but not the first presentation), and "spontaneous" (used formal operations on both presentations).

The important thing here is that there is a vast difference between one's developmental cognitive ability and the likelihood of one's performing at that level. Perhaps many persons are capable of formal thinking who typically resort to concrete logic. A similar conclusion was reached by Kuhn, Ho, and Adams (1979), who compared a group of preadolescents with a group of first-year college students in an effort at understanding in what ways young adults could be said to lack formal reasoning ability. The college students were nonformal on initial screening, as were the preadolescents. However on reassessment, after having a weekly opportunity over a three-month period to encounter problems requiring formal reasoning, the college students demonstrated formal logical ability immediately, while the preadolescents made only slow and modest improvement. The researchers suggest cautiously that perhaps "the absence of a formal operational level of performance on the part of many older adolescents or adults may, to a large extent, reflect cognitive processing difficulties in dealing with the problem formats, rather than absence of underlying reasoning competencies." (Kuhn, Ho & Adams, 1979, p. 1128).

Cognitive correlates of the transition to formal logic

It has been demonstrated that the onset and use of formal operational reasoning correlates with other logical abilities. For example, Palmquist (1979) found that among eighth graders, there is an important relationship between level of "objective" cognitive ability, and one measure of "social" cognition. Palmquist studied impression formation in these youngsters. We know from earlier research that people differ in the tenacity of their first impressions of other people. Some people stick with those early impressions despite evidence to the contrary. This is called the "primacy effect," that is, emphasizing the importance of the first information one gets. Palmquist figured that people who functioned at a concrete operational level would be more susceptible to this primacy phenomenon than those at a formal level. It makes sense. Nonformal thinkers are reality oriented. They take the information they receive as factual. Additional confirming information makes the possibility of any future disconfirmation very unlikely. Formal thinkers, on the contrary, are concerned with the possible, not just concrete reality. They would be less likely to form rigid first impressions which are resistant to change. The results of Palmquist's study supported her hypothesis. Nonformal thinkers maintained their early evaluations in the face of contradictory evidence more than formal thinkers did. The same reasoning abilities involved in objective cognition seem to apply to social cognition.

Another variable that correlates with the use of formal reasoning is cognitive style. Two important dimensions of cognitive style are reflective versus impulsive and field dependent versus field independent. The first dimension refers to the fact that on a simple perceptual task some individuals rush through (and maybe get half the answers wrong), while others take their time and get them all right (but maybe only get half done within the time limit). The first style is called impulsive; the latter reflective. Neimark (1975) has found that reflectivity is associated with more advanced cognitive development. She has also found that cognitively more advanced subjects are more likely to be field independent. This dimension refers to an ability to respond distinctively to the various components of the visual field without fusing them into a global whole. A good example of the difference between field-dependent and field-independent persons can be seen in their performance on the embedded-figures test. When a diagram of a common object is hidden in a pattern of criss-crossing lines and other figures, the field-independent person is more able to isolate the important figure from its irrelevant background. The field-dependent person cannot as easily separate the figure from its confusing field. It was this ability, as well as reflectivity, which Neimark found formal thinkers to possess to a greater extent than nonformal thinkers. In other research (Linn, 1978), it has been suggested that field independence interacts with some aspects of formal reasoning and not others. Particularly, it appears that field-dependent individuals are less likely to be able to apply formal logic in an experimental context in which some of the necessary information is withheld. In such a situation, the individual must be able to indicate the hypothetical circumstances under which different results can be expected. Linn argues that cognitive style interacts with "task context" rather than with formal reasoning overall.

Other researchers (Cloutier & Goldschmid, 1976) have found that formal reasoning is related to such other cognitive variables as intelligence, quickness of response, systematic logical reasoning, and ability to generate original ideas. The issue of relationship between formal thinking and creativity needs further examination. In at least one study (Ross, 1976), children were found to improve in formal reasoning ability from the 6th to the 10th grade but to decrease in their capacity for creativity. What other variables are involved remains unexplored.

Sex differences in cognitive development

Sex differences in cognitive development begin to emerge during adolescence (Maccoby & Jacklin, 1974; Petersen & Wittig, 1979). Not surprisingly, boys do better on tests of mathematics and spatial ability, and girls get better scores on tests of verbal ability. Why this is so isn't clear, however. Some have suggested that females' lower scores in math may result from the fact that they choose fewer math courses in high school than boys do (Sherman & Fennema, 1977; Petersen & Wittig, 1979). This doesn't seem to be the whole answer, however. Maccoby and Jacklin (1974), reviewing the research in this area, observed that when high school seniors' math scores were analyzed with previous math courses equated, boys still did better than the girls. Boys who do well in math also do better in science and express a higher interest in science. It may be that girls tend to write these areas off as "male" topics and downplay their own ability in these areas. We know from a study of much younger children (Montemayor, 1974) that when a task is perceived as sex-inappropriate, children express less interest in the task and do less well, all other things held constant.

Most studies examining sex differences in verbal ability have demonstrated a superiority for females, but the differences cited in the early studies among very young children are open to question. By 10 or 11, however, girls clearly begin to demonstrate superior language skills. Maccoby and Jacklin (1974) are careful to note that these differences don't refer simply to spelling or punctuation, but "included as well are considerably higher-level skills, such as comprehension of complex written text, quick understanding of complex logical relations expressed in verbal terms, and in some instances verbal creativity of the sort measured by Guilford's tests of divergent thinking" (p. 84).

The reasons for sex differences in cognitive development aren't completely clear. An excellent brief review of endocrine, genetic, neurological, and social influences is contained in a chapter by Petersen and Wittig (1979). Their conclusion is that each of these factors undoubtedly interact with the others, in ways as yet unknown, to produce sex differences in cognition.

An interesting line of study has led one researcher (Waber, 1976, 1977) to speculate on the possibility that these sex differences in cognition are related to differences in the organization of male and female brains. Waber noticed that females mature earlier than males and that they also do better at verbal tasks, especially beginning around puberty. Maybe there is a connection, she thought. Indeed, regardless of sex, she found that early maturers are better at verbal abilities than they are at spatial skills, and vice versa for late maturers. So maybe the sex difference in cognition is really a maturation rate difference. It was the spatial scores that really made the difference with late maturers doing significantly better than early maturers. There did not seem to be any difference on verbal scores. Furthermore, late maturers were found to have more lateralized brains on a dichotic listening test. That is, for late maturers, the side of the brain which processes auditory material has a greater superiority over the opposite side of the brain. All of this led Waber to conclude: first, sex differences in cognitive ability are related to a continuum (e.g., maturation rate) rather than a single category (male versus female); secondly, the sex differences in verbal ability and spatial ability may have very different causes, since the sex difference in spatial ability (but not verbal) is related to maturation rate; finally, it is possible that maturation rate "may play an important role in the organization of higher cortical functions" (Waber, 1976, p. 574).

An excellent review of the sex-related differences in spatial ability is contained in a chapter by Harris (1980), who questions Waber's early (1976) explanation of sex differences in spatial skills. A basic assumption of that rationale, as Harris saw it, was that puberty somehow slowed down or stopped the lateralization process (just as it is responsible for the ossification of the bones and thus the ending of the growth process). Thus, late maturers have a longer time for lateralization to occur, and therefore, they become more lateralized. Harris observes that in a later formulation, Waber (1979) takes into account studies which indicate that lateralization doesn't increase with age as was previously thought. Although the increase-of-lateralization-with-age hypothesis may be inadequate, Waber has pointed to important physiological correlates of sex difference in cognition.

Some personality correlates of the transition to formal logic

Although Piaget's theory deals primarily with cognitive development, it has been noted by some authors that underlying personality changes accompany the changes in cognitive structure. Elkind (1967), for example, has drawn attention to the "egocentrism" that accompanies each of the transitions from one logical stage to the next. Egocentrism refers to an inability to differentiate between subject and object. It takes a somewhat different form at each transition stage. During the sensorimotor stage, for example, the child does not differentiate between his or her own behavior and the existence of external objects. The child will stop looking for a hidden object, for example, when he can no longer see it. Later in the sensorimotor stage, the child might look for an object where he last dropped it even though he may have seen a subsequent displacement of the object.

Still later, during the preoperational stage, egocentrism takes a somewhat different form. Since the major task of that stage is the development of a language, the child expresses egocentrism in his or her speech. He may identify a word so completely with the object for which it stands in his mind that no object can seem to have more than one name. Some have observed that at this stage the child is confused by nicknames and does not like to be called by a name other than the one with which he is most familiar. It is difficult for a child at this stage to take the point of view of another or to decenter and take more than one point of view at a time. For example, the child cannot simultaneously consider both height and weight in judging the amount of water in a beaker. Thus, the task of conservation of volume when the shape of the container is changed, is an impossible task for him.

The egocentrism of the concrete-operational stage takes on yet a different form. Although the child is capable of conservation of volume at this stage, he assumes that the operations which he perceives are analogous to the mental operations necessary for the understanding of conservation.

During adolescence, as pointed out above, the individual can deal with his or her own mental operations as objects of consideration. He can consider not only the perceptions of others but also his own logical operations. Thus, he can think about himself in a way that others might think of him, that is, consider himself as an object of others' perceptions and thoughts. The egocentrism of adolescence, then, as Elkind describes it, amounts to the adolescent's belief that he or she is somehow uniquely the focus of others' concern, which extends to behavior as well as to appearance.

Two aspects of this egocentrism cited by Elkind are the adolescent's concerns about an *imaginary audience* and the *personal fable*. By imaginary audience, Elkind is referring to the fact that during this period the youngster may consider that he or she is being watched by others and is somehow the center of their attention. The self-consciousness of the pubescent child, which many observers have noted, is undoubtedly related to this type of egocentrism. The increased conformity demonstrated in a study by Costanzo and Shaw (1966) is also undoubtedly a function of this egocentrism. Thus, a youngster who is very aware of the reactions of others to his or her behavior may conform in an attempt to assure that those reactions will be positive. Recall that Costanzo and Shaw demonstrated that the developmental peak of conformity occurs in the 11- to 13-year-old group, or at about the time when formal operations are beginning.

It should also be obvious that the physical changes which adolescents are undergoing at this time would make them more aware of their own development and would preoccupy them to some extent. They thus become objects of their own consideration. Since the changes are uniquely their own, that is, they do not occur simultaneously with the changes in their friends, these changes may also make them appear somewhat different. This differentiation or individuation of self from others is synonymous with objectification. The awareness of separateness must now be overcome in a new way. The separateness from its mother which the infant felt after weaning was overcome by the development of language and the onset of a new stage of logical thinking once it was able to walk. The separateness which occurs in puberty is overcome by the development of yet another logical stage. One element of this separateness stems, of course, from the increased differentiation between the sexes at puberty.

The self-consciousness of the adolescent which accompanies this separateness of puberty and the adolescent's related concern about an imaginary audience may lead to both self-criticism and self-praise. Thus, at one time the young adolescent may appear to be highly narcissistic, at another time extremely self-abasing. Although these behavioral manifestations may seem to be antithetical, it appears that they both have a similar cognitive basis.

A second personality correlate of the egocentrism which occurs at the formal operational stage is the experience of the *personal fable*. Elkind uses this term to refer to the adolescent's notion that his or her own feelings and experiences are unique. It seems impossible to the adolescent that an adult might know what he is experiencing or how he feels. What looks like defiance or negativism in an early adolescent may often be the result of such an adherence to a personal fable. A refusal to obey legitimate school authorities, for example, or failing to turn in assignments on time may result from the feeling that one's own situation is unique. Although the adolescent may recognize that others may be punished for such infractions, he may also maintain the belief that the laws do not apply in his unique case.

The effect of an imaginary audience is exemplified by the tendency of many adolescents to fantasize about what might occur if they were to engage in some daring or unusual activity. One of us, for example, recently had the experience of treating a disturbed young adolescent whose first love was fast cars and motorcycles. He worked in a garage and looked forward to the day when he would have his own motorcycle. In the meantime he occasionally used his father's trailbike, but he spoke to his therapist about it as through it were a racing cycle. He talked about such daring exploits as going off high bumps, over ravines, and so on. Finally, one afternoon, he mumbled almost inaudibly, "I wish somebody would watch me race my bicycle."

Other personality correlates of the change to formal operations

One consequence of the egocentrism which occurs during this period is the sometimes unrealistic idealism of the early adolescent. Piaget states that "the adolescent not only tries to adapt his ego to this social environment but, just as emphatically, tries to adjust the environment to his ego" (Inhelder and Piaget, 1958, p. 343). Thus the adolescent may be highly interested in political, religious, or educational reform and may develop ideas of a rather egocentric nature as solutions to problems in these areas.

The adolescent's heightened sensitivity to political reform is documented by Adelson and O'Neil (1966). Basically, these authors have studied the growing sense of community during adolescence. By interviewing 120 youngsters between the 5th and the 12th grades, they found that the child moves from a markedly personalized view of the political order to a more highly socialized view. The early adolescent view of government stresses its negative coercive qualities, whereas the more mature later adolescent view includes its more positive administrative functions. The view of the younger child stresses immediate needs and concerns of a political nature, whereas the later adolescent view includes a more extensive time perspective and a greater future orientation.

In sum, it is clear that the idealism of youth, which has been cited by literary observers (Michener, 1973) as well as by social scientists (Keniston, 1968), is based on an ability related to formal operational logic. The involvement of adolescents in revolutionary movements, their interest in alternative life-styles, and their religious conversions can occur because adolescents are capable of imagining what might be and of contrasting it with what is. This ability to speculate and to consider alternatives simultaneously is as characteristic of the "Jesus freak" as of the modern political activist.

THE DEVELOPMENT OF INTELLIGENCE

Quantitative changes

In the foregoing section we have dealt primarily with the qualitative changes which occur with the development of the formal operational stage of thought. In this section we shall deal briefly with the more quantitative aspects of adolescent intellectual functioning.

Although the measurement and the theory of intelligence were described in some detail in the two earlier volumes of this series, it may be helpful to briefly review some of that material here. Intelligence has been one of the most difficult concepts for psychologists to define, and yet it has been the psychological construct which the public has been quickest to adopt as a tool, as a method of classification, and as a diagnostic device. The definitions of intelligence range widely and depend on the assumptions that one makes about ability. Intelligence, then, refers to ability in its most general sense. In defining intelligence, learning theorists (Thorndike, 1903) have traditionally emphasized that what one learns in one situation can be transferred to another situation. The notion of a general factor of intelligence has come rather from psychometrically oriented psychologists who have noted the correlation among a variety of specific abilities.

There has also been a difference of opinion among psychologists as to whether intelligence is primarily an innate ability (Galton, 1870; Woodworth, 1910; Garrett, 1961) or an environmentally influenced construct (Liverant, 1960; Hunt, 1961). Still others have defined intelligence in terms of the measuring instrument (Spiker & McCandless, 1954). The inability of psychologists and educators to reach agreement on the best methods of measuring intelligence is undoubtedly the result of the many widely differing definitions of the construct (Wesman, 1968). Nevertheless, scientists have continued to explore both the theory and the measurement of intelligence. One of their main concerns in recent years has been the relative importance of heredity and environment. The age-old nature-nurture issue is not dead. These continued attempts to redefine and find better measures of intelligence suggest the central importance which both teachers and psychologists have attached to this fundamental construct of human behavior. If anything, we have expected too much of the construct of intelligence (McKinney, 1962). Too often, we have assumed that intelligence is an entity, or at least a unitary construct, that can account for a tremendous variety of behaviors and have tended to overlook the many dimensions which are involved in competent behavior.

Heredity and environment

There have been a number of other criticisms of intelligence and its measurement. One major difficulty is that many of the criticisms have been expressed in an either-or fashion. This has been particularly true of the controversy around the nature-nurture issue. One exception is Anastasi's (1958) excellent paper. Although somewhat older than many current versions of this controversy, Anastasi's paper deserves our attention since it emphasizes as most fundamental the interaction between heredity and environment rather than considering these two components of intelligence in an either-or fashion. In other words, Anastasi acknowledges that a child's mental capacity will be determined by both hereditary endowment and environment. However, she then argues that the important scientific question is not *how much* variance in intelligence is attributable to heredity or to environment but rather how the two interact and how their interaction is related to intellectual behavior.

Anastasi has correctly observed that the nature-nurture issue with respect to intelligence has been clouded by the fact that investigators have typically asked the wrong questions. They have asked whether ability is determined *either* by heredity *or* by environment, or they have asked the equally unanswerable question, "How much is ability determined by heredity?" The assumption of such a question is, of course, that some constant amount of variance in ability is attributable to heredity. It should be obvious, however, that when environmental experiences vary greatly the variability in behavior which can be attributed to genetic differences will be less than when the differences in environmental experiences are slight. A simple example may help to demonstrate this point. Let us say that we are interested in studying the effect of heredity and environment on broad jumping among high school boys. We might find a group of high school boys who have all had exactly the same experimental treatment, for example, no physical education classes, no gym, no playfields, and no toys. They have always lived in highly similar environments. If such a group of boys were tested in high school for broad jumping ability, the differences among them would undoubtedly reflect differences in genetic makeup, hereditary constitutional differences. If, on the other hand, a similar group of students had been given a wide variety of experiences, some being raised in an environment rich with gym equipment and training, others being raised in an athletically impoverished environment, and still others being raised in an athletically neutral environment, we would expect that by adolescence the differences in their broad jumping ability would be more related to environment than was true for the first group of subjects. In one study we would have demonstrated that broad-jumping ability is primarily a function of heredity, and in the second study we would have demonstrated that broad-jumping ability is influenced by environmental experiences. But which study is correct? The difficulty here is not with the research but with the way in which the question is formulated. Anastasi argues that instead of asking to what extent intelligence or ability is innate, the more appropriate question is, "How do heredity and environment interact in the production of meaningful behavior?" Other research (Scarr-Salapatek, 1971) supports this interactionist view.

Other difficulties have plagued the construct of intelligence. Many of these were summarized in a paper by Liverant (1960) in which he proposed that the construct of intelligence was in need of a careful reexamination: "The importance of the concept of intelligence in understanding and predicting human behavior appears so obvious that the value of this term in a science of behavior has seldom been questioned by psychologists. . . . By leaving open the possibility that the concept may be unnecessary, and even an obstacle in explaining behavior, perhaps we can arrive at a better solution to the problems now subsumed under the rubric of intelligence" (p. 101). This same point has been made in a number of ways. Some psychologists have argued that whatever actually exists should be measurable. However, the converse is not necessarily true. That is, it does not necessarily follow that because we can measure something, it therefore exists as an entity. The notion that intelligence is a separate entity has been with psychological thinking far too long.

Ability and achievement

Another dichotomous assertion about intelligence has been the distinction between ability and achievement. *Ability* is the term generally used in referring to capacity for future learning, that is, to some potential. *Achievement* is the term that has been used primarily to designate past accomplishments. Implicit in this distinction is the idea that ability is innate and somehow dependent primarily upon physiological structures, whereas achievement is based on environmental factors and has more to do with socioeconomic status, experience,

FIGURE 4–1   Achievement can take many forms.

Photograph courtesy of J. P. McKinney

education, and so on. In at least one neuropsychological theory (Hebb, 1949), however, attention is paid to developmental changes in the central nervous system which occur as the result of environmental experience. It would seem that such psychological theorizing should go a long way in helping us to overcome the senselessness of a physiological-environmental dichotomy in understanding intelligence.

The development of intelligence during adolescence

It is fairly apparent from a number of studies that the growth of intelligence is not an even and uninterrupted phenomenon. There are periods of rapid growth, periods of slower growth, and periods of decline. In general, the curve of mental growth and decline is given in Figure 4–2. It can be seen that intellectual growth is greatest during early childhood, tapers off somewhat in late adolescence, and then actually declines into old age. Figure 4–2 is based on data obtained with the Wechsler-Bellevue Intelligence Scale. Similar results were obtained by Jones and Conrad (1933), who administered the Army Alpha Intelligence Test to 1,191 persons between the ages of 10 and 59. It is important to remember, however, that these curves represent total IQ scores and that the subtests on which these scores are based do not all show uniform growth or uniform decline into maturity and old age. Second, the overall decline of intelligence is related to the educational level of the subjects. The longer an individual continues in school, the less likely he or she is to show early decline in intellectual functioning,

FIGURE 4 – 2   Curve of mental growth and decline—Bellevue Full Scale: Ages 7–65.

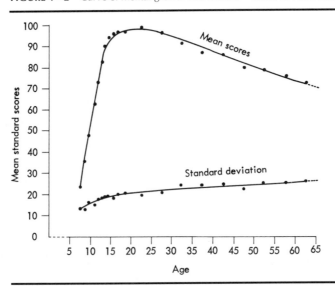

Source: Adapted from D. Wechsler, "The measurement and appraisal of adult intelligence," 4th ed. (Baltimore: Williams & Wilkins, 1958), p. 31. Copyright 1958 by David Wechsler. Used by permission of the author and Williams and Wilkins.

specifically in those areas which are related to his or her education. Teachers, for example, show very little decline in verbal skills, such as vocabulary (Burns, 1966).

The age differentiation hypothesis

It has been mentioned that intelligence can be regarded as a general ability which is basically the correlation between a number of more specific abilities. One question which has intrigued investigators of the development of intelligence is whether the specific abilities become more differentiated or more integrated with age. It has been shown in a number of studies that the correlation among the specific abilities decreases with age. That is, there is an increasing differentiation among the abilities as a function of development.

One way of examining this hypothesis is through the statistical procedure known as factor analysis. The factor analytic technique allows the investigator to examine the relationship among a set of correlations so that he or she can logically reduce a large number of variables to a smaller number of meaningful factors. One of the first persons to use the factor analytic technique in the study of human ability was the British psychologist Spearman (1904). Essentially, Spearman advanced a two-factor theory which stated that intelligence was composed, first, of a general factor, that is, an innate ability not specific to any task but general to all tasks, and second, of a set of specific factors, that is, one factor for each ability.

Later, in the 1930s, Thurstone, an American psychologist, proposed a multiple factor theory (Thurstone, 1938). Thurstone's group factors were considered to be more specific than Spearman's general factor and more general than his specific factors. They included such abilities as verbal comprehension, number skills, word fluency, perceptual flexibility and speed, inductive reasoning, rote memory, and deductive reasoning. Other factorial approaches have been described by Cattell (1961), who proposed two kinds of general intelligence, namely, fluid and crystallized intelligence. By fluid intelligence, Cattell means that group factor which is "a *general* relation-perceiving capacity." By crystallized intelligence, he means "a sum of *particular* relation-perceiving skills required in *specific* fields" (p. 743; italics added). A still more complex model of the structure of intellect has been provided by Guilford (1959), who proposes three basic and independent intellectual dimensions, namely, operations, content, and products. As can be seen in Figure 4–3, each of these can be further subdivided into categories, such that a three-dimensional solid with 120 components would result.

For the developmental psychologist, an important aspect of the factor analytic approach to the study of intelligence is that it allows him to examine the age differentiation hypothesis mentioned above. What this hypothesis suggests is that the structure of intellectual functioning changes with age, such that the young child possesses one general ability, as compared to the older child, the adolescent, and the adult, in whom the structure is more complex and in whom a network of specific abilities can be identified.

FIGURE 4–3 A cubic model representing the structure of intellect.

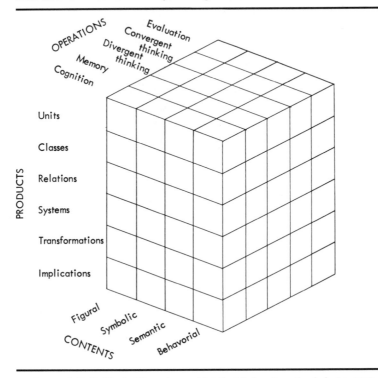

Source: J. P. Guilford, "Three faces of intellect," *American Psychologist*, 1959, *14*, 470. Copyright 1959 by the American Psychological Association. Reprinted by permission.

Although not all of the research has supported this hypothesis, some relatively recent data (Dye & Very, 1968) suggest that the hypothesis may, indeed, be an adequate representation of the nature of intellectual development. Dye and Very tested over 500 subjects from 9th-grade, 11th-grade, and university classes. They used a battery of 20 tests designed to assess numerical facility, perceptual speed, verbal ability, mathematics achievement, inductive reasoning, deductive reasoning, arithmetic reasoning, general reasoning, and estimative ability. Each of these nine factors was measured by one or more tests which were known from previous research to load on the given factor; that is, the specified tests for each factor were known to correlate highly with one another and thus to define the factor.

Like others before them, Dye and Very found that females tended to be superior in verbal and perceptual ability, whereas males tended to be superior in mathematical ability. They also found, however, that these differences tended to decrease with increasing age. In terms of their factor analytic results, Dye and Very found, as they had predicted, that the correlations among the tests resulted in a greater number of factors at the older age level, compared to the younger age levels. That is to say, there was greater differentiation in abilities among the college students than among the high school students. These data would support the age differentiation hypothesis of human ability. Table 4–1 summarizes the results of Dye and Very's study. Note, for example, that numerical facility in the 9th-grade group has been further differentiated into numerical facility and perceptual speed in the 11th-grade and college groups.

TABLE 4–1
Summary of comparative factorial structure*

9th grade		11th grade		College	
Males	*Females*	*Males*	*Females*	*Males*	*Females*
Numerical facility	Numerical facility	Numerical facility	Numerical facility	Numerical facility	Numerical facility
		Perceptual speed	Perceptual speed	Perceptual speed	Perceptual speed
Arithmetic reasoning	Arithmetic reasoning	Arithmetic reasoning	Arithmetic reasoning	Arithmetic reasoning	Arithmetic reasoning
		Inductive reasoning	Inductive reasoning	Inductive reasoning	Inductive reasoning
Symbolic-inductive reasoning		Symbolic-inductive reasoning		Symbolic-inductive reasoning	
Verbal reasoning	Verbal reasoning	Verbal reasoning	Verbal reasoning	Verbal ability	Verbal ability
Reasoning	Reasoning	Reasoning	Reasoning	General reasoning	Reasoning
Estimative ability		Estimative ability		Estimative ability	Estimative ability
"Deductive" reasoning			"Deductive" reasoning	"Deductive" reasoning	"Deductive" reasoning
				Mathematics achievement	

* Where a particular factor was found for some groups but not for others, a blank space has been left to make differences in factorial structure more evident.
    Source: N. W. Dye and P. S. Very, "Developmental changes in adolescent mental structure," *Genetic Psychology Monographs*, 1968, *78, 72*. By permission of the author and The Journal Press.

Another way to test the age differentiation hypothesis is via the differentiation of social cognitions. One can examine individuals' descriptions of other people for the content of those descriptions or for the conceptual categories which are used in arriving at the descriptions. A recent review of such research (Hill & Palmquist, 1974) concludes that the greatest increase in differentiation takes place in early childhood and that adolescent changes in this aspect of cognitive functioning are less impressive (Gates, 1923; Kohn & Fiedler, 1961; Peevers & Secord, 1973; Rosenbach, Crockett, & Wapner, 1973; Signell, 1966; Yarrow & Campbell, 1963).

The work of Peevers and Secord (1973) is an example of this sort of research. Peevers and Secord studied descriptions of people whom subjects of various ages liked and disliked. By interviewing subjects from kindergarten through college, they discovered interesting developmental changes in such "person perception." For one thing, they found that adolescents and young adults were far more differentiating in their descriptions than were the younger subjects. That is, adolescents and young adults, unlike the younger subjects, used terms which described others as unique. The age differentiation hypothesis is confirmed here, not by the number of concepts the subjects use or by the subcategories within those concepts, but by the descriptive terms themselves. Terms which give more information about a person as a unique individual (for example, "is an amateur astronomer" rather than "has blue eyes") reveal a greater cognitive differentiation in the perception of other persons.

Development of creativity during adolescence

Like intelligence, *creativity* has been a difficult term to define. Guilford (1967), for example, equates creativity with divergent thinking, which is one of the operations in his model of the structure of intellect. This he contrasts with convergent thinking, that is, the logical processes of induction and deduction. Getzels and Jackson (1963) view creativity as something quite distinct from intelligence as traditionally measured by IQ tests. They argue that the notion of intelligence has been required to carry too heavy a burden in dealing with all the cognitive constructs which have been traditionally assigned to it, creativity being one of these. They point out that the term *gifted child* has come to mean a child of very high IQ, whereas the term *creative child* has generally been used to refer to the artistically gifted child. They consider such a definition to be unduly restrictive because it precludes the recognition or measurement of creative attempts elsewhere than in the arts. Moreover, Getzels and Jackson question the assumption that giftedness has been valued equally by parents, teachers, and peers.

To examine whether there was a real difference in the dimensions of intelligence measured by IQ and creativity tests, Getzels and Jackson tested a large number of adolescents both on standard IQ tests and on some creativity measures. They then compared the high-IQ group with the high-creativity group on a number of variables. They defined their high-intelligence group as those same-sex subjects who were in the top 20 percent on the IQ measures but not in the top 20 percent on the creativity measures. The high-creativity group, by contrast, comprised those subjects who were in the top 20 percent on the creativity measures, compared to their same-sex peers, but not in the top 20 percent on the IQ measures. The authors found some interesting and striking differences between the two groups, as can be seen in Table 4–2.

The IQs of the high-creative group were similar to those of the general population. It is interesting that the high-creative group, like the high-IQ group, had significantly higher school achievement scores than did the general population. Both of the two experimental groups had almost the same school achievement scores, and both had almost the same need for achievement scores when tested on a projective technique. In other words, the differences in teachers' preferences for the two groups could not be related to differences in scholastic achievement. The researchers speculated that there must be some other dif-

TABLE 4–2

Means and standard deviations of highly creative and highly intelligent groups on experimental variables

		Total population* (N = 449)	High IQ (N = 28)	High creative† (N = 24)
IQ	X̄	132.00	150.00§	127.00
	s	15.07	6.64	10.58
School	X̄	49.91	55.00§	56.27§
achievement	s	7.36	5.95	7.90
Teacher-preference	X̄	10.23	11.20‡	10.54
ratings	s	3.64	1.56	1.95
Need for achievement	X̄	49.81	49.00	50.04
(T-scores)	s	9.49	7.97	8.39

*For purposes of comparison the scores of each experimental group were extracted from the total population before t-tests were computed.

† Two subjects omitted because of incomplete data.

‡ Significant at the .01 level.

§ Significant at the .001 level.

Source: J. W. Getzels and P. W. Jackson, "The highly intelligent and highly creative adolescent: A summary of some research findings," in C. W. Taylor and F. Barron (Eds.), *Scientific creativity: Its recognition and development* (New York: John Wiley & Sons, 1963), p. 165. By permission of the author and John Wiley & Sons, Inc.

ferences between the two groups which formed the basis for teachers' differential reactions to them. Such factors as differences in aspirations, values, and so forth might have been accountable. Indeed, on careful examination the researchers did find differences in the values of the two groups. The high-creative and high-intelligence groups perceived equally well the set of values required for adult success. The correlation between the two groups on this question was almost perfect. So too was the correlation between the groups on the question asking for their perception of their teachers' preferences or set of values. Where the two groups differed, however, was in what they considered ideal values for themselves. Although both groups perceived the same qualities as essential to success in adult life and perceived the same qualities as being favored by their teachers, they differed significantly in the qualities they perceived as being ideal for themselves. For the high-IQ group, as can be seen in Table 4–3, there was a high correlation between the qualities they perceived as ideal for themselves and those they perceived as predictive of adult success. There was also a high correlation between the qualities they perceived as ideal for themselves and those they thought the teachers favored. This was not true for the high-creative subjects. There was a negative correlation, in fact, between what these subjects favored for themselves and what they assumed the teachers favored. There was a very low—and insignificant—correlation between what they preferred for themselves and what they realized was important for adult success. The difference, then, in their teachers' reactions to the two groups undoubtedly lay in these value differences. High-creative individuals here revealed themselves as persons

TABLE 4–3
Rank order correlations among subsections of the Outstanding Traits Test

	Subjects	
Components of correlations	IQ (N = 28)	Creative (N = 26)
"Personal traits believed predictive of success" and "Personal traits believed favored by teachers"	.62	.59
"Personal traits preferred for oneself" and "Personal traits believed predictive of adult success"	.81	.10
"Personal traits preferred for oneself" and "Personal traits believed favored by teachers"	.67	−.25

Source: J. W. Getzels and P. W. Jackson, "The highly intelligent and highly creative adolescent: A summary of some research findings," in C. W. Taylor and F. Barron (Eds.), *Scientific creativity: Its recognition and development* (New York: John Wiley & Sons, 1963), p. 168. By permission of the author and John Wiley & Sons, Inc.

who rejected the values of their teachers and of the society at large in favor of some unique set of values which were their own.

The stories that the students gave to a set of pictures, which were used in arriving at their achievement scores, were also analyzed for a variety of other qualities. The researchers found that the stories of the high-creative subjects differed significantly from those of the high-IQ group in a variety of ways. The high-creative group were less bound to the stimulus picture itself, were more likely to give unexpected endings and to use humor and incongruity, and took a more playful attitude toward the task. This childlike playfulness has shown up in a good deal of other research with creative children and adolescents. An interesting example of this difference is given in the following stories, which are provided by the authors (p. 52–53).

Here, for example, in response to the picture-stimulus perceived most often as a man sitting in an airplane reclining seat returning from a business trip or a professional conference, are case-type stories given by a high I.Q. subject and a high Creative subject.

THE HIGH I.Q. SUBJECT: "Mr. Smith is on his way home from a successful business trip. He is very happy and he is thinking about his wonderful family and how glad he will be to see them again. He can picture it, about an hour from now, his plane landing at the airport and Mrs. Smith and their three children all there welcoming him home again."

THE HIGH CREATIVE SUBJECT: "This man is flying back from Reno where he has just won a divorce from his wife. He couldn't stand to live with her anymore, he told the judge, because she wore so much cold cream on her face at night that her head would skid across the pillow and hit him in the head. He is now contemplating a new skid-proof face cream."

Or one more, this in response to the stimulus-picture most often perceived as a man working late (or very early) in an office.

THE HIGH I.Q. SUBJECT: "There's ambitious Bob, down at the office at 6:30 in the morning. Every morning it's the same. He's trying to show his boss how energetic he is. Now, thinks Bob, maybe the boss will give me a raise for all my extra work. The trouble is that Bob has been doing this for the last three years, and the boss still hasn't given him a raise. He'll come in at 9:00, not even noticing that Bob had been there so long, and poor Bob won't get this raise."

THE HIGH CREATIVE SUBJECT: "This man has just broken into this office of a new cereal company. He is a private-eye employed by a competitor firm to find out the formula that makes the cereal bend, sag, and sway. After a thorough search of the office he comes upon what he thinks is the current formula. He is now copying it. It turns out that it is the wrong formula and the competitor's factory blows up. Poetic justice!"

In a study comparing creative high school students with an unselected group of job applicants of about the same age and socioeconomic level, Torrance and Dauw (1966) found significant personality as well as cognitive differences between the two groups. Some of the most interesting results are summarized in Table 4–4. The researchers gave an attitude test to both groups of subjects and found on the basis of factor analysis that five different orientations could be used to account for a large variety of attitudes that were measured by the test. The attitudes of the two groups were strikingly different on all orientations.

In comparing Torrance and Dauw's results with those of Getzels and Jackson, it is important to remember that Torrance and Dauw tested an unselected group of job applicants as the control group, whereas in the Getzels and Jackson study

TABLE 4–4

Comparison of high patterns of highly creative high school seniors and a similar unselected group on the Runner Studies of Attitude Patterns

Attitude or orientation	Creative seniors (N = 115)		Unselected (N = 100)	
	Number	Percent	Number	Percent
Experimental	94	82	23	23*
Intuitive	105	91	56	56*
Rules and tradition	22	19	40	40*
Planfulness (structure)	17	15	44	44*
Power and authority	18	17	18	18
Passive compliance	38	33	56	56*
Extraversiveness	51	44	44	44
Hostility and blame	47	41	59	59†
Resistance to social pressure	76	66	35	35*
Social anxiety	91	79	70	70
Pleasure in tool-implemented hand skills	66	57	78	78
Performance anxiety	88	76	70	70

* Difference in percentages is significant at better than .01 level.
† Difference in percentages is significant at better than .05 level.
Source: E. Torrance and D. C. Dauw, "Attitude patterns of creatively gifted high school seniors," *Gifted Child Quarterly*, Summer 1966, 53–57. By permission.

one group consisted of high-creative subjects and the other of high-IQ subjects. Torrance and Dauw found, for example, that the high creatives had a significantly higher achievement orientation than the unselected control group. Getzels and Jackson, on the other hand, found that the high-creative and high-IQ groups had approximately the same need for achievement. It is important, then, to remember how the two groups were selected in the Getzels and Jackson study. The high-IQ group consisted of subjects who were in the top 20 percent on the IQ measures but not in that high a percentile on the creativity measures. Conversely, the high creatives were defined as those in the top 20 percent on the creativity measures but not in the top 20 percent on the IQ measures. Their high-creative subjects, in other words, were being forced by the process of selection to be subjects without high IQs, whereas their high-IQ subjects were being forced by the process of selection to be persons who were not especially creative. This arbitrary distinction may not in fact reflect the distribution of intelligence and creativity in the general population. That is to say, there may be a higher correlation between the two dimensions than Getzels and Jackson's selection would reflect. One wonders to what extent the most intelligent subjects in Getzels and Jackson's population were also the most creative, and vice versa.

This question of the actual independence of the two cognitive styles of intelligence and creativity is attacked in a study by Wallach and Kogan, which is reported in their book *Modes of Thinking in Young Children* (1965). By reviewing not only Getzels and Jackson's work but also a large number of other studies dealing with creativity, Wallach and Kogan found that the instruments used to measure intelligence and those used to measure creativity were generally almost as highly correlated with one another as they were with themselves. In other words, the creativity measures in the Getzels and Jackson study were almost as highly correlated with the intelligence measures as they were with other creativity measures. From the results of these correlations, there would be no evidence for assuming that the two dimensions are independent. Wallach and Kogan were able to overcome this problem by selecting a set of creativity measures and a set of intelligence measures so that the correlation within each set was high whereas the correlation between the two sets was low. Although their study was conducted on fifth-grade children rather than on adolescents, they too found important personality differences between their high-creative and high-intelligence groups.

One of the main differences between Wallach and Kogan's study and earlier studies on intelligence is that Wallach and Kogan examined four groups: a high-creativity–high-intelligence group, a high-creativity–low-intelligence group, a low-creativity–high-intelligence group, and a low-creativity–low-intelligence group. Wallach and Kogan found the group which was high on both dimensions to be the most flexible—able to use both adultlike and childlike modes of thinking. They found that the high-creativity–low-intelli-gence children were in conflict with school and other authorities and were concerned about feelings of unworthiness and inadequacy; that the low-creativity–high-intelligence children were striving, ambitious, and fearful of failure; and that the low-creativity–low-intelligence group were bewildered and somewhat defensive in their attempts to adapt to an environment which was at best difficult for them.

In summary, it appears that there is an aspect of cognitive development which can be labeled creativity and that it is independent to some extent of the sort of intellectual functioning which is measured by IQ tests. In their dealings with students, teachers should recognize both of these dimensions as well as the personality correlates of these dimensions. Judging from the Getzels and Jackson study, it would seem all too easy for a teacher to reject, or at least neglect, the development of creativity in students in favor of the more convergent thinking of the highly intelligent students. The convergent thinker single-mindedly goes about arriving at the "correct" answer, that is, the expected answer. The divergent thinker tends to come up with different, original, and sometimes creative answers. Unfortunately, according to our usual standards, these answers are frequently wrong. The teacher who pays attention to the product only, that is, to the final answer, may overlook the quality of the process by which the student arrived at that answer. Sigel (1963) made the same argument about intelligence tests, namely, that they restrict our understanding of intelligence. His main point was that intelligence tests seem to focus our attention on the answers rather than on the cognitive style and the process by which the child arrives at those answers.

In more recent research, Milgram, Milgram, Rosenbloom, and Rabkin (1978), have used the Wallach and Kogan creativity measures and have found that there is a relationship between the quantity and quality of creative thinking. In other words, those adolescents who come up with a large number of unusual ideas, including some poor ideas, are the ones who also have the best unusual ideas. This result fits with the earlier finding (Milgram & Milgram, 1976) that there is a strong relationship between the quality and quantity of creative activities. Those adolescents who participate in a wide variety of creative endeavors, such as music, art, writing, drama, even though superficially in some instances, are the students whose creative productions are of the highest quality.

There are also some important developmental changes in creative thinking occurring during adolescence. Twelfth graders have been found, for example, to produce more unusual responses than sixth graders on measures of creativity. They do not, however, produce more common responses (Milgram, Milgram, Rosenbloom & Rabkin, 1978).

SUMMARY AND CONCLUSIONS

In this chapter we have briefly outlined Jean Piaget's developmental theory of cognition and have examined some of the issues and data concerning intellectual growth during adolescence.

Piaget came into psychology via biology and philosophy. His basic theoretical concepts reveal his indebtedness to the former as much as his methodology reveals his indebtedness to the latter. Piaget compares intelligence to biological adaptation and demonstrates that the processes of assimilation and accommodation occur at various stages of cognitive development.

The cognitive stage of interest to the adolescent psychologist is the stage of formal operations. Individuals who have attained this stage of reasoning are no longer tied to specific concrete examples in their problem solving. They can abstract, and because of their added ability to decenter, they can consider several alternative solutions simultaneously. They are able to consider possibilities as well as realities, and to examine the relationships among relationships.

Recent work in the area of cognitive development suggests that the Piagetian tasks for the formal operations stage tap only a small range of the domain of abstract reasoning. However, it has been demonstrated that the onset and use of formal operational reasoning correlates with other logical abilities. For example, those people who function at the level of formal operations have been shown to be less susceptible to the primacy effect.

It would appear that the acquisition of formal thought is not an all-or-none affair but rather occurs in stages. These stages are largely based on the distinction between competence at a task and performance. While the sequential manner in which formal logic develops has been observed, it would appear that not all adolescents rely on formal reasoning and probably no adolescent relies on it completely.

Some researchers argue that most adolescents have a sort of latent ability to do formal reasoning, which can be elicited if proper attempts are made. It is important to realize that there is a vast difference between one's developmental cognitive ability and the likelihood of one's performing at that level.

Several personality correlates of this cognitive stage have been cited, including, at its outset, a new egocentrism which includes both a personal fable ("It could only happen to me") as well an imaginary audience ("Everybody is probably watching; I wonder how I look to them"). The idealism of adolescents also depends on formal logic and the ability to consider the possible as well as the real.

The study of the intellectual development of adolescents has been plagued by the same problems that have historically surrounded the construct of intelligence: the heredity-environment controversy, making an entity of the construct, and the difficulties in distinguishing between ability and achievement. It is clear that the structure of intellect becomes more complex and differentiated with age, though the greatest increase in differentiation seems to occur before adolescence.

Sex differences in cognitive development begin to emerge during adolescence. Boys do better on tests of mathematics and spatial ability while girls get better scores on tests of verbal ability. The reasons for sex differences in cognitive development aren't completely clear. At this point in time, it is believed that an interaction of endocrine, genetic, neurological, and social influences work, in ways as yet unknown, to produce sex differences in cognition.

One aspect of cognitive functioning which deserves the attention of parents and teachers is the development of creativity. When highly creative youngsters are compared with those who are highly intelligent but not especially creative, some interesting personality differences emerge. Highly creative students are able to perceive the values of their teachers but do not favor the same values for themselves. There is, in addition, a certain playful quality in much of the responding of creative adolescents. It was argued in this chapter that creativity, like the more traditional convergent thinking of the high achiever, is an independent aspect of cognitive growth which can be nurtured.

SUGGESTED ADDITIONAL READING

Flavell, J. *The developmental psychology of Jean Piaget.* Princeton, N.J.: Van Nostrand, 1963.

Ginsburg, H., & Opper, S. *Piaget's theory of intellectual development: An introduction.* Englewood Cliffs, N.J.: Prentice-Hall, 1969.

Inhelder, B., & Piaget, J. *The growth of logical thinking: From childhood to adolescence.* New York: Basic Books, 1958.

Wallach, M. A., & Kogan, N. *Modes of thinking in young children.* New York: Holt, Rinehart & Winston, 1965.

BOX 5–1
Study questions

How does a child psychologist's own social history influence what Elkind calls his or her "child sense"?

Why has Erikson's theory of psychosocial development been called an "ego psychology" when compared to earlier psychoanalytic writings?

Which one of Erikson's psychosocial stages is particularly relevant to adolescent psychology? How does this stage integrate the many developmental problems of the adolescent into one task?

Name the four identity statuses used by Marcia in his measure of identity. Give an example of each status as it would relate to an individual's religious identity.

In what ways do identity achievers differ from persons with the other statuses?

What types of personal changes are needed in achievement of a firm identity?

How do identity achievers differ from persons in the other statuses on measures, such as self-esteem, cognitive style, use of formal operations, and values?

How do males differ from females on Marcia's measure of identity status?

CHAPTER 5

THE SOCIAL AND EMOTIONAL DEVELOPMENT OF ADOLESCENTS

The transition from childhood to adulthood is marked by personal and social change of exciting and important dimensions. In the previous chapters, we have concentrated on adolescents' physical and cognitive growth. As important and apparent as these changes are, they are paralleled by equally forceful and personally relevant changes in self-perception and social relations.

The way in which the adolescent views his world and his place in it; the way in which she recalls her past and sees herself then and now as the same person despite change; the way in which he perceives his own personal future, and the relevance of his life now to that distant tomorrow; her eagerness, willingness, or reluctance even to take that step into an adult future; these are some of the personal and social concerns of the early adolescent. In the next several chapters, which are concerned with cultural differences, family changes, peer relations, and values, we will be dealing with the research around these issues. First, though, it will be useful to examine the concepts themselves and a theory which should help us to organize the data.

Identity: The search for sameness

If one were to talk about the psychological theory of Erik Erikson, and had for some unfortunate reason, to confine oneself to one word, the word would have to be *identity*. As mentioned in the first chapter, this term is rich with meaning in Erikson's theory, and it is particularly useful in unraveling the meaning of the psychosocial events of adolescence.

Erik Erikson

Before going into detail about Erikson's theory, however, it would be helpful to examine the history of the man. We can gain insight into a theory by understanding the theorist, and one way to do that is by examining his personal history. Nor is this approach foreign to Erikson. In fact in one sense, personal histories are his stock in trade. His major works include *Young Man Luther* (1958), a biography and psychoanalytic study of Martin Luther, and *Gandhi's Truth* (1969), a psychoanalytic study of the life and political strategy of Mahatma Gandhi.

In a recent address on "Child Sense and Child Development Research," David Elkind (1979) comments on this psychohistorical approach of Erikson's which "tries to relate the achievements of a given individual to personal history and social milieu" (p. 1).

Elkind deomonstrates, very persuasively, that among the famous child psychologists their own social history has had a powerful influence on what he calls their, "child sense," that is, their unique conception of childhood, their special contribution to our understanding of development. We will shortly examine Erikson's child sense, or adolescent sense, and I believe we will find some important correlates of that conception to his own personal history.

Erikson was born in 1902 of Danish parents. Before his birth his parents separated, and his mother then moved with Erik to Germany. Three years later she married the man who was her son's pediatrician. In talking about this, Erikson is quoted in a biography by Robert Coles (1970) as saying that his own identity crisis was "central and long drawn:"

> To begin with I never knew my father. Both my parents were Danish, but they were separated when I was born and my mother first raised me among strangers in Germany. Eventually, she married my pediatrician and I grew up in Karlsruhe in Baden. He was Jewish. I was blond and grew tall and the Jewish boys nicknamed me "the goy." In school, I became a German superpatriot to live down my Danishness

(the Danes wanted to steal Schleswig-Holstein, you remember) and then found that my Jewishness was too much for the patriots, and their antisemitism too much for me (quoted in Coles, 1970, p. 180).

From the point of view of Elkind's concept of child sense it isn't surprising that this is the man who most forcefully introduced the concept of identity to the psychological world as well as to the lay public.

Erikson's theory of psychosocial development

The concept of identity is embedded in a theory of psychosocial development, as rich as it is complex. Like Freud's theory, Erikson's is also a psychoanalytic view. (He was psychoanalyzed in Vienna by Freud's daughter, Anna). Unlike Freud, however, Erikson is more concerned with the rational, logical aspects of personality, that is, those conscious components of mental life, and less with the unconscious. His theory has been called an "ego psychology" in contrast to the emphasis on the id in earlier psychoanalytic writing. Erikson is more concerned with normal development than with pathological and developed a theory of psychosocial stages of development, in contrast to Freud's developmental theory of psychosexual stages.

Erikson's stages of psychosocial development are eight. Each reflects a dilemma or conflict which must be met and, at least to some extent, resolved before going on to the next stage:

1. Basic trust versus basic mistrust   This is the first conflict to be resolved in the healthy personality, and on its resolution are based all the future stages of psychosocial development. The interactive task for the infant, according to Erikson, calls for the ability and willingness to reach out to one's social environment for nurturance with the expectation that one's longing will be satisfied. Not to resolve this conflict leads in adulthood to a basic fear and withdrawal from interpersonal contact, and a dread that one's social needs cannot or will not be met. Extremes of such regression can be seen in psychotic persons who refuse comfort, help, and sometimes even food.

2. Autonomy versus shame and doubt   The psychosocial task of the toddler is to establish a will of one's own (a precursor of identity to appear much later). Just as the stage of basic trust versus mistrust can be compared to the oral stage in Freud's theory, the stage of autonomy versus shame and doubt can be compared to the anal stage. Erikson embellishes that notion to encompass not just the retention and expulsion of feces, but also the "holding" and "letting go" which is exercised muscularly by the toddler, as well as symbolically in his or her autonomous social interaction and mutual regulation. Not to develop autonomy can lead to shame, a sense of unworthiness, the result of a parental restriction on one's freedom of movement whenever the "I" or "mine" are asserted independently.

3. Initiative versus guilt   Just as autonomy cannot be acquired without a sense of basic trust, so the conflict of initiative versus guilt cannot be resolved without a prior foundation in autonomy. This is the stage in a child's life when the child separates even more from family, widens his or her social world, and does so on one's own. In discussing the goals of this period, Erikson (1959) refers to the tripartite achievements of increased social mobility, language development, and the expansion of imagination. While he or she is learning to make and do things for him or herself, the child also develops during this stage a conscience, which Erikson refers to as "the great governor of initiative" (1959, p. 80).

4. Industry versus inferiority Once again, built on the preceding stage, this era in a child's life reflects the psychosocial dilemma of mastering tasks which are essential for functioning in society. Erikson contrasts this with earlier stages by suggesting that in the first stage, personality consisted of "I am what I am given;" in the second stage, "I am what I will;" in the third, "I am what I can imagine I will be;" and now "I am what I learn" (Erikson, 1959, p. 82). This is the period of the schoolgirl or schoolboy where mastery is learned, as well as the satisfaction that comes from mastery. Mastering experience, with newly developed cognitive skills, is as important in this era as the mastery of things. Erikson mentions meditating, experimenting, planning, and sharing, all of which require the cognitive level of concrete operations with its attendant decentering. Although Erikson doesn't deal explicitly with the child's cognitive capacity at each period, notice how important the Piagetian stages are to the child's ability to master these psychosocial dilemmas.

5. Identity versus identity diffusion Now we come to the crux of Erikson's contribution to adolescent psychology. His definition of the conflict of this period revolves around the rich concept of identity which underlies the "sameness" of self. In other words, the sense of continuity with previous experience, as well as the sense of hope for the future, rest on an awareness of oneself as an integrated person spanning those three eras in time: past, present, and future. In reference to the identity crisis at this age, Erikson points to the relatively sudden body changes, both absolutely and proportionally, genital growth, and the onset of sexual drives. Each of these represents a discontinuity with previous experience. To the extent that inner sameness (despite these external changes) is guaranteed by ego-identity, the crisis will be resolved. Notice, however, that in the solution of this crisis, a commitment is required. That is, if the adolescent sees himself or herself as an American, a scholar, a Jew or a black, identity can only be achieved to the extent that these identifications are freely chosen or assented to, not simply accepted or passively acknowledged in a spirit of resignation. Just as in the earlier stages, the individual must be an agent as well as a patient. However, to choose among alternatives, to the extent demanded of full identity achievement, requires some ability to separate variables, considering one at a time while holding the others in abeyance. In other words, some formal reasoning is necessary.

Once again, Piaget's cognitive stages and Erikson's psychosocial stages complement one another in the development of the total person. We will return to the topic of identity versus identity diffusion after a discussion of Erikson's last three stages of development.

6. Intimacy versus self-absorption or isolation Erikson is less explicit about the stages of adulthood. However, he describes the young adult era as characterized by a conflict between intimacy and isolation. Once identity is achieved, the individual can experience true psychological intimacy with the opposite sex. Physical and sexual closeness are only one component of this interpersonal intimacy. Erikson is referring also to a mutual sharing based on trust. The lack of such a relationship leads to isolation or, at best, superficial relations, a pseudointimacy which is formal and stereotyped, (i.e., lacking in spontaneity and warmth).

7. Generativity versus stagnation Middle adulthood, too, has its developmental crisis. Erikson expresses it, in a word coined for this purpose; in terms of the ability to generate. While he refers to the generation of children, the term isn't used exclusively in that sense. Generativity refers equally to the spawning of ideas, to creativity, and to altruism in the guiding of the young, whether biologically one's own or not.

In describing the middle-adult stage, Erikson (1963) takes a backward glance and says:

> In this book the emphasis is on the childhood stages, otherwise the section on generativity would of necessity be the central one, for this term encompasses the evolutionary development which has made man the teaching and instituting as well as the learning animal. The fashionable insistence on dramatizing the dependence of children on adults often blinds us to the dependence of the older generation on the younger one (p. 266).

One cannot fault Erikson or his contemporaries for focusing on the early years of development, though it is not entirely clear to us why this has been fashionable. Perhaps we have been limited by our adherence to a physical development model. Perhaps that model causes us to misperceive all development, psychosocial as well as physical, as slowing down and ending after adolescence.

In any event, Erikson's term *generativity* connotes social as well as physical characteristics. It comprises, but is not restricted to, "creativity" and "productivity." A person in the middle-adult stage is said to be in the prime of life, a producer of ideas as well as children, whose task it is to nourish both to fulfillment.

8. Integrity versus despair and disgust The interpersonal task of the elderly is the maintenance of integrity despite the objective evidence of old age. Once again, the internal commitment to an integrated old age cannot belie the biological facts. Neither does it succumb to them. The healthy personality is characterized by a sense of self-worth and a readiness to defend the dignity of one's own lifestyle despite physical change, possible mental decline, possible economic hardship, and often a callous disregard from the more youthful members of the society.

This is the stage of life when the main task is to remain, without despair, an integrated human being, despite physical and environmental pressures toward disintegration. The psychology of the elderly is almost as sparse as that of middle adulthood. Even the terms used to describe this stage of life have a phony ring. Friedenberg (1959) complains that the strained language surrounding the whole area of adolescence betrays a society's ambivalence about this age group. If such sweeping generalizations have any merit whatever, the same could be said of the language surrounding old age. *Senescence* is as academic and pedantic a

FIGURE 5-1   . . . when the main task is to continue to be—without despair—an integrated human being.

Photograph courtesy of J. P. McKinney

word as *adolescence,* and surely *senior citizen* is as condescending as youngster. The terms *elderly* and *teenager* are both fraught with emotional implications.

Semantic studies of terms like these may give us clues to such ambivalence as may exist, and thus may give us further clues to the reasons why neither adolescence nor old age has been studied adequately. In the meantime, one hypothesis may be ventured: namely, that like adolescence, old age signals a leaving, an exit. Leaving life, like leaving childhood, means entering into the unknown. It appears to us that hypotheses arising from the semantic study of the language about developmental periods would be worth exploring in the clinic and in the laboratory of the developmental psychologist.

Like Shakespeare's stages of life, Erikson's psychosocial stages appear all encompassing. The beginning student may well wonder how explicit it is possible to be about the stages and how well one can predict behavior in any given stage. In an attempt to answer such questions, we shall look more closely at the research dealing with the adolescent stage of identity versus identity diffusion.

A measure of identity status

Undoubtedly the most comprehensive empirical exploration of Erikson's concept of identity has followed from the seminal work of Marcia (1966, 1967). In developing a measure of identity, Marcia distinguished among four possible statuses. The first two were naturally the extremes in Erikson's conceptualization: Identity achievement and identity diffusion. The other two, also derived from Erikson's theory and somewhere between the two extremes, are identity foreclosure and moratorium.

Before examining the research on identity formation, it would be useful to examine each of these statuses in turn. Marcia defined these statuses in terms of an individual's position on three issues that seemed to be centrally related to the psychosocial tasks of adolescence: occupational choice, religion, and political ideology. An individual's position on these tasks could be described along two dimensions: crisis and commitment. Crisis refers to that period of time during which an individual is choosing among alternatives (i.e., wrestling with a decision). Commitment means the level of emotional assent, engagement, or agreement an individual gives to a particular position. Using the example of occupational choice, we can see how each of the statuses derives from an individual's position as defined by these two dimensions:

1. Identity achievement. This person will have had a period of crisis, that is, will have struggled with the choice of alternative occupations, and will now be firmly committed to his or her chosen occupation.
2. Identity diffusion. This position implies a lack of commitment regardless of whether or not there has been a crisis. In other words, the individual hasn't made an occupational choice and isn't much worried about it.
3. Identity foreclosure: The person with this status is firmly committed to an occupation but without ever having considered alternatives. In other words, there's never been a crisis, and the choice is often as much the parents' as it is the individual's.
4. Moratorium: This status is characterized by an ongoing crisis without clear commitment as yet. Moratorium is distinguished from diffusion by the fact that in the moratorium status, while there isn't yet commitment, there is at least the struggle of considering alternatives.

Marcia's method of assessing these statuses in an individual was through a semistructured interview. It might make the statuses clearer to read some typical answers given by students in the four statuses to questions about their occupation and religion:

A sample question in the occupational area was: How willing do you think you'd be to give up going into _____ if something better came along?

Examples of typical answers for the four statuses were:

Identity achievement. Well, I might, but I doubt it. I can't see what "something better" would be for me.

Moratorium. I guess if I knew for sure I could answer that better. It would have to be something in the general area—something related.

Foreclosure. Not very willing. It's what I've always wanted to do. The folks are happy with it, and so am I.

Identity diffusion. Oh sure. If something better came along, I'd change just like that.

A sample question in the religious area was: Have you ever had any doubts about your religious beliefs?

Identity achievement. Yeah, I even started wondering whether or not there was a God. I've pretty much resolved that now, though. The way it seems to me is . . .

Moratorium. Yes, I guess I'm going through that now. I just don't see how there can be a God and yet so much evil in the world or . . .

Foreclosure. Not, not really, our family is pretty much in agreement on these things.

Identity diffusion. Oh, I don't know. I guess so. Everyone goes through some sort of stage like that. But it really doesn't bother me much. I figure one's about as good as the other! (Marcia, 1966, p. 553)

In what ways do identity achievers differ from persons with the other statuses? When Marcia gave his subjects a cognitive task ("concept attainment") to be performed under stressful conditions, the identity achievement group did best. They also had the most realistic expectations, or level of aspiration. When given negative feedback about themselves, this group was most able to maintain their self-esteem. The identity achievers were also least likely to subscribe to authoritarian values.

Surprisingly, Marcia found that the group most unlike the identity achievers were not the identity diffusers, but rather the foreclosure group. It was the foreclosure group that had the highest authoritarianism scores, who did the poorest on a concept attainment task under stress, and whose self-esteem was most shaken by a negative appraisal. This group also had the most unrealistic expectations, or level of aspiration, for their performance on the cognitive task.

The moratorium group was fairly close to the achievers except that they did not do so well on the concept attainment task under stress. The diffusion group in Marcia's sample may not be a good example of what Erikson meant by identity diffusion. After all, Erikson was referring to a diverse group, some of whom could be quite disturbed. One isn't likely to find a complete range of such people on a college campus, at least to the extent that one could find a range of persons in the other three statuses. Marcia speculated that there may be a spectrum of diffusers ranging from the playboy variety at one end, to the schizoid personality at the other. All of Marcia's subjects, by the way, were male.

The achievement of identity, then, is a conditio sine qua non for the attainment of social adulthood. When somebody talks about a 30- or 40-year-old who is still an adolescent, they generally mean someone who has not achieved a clear or firm identity. As we have seen, that achievement involves both a struggle or at least real choosing among alternatives (crisis) and also a commitment to one's choice. It is not enough to have a commitment, for example, to a political party, one's spouse, or religion without having gone through the process of choosing among alternatives. It is this process that, in psychosocial terms, distinguishes the child from the adult. Perhaps, in the religious area, a symbolic representation of that transition is seen in the Christian rite of confirmation. As an infant, the child was sponsored or spoken for by godparents in baptism. Any commitment to his or her religion was made for the child by the godparents. As an adolescent growing into adulthood, however, the individual is presumably required to make his or her own choice, after considering the alternatives of not making that commitment, or of making a different choice, and the implication of each potential decision. It's easy to understand why this couldn't happen until adolescence. A certain level of formal reasoning is obviously required to separate all the potential variables and to consider several alternatives simultaneously.

The Jewish ceremony of bar mitzvah (or bat mitzvah, for girls) provides an analogous situation. While the parents spoke for the boy at circumcision, or for their girl at the naming ceremony, at bar mitzvah the child must speak for himself. A rabbi recently told the son of one of our colleagues as he participated in his own bar mitzvah, "Before, you did what your parents expected. It reflected well on them when you did well and poorly on them when you didn't. Now, you must choose for yourself between right and wrong, just and unjust. Your decisions will now reflect on you and not on your parents." No identity foreclosure is allowed, in other words. The rabbi went on to say that the young man was a member now of the adult community. He could, for example, be a member of the minyon (the minimum number of people required in order to meet as a congregation). He had, by his committed perseverance in study and his wrestling with alternatives, achieved an adult psychosocial status in the community, one mark of identity achievement. The parents too acknowledge this new status. After the child had demonstrated the necessary cognitive qualities by reading from the prophetic texts, the father went with the rabbi and cantor to the podium to pray, "Blessed is He who has relieved me of responsibility for all this." In the community he has spoken a public disavowal of responsibility for the sins—or meritorious acts—of his son or daughter. As we shall see when we return to the topic of adolescent rites in the next chapter, bar mitzvah and confirmation do not carry, however, the universal significance of puberty rites in so-called primitive groups. The community addressed at these religious ceremonies is simply the community of believers.

Research on identity status

Subsequent research involving Marcia's measure of identity status has supported both the utility of the identity construct as well as the reliability and validity of Marcia's method of assessing it. For example, in identity achievers self-esteem is less vulnerable to external evaluation, whether favorable or unfavorable, than for persons in the other statuses (Marcia, 1967). The moratorium, or "in-crisis," group scored highest on measures of anxiety.

There are also differences in cognitive style among the status groups. Achievers and moratorium persons have a more reflective conceptual tempo, and diffusers and the foreclosure group have an impulsive style (Waterman & Waterman, 1974). The reader will recall from Chapter 4 that a person with a reflective tempo is one who takes his or her time in answering a problem. While they may get less done than a person with an impulsive style, they tend to do better on what they finish. It isn't surprising then, that the identity achievers are more likely to have a reflective style, and diffusers and foreclosures an impulsive style. Intelligence, however, has not been shown to relate to identity status. Once again, both of the studies just outlined were conducted with male subjects only. We will return to the issue of female identity shortly.

Other correlates of identity achievement have included level of moral judgment (Podd, 1972; Rowe & Marcia, 1980), the use of formal operations (Rowe & Marcia, 1980), and values (St. Clair & Day, 1979). In the latter study, done with high school females, the authors found that students in identity achievement, moratorium, and foreclosure categories had higher scores on a religious value scale than did the diffusion group. The trend did not hold up, however, for political values.

While the construct of ego identity was not intended to be a primarily masculine notion, little of the early theorizing and research revolved around the idea of identity formation in women. Marcia's constructs of identity status were initially validated with men only. During the past 10 years, however, a number of studies (Marcia & Friedman, 1970; Toder & Marcia, 1974; St. Clair & Day, 1979; Schenkel & Marcia, 1972) have focused on sex differences in identity achievement and, more importantly, the distinctive way in which women resolve the issue of identity.

One important finding regarding female identity relates to the issue of foreclosure. Marcia and Friedman (1970) found that foreclosure women had the highest self-esteem and lowest anxiety scores, not identity achievers. The researchers speculated that possibly ". . . the foreclosure identity status is a particularly adaptive one for women" (p. 260). They point to the traditional pressure on women to be the culture-bearer, or the caretaker; in other words, to be what has already been planned for them. Men, on the other hand, have traditionally been expected to have a crisis, to rebel, to strike out on their own, or to pioneer. (Don't forget, this study was conducted prior to 1970). Marcia and Friedman argued that perhaps identity achievement was threatening for women and suggested, "whatever the threat achieving—as opposed to foreclosing—an identity poses to women, it would seem from diffusions' high anxiety scale that just having some identity, achieved or foreclosed, is better than remaining diffuse" (Marcia & Friedman, 1970, p. 261).

Some support for the idea of a relationship between identity achievement and identity foreclosure in women came in a later study done by Toder and Marcia (1974) with college females. They found that identity achievers and foreclosures are less conforming than those in the moratorium and diffusion groups, which the authors called the unstable identity statuses. That is, the achievers and foreclosures were less swayed in their own perceptual judgments by the erroneous responses given by their peers. Even though the moratorium group may be chronologically closer to identity achievement, it was the foreclosure group (which is another stable status) which was similar to achievement in being less conforming. Another similarity between the achievement and foreclosure women concerned the social perceptions the women had of themselves. While diffusion and moratorium women described themselves as "hip," achievement and foreclosure women saw themselves as more "straight" or "indeterminate." The life patterns of women who have acquired a stable identity, whether by achievement or foreclosure, seem to be more conventional. Whether these results will hold up over time, as sex roles become less stereotypical, remains an open question.

Intimacy versus isolation: The next psychosocial stage

Once a person has established some sense of ego identity, he or she is confronted with the dilemma of psychological intimacy or isolation. The idea of intimacy in Erikson's writings refers clearly to psychological closeness not simply physical familiarity, although that may be involved. When Marcia followed up on some of his early subjects after six years (Marcia, 1976), he found that those who had established patterns of intimacy were those who had also achieved identity. Furthermore, there was a correlation between those who were already identity achievers in his early study and those who later had developed a capacity for intimacy. This is not to say that all college students arrive at this point. While there is an increase in identity achievement during the college years, some students still end up in the diffusion category (Waterman, Geary, & Waterman, 1974). The identity status of college students appears to be unrelated to overall academic performance (Waterman & Waterman, 1972), although there is significantly more changing of academic programs among the moratoriums. Further data on withdrawal from college suggests that achievers who withdraw are more likely to withdraw in good standing, while foreclosures and diffusions are more like to withdraw because of academic difficulty. Once again, however, those who remain in college have not been found to have different academic records as a function of identity status, although among women, identity achievers are more likely to take difficult college courses compared with the other statuses (Marcia & Friedman, 1970).

It would appear that identity achievement, however, is a prerequisite for the establishment of intimacy. In their study of 88 college students, Kacerguis and Adams (1980) concluded, "Identity achievement males and females were observed to have more depthful and committed intimate relationships than their diffused, foreclosed, or moratorium peers" (p. 124).

SUMMARY AND CONCLUSIONS

Erikson's theory of psychosocial development provides one of the best frameworks for understanding the social and emotional development of adolescents. Erikson's own early life gives us some clues into the basis for his including identity as a central theme in his theory. In this chapter we have outlined the stages in Erikson's theory and have concentrated on subsequent research on those stages which deal primarily with adolescence: identity versus identity diffusion and intimacy versus isolation. The research on identity has derived largely from the seminal work of Marcia (1966, 1976) who has distinguished four identity statuses: identity achievement, identity diffusion, identity foreclosure, and moratorium. These statuses are defined in terms of the presence or absence in an adolescent's life of a crisis and a commitment to such issues as a vocational choice or a religious preference.

Once identity is established, the adolescent has the basis for resolving the next dilemma, that of intimacy versus isolation. We shall return to this later stage in Chapter 8, where we deal with late adolescent friendships and peer relations.

CHAPTER 6

THE EFFECTS OF CULTURE AND SOCIAL CLASS ON ADOLESCENT DEVELOPMENT

In the first section of this book we were concerned with adolescence as a biological phenomenon. The last two chapters have dealt with the adolescent's physical development and sexual behavior, attitudes, and values. The present chapter will deal with the adolescent in a social and cultural context. We saw earlier that psychological interest in adolescence began with G. Stanley Hall, who was particularly interested in the biological changes surrounding puberty. This same biological orientation could be seen in the work of Freud, whose theory of psychosexual development was quite compatible with Hall's view of adolescence. Freud, too, regarded adolescence as mainly a biological phenomenon. That is, he believed that the biological changes of puberty, and their associated drives, rekindled the conflicts of earlier psychosexual stages. It was not until the 1920s that the important work of cultural anthropologists, especially Margaret Mead and Ruth Benedict, questioned some of the earlier assumptions about adolescence. As a result of the anthropologists' theories, supported by field observations, it became obvious that Hall's period of storm and stress and Freud's resurgence of the Oedipus complex and "onanism of necessity" were simply not as universal as had been thought.

Cultural relativism in the training of children

One of the main theoretical statements of the cultural anthropologists concerning human development is contained in a paper by Ruth Benedict (1938) entitled "Continuities and Discontinuities in Cultural Conditioning." Benedict asserts that the role of the anthropologist is not to question the facts of nature, such as the physiological changes of puberty, but rather to examine the ways in which different cultures add their special nuances to the phenomena of development. She says, "Although it is a fact of nature that a child becomes a man, the way in which the transaction is effected varies from one society to another, and no one of these particular cultural bridges should be regarded as the 'natural' path to maturity" (p. 161).

By contrasting the roles of the father and the son, Benedict demonstrates that over and above the basic facts of nature which differentiate the father from the son, the specific ways in which the young are trained differ from one culture to the next. She notes that in all cultures there are certain continuities in training, that is, ways in which children are conditioned so that their later behavior will not be at variance with the things that are expected of them as children. An example of this is conditioning to a mealtime schedule. Although such conditioning is not universal, within the first few years of life children in our culture are trained to eat three meals a day on a schedule that they generally follow for the rest of their lives. Another example is modesty training. In our culture children are taught to keep themselves clothed from a very early age, and this is as much a social requirement of adulthood as of childhood.

However, there are also certain discontinuities in the cultural conditioning of children. Benedict points to three such discontinuities which are prominent in our culture but which again are not universal. One of these is the distinction between the responsibility expected of an adult versus the nonresponsible status of the child. The second is the expectation that adults will be dominant and children submissive. The third discontinuity is the expectation that children will be nonsexual, whereas adults have the potential of being sexually active human beings.

With respect to the responsible-nonresponsible discontinuity, Benedict provides several examples of cultures in which there is no such clear-cut distinction between the play of the child and the work of the adult. In our culture, children are expected to play and not to be held responsible for serious work; adults, on the other hand, are expected to be responsible in a work life. Some cultures, however, perceive the play of the child as more analogous to the work of the adult. In this connection Benedict mentions the Canadian Ojibwa:

> This tribe gains its livelihood by winter trapping and the small family of father, mother and children live during the long winter alone on their great frozen hunting grounds. The boy accompanies his father and brings in his catch to his sister as his father does to his mother; the girl prepares the meat and skins for him, just as his mother does for her husband. By the time the boy is 12, he may have set his own line of traps on a hunting territory of his own and return to his parent's house only once in several months—still bringing the meat and skins to his sister. The young child is taught consistently that it has only itself to rely upon in life and this is as true in the dealings it will have with the supernatural as in the business of getting a livelihood. (p. 163)

This, of course, is in marked contrast to the traditional educational pattern in our culture, in which the child's role as learner is distinctly different from the adult's role as teacher. Related to this is the fact that in our society children are expected to be submissive. They are punished for displays of disobedience and rewarded for compliance and obedience to the demands of their parents. On the other hand, according to Benedict, "many American Indian tribes are especially explicit in rejecting the ideal of a child's submissive or obedient behavior" (p. 164). She points out that in many tribes parents are proud of their children when they seem to be disobedient or flaunt their parents' authority.

A third nonuniversal discontinuity in the training of children in our culture concerns the contrasted sexual roles of children and adults. In our culture, children are taught to be modest and to avoid open displays of sexuality. This privacy and the punishment of children for sexual experimentation would seem to be consistent with the fact that children are physiologically asexual, whereas adults are sexual. Still numerous cultures are far more permissive than ours in dealing with the innocuous sexual play and experimentation of young children. The point that Benedict makes here is that as long as children do not have to unlearn something that they learned as children, there need be no discontinuity in their sexual experience. The fact that children may experiment with sexuality and not be punished for doing so is not discontinuous with their sexual lives as adults. In our culture, on the other hand, punishing children for sexual experimentation is discontinuous with the learning of appropriate sexual responses as adults. Benedict points out that "the adult in our culture has often failed to unlearn the wickedness or the dangerousness of sex, a lesson which was impressed upon him strongly in his most formative years" (p. 165).

Benedict, then, interprets the *Sturm und Drang* of adolescence as the result not so much of physiological changes as of discontinuities in the training of children. That is, in order to become adults adolescents must unlearn some of the very basic things that they were taught as children. It is this relearning process, according to Benedict, which forms the struggle of adolescence.

Puberty rites: Making discontinuities explicit

Some societies clarify the adolescent's change in status and role expectations through puberty rites. There have been a variety of interpretations of the basis and function of such rites. Some have suggested that the severity of these initiation rites is based on the need to overcome the results of paternal permissiveness during earlier childhood and also to help the male initiate to identify closely with his maleness. Muuss (1970) suggests that "societies that indulge infants are more demanding of their adolescents and those that place greater restrictions on the infant are more indulgent of their adolescents" (p. 115). This notion was derived largely from the work of Whiting, Kluckhohn, and Anthony (1958), who, guided by a set of psychoanalytic hypotheses, studied the initiation rites of a number of tribes and came to the conclusion that the revival of the Oedipus complex in adolescence was the primary reason for the severe puberty rites in some groups. Others have viewed the function of initiation rites more in terms of stabilizing the sex role of the adolescent male (Young, 1962) or simply of clarifying his new expectations, that is, his induction into adult society with relevant associated responsibilities.

In reviewing the later research relative to the psychoanalytic interpretation, J. K. Brown (1969) cites a number of studies which have offered evidence counter to the basic assumptions of Whiting, Kluckhohn, and Anthony. Brown argues that in the societies in which female puberty rites occur, they have a quite different significance. They are rarely severe and generally do not include painful operations or harsh treatment. More often they revolve around the girl's menarche and include such things as training in the cleanliness of her body and preparation for courtship and marriage. Brown finds that initiation rites for girls are more characteristic of societies in which women carry out much of the subsistence activity of the group, or, as she puts it, "where women do a major share of the breadwinning."

An alternative interpretation of puberty rites based on cross-cultural studies of several societies has been suggested by Cohen (1964). He found that puberty rites exist chiefly in societies in which children are brought up to be anchored in the clan or lineage and are lacking in societies which emphasize the nuclear family. Cohen hypothesized from this finding that puberty rites function as a means of perpetuating the interdependence of the members of a society by strengthening social-emotional ties to the group and by eliminating dependence upon the nuclear family. He states, "There is no more effective way to deflect a child's emotional dependence away from his nuclear family than to traumatize him and at the same time forbid him to turn to the well-established security and comfort of his family for protection" (p. 104).

If initiation rites serve to clarify one's new role in society, to signify induction into the adult group, or to stabilize one's sex identification, how does this occur in our culture? We have noticed a number of discontinuities in the cultural conditioning of Western children. It would seem, therefore, that something like an initiation rite would be helpful in clarifying their new status. However, it appears that there is nothing directly resembling an initiation rite for American children. If one were to accept the psychoanalytic interpretation presented by Whiting, Kluckhohn, and Anthony, this would be reasonable, since in our culture there is no long period of close association between the mother and the child. That is, in our culture there is nothing comparable to those cultures, for example, in which Whiting, Kluckhohn, and Anthony found that the child slept with the mother during the first year after birth while sexual intercourse between the parents was prohibited. In such cultures, incestuous attachments would be more likely, and a resurgence of the Oedipus complex in adolescence would be a more threatening event. On the other hand, since there is no such period of close attachment to the mother in our culture, we would seem to have less need for an initiation rite which would clarify the child's responsibilities and repress incestuous attachments.

However, as we have seen, this psychoanalytic interpretation has been brought into question. Moreover, the clarification of one's new role in a variety of nonsexual matters might be aided by such a rite. However, though such ceremonies as the bar mitzvah, confirmation, initiation into sororities or fraternities, and "coming out" balls occur in our culture at approximately the same time as do puberty rites in primitive cultures, they do not always serve the same function. For one thing, they do not carry with them the universal recognition of induction into adult society. For example, though the confirmation of a Christian boy may have great meaning for himself, and perhaps for his family and close friends, as a mark of a new responsibility to himself and his community, as mentioned in Chapter 5, this view of his new status is not universally shared.

One initiation rite which does appear to be similar to the initiation rites of primitive groups, and which deserves far more study than it has received so far, is initiation into religious orders. In the past this has been associated with putting on a new uniform or habit, taking on a new name, pledges of obedience and fidelity to an authority within the group, and so on. As an initiation rite, this has been described very interestingly by Arnold Van Gennep (1960) in his book *The Rites of Passage*.

But for the average American boy and girl there appears to be no single, dramatic induction into adult society which would be analogous to the initiation rites of preliterate people. Muuss (1970) suggests that perhaps there are a series of inductions which might include graduation from grade school, high school, and college, as well as time points serving to mark changes in legal status—for example, the age at which a youngster can acquire a driver's license, or has the right to purchase alcohol, or must pay adult admission at theaters, or can marry, or can agree to have intercourse without its being legally considered rape. However, though each of these constitutes a change in social status, no one of them taken alone could be considered as the point at which the child has become a member of the adult society. Perhaps the ambiguity in the life space of the adolescent rests in the fact that there are discontinuities in the training of children and that there is no single point that distinguishes the status of the child from that of the adult. Put simply, it may appear inconsistent that from the time children are 12 years old they are required to pay adult admission, and yet they are not allowed to vote until they are 18.

Cultural differences in the treatment of adolescents

As may be seen from the discussion above, there are wide differences in the ways different cultures regard and treat adolescents. Among many preliterate peoples, the role of adolescents is clarified through an elaborate ceremony. Whiting, Kluckhohn, and Anthony (1958) give an example of such a ceremony of the Thonga tribe of Africa, in which the younster undergoes severe hazing and sometime between his 10th and 16th year is sent to a "circumcision school." Boys are expected to run the gauntlet between rows of men who beat them; during the initiation ceremony they are stripped of their clothes and their hair is cut off. The aggressive behavior toward the boys includes a ritual circumcision, and the boys are expected to have no interactions with women during this period. An example of an initiation rite for girls among the Cheyenne Indians is given by Grinnell (1923). He states that a Cheyenne girl's first menstrual period was a time of rejoicing. After the girl told her mother what had happened and the mother told the father, the father would make a public statement announcing the news from the lodge door. In addition, if he could afford it, he would give away a horse in his daughter's honor.

Afterwards, the girl was bathed and painted in red by the older women.

Dressed only in a red robe, she sat among the women before a ritual fire. A coal from the fire was placed in front of her and juniper needles were put on the coal. The girl would open her robe so the smoke could encircle her naked body. After the ceremony, she and her grandmother retired to a separate lodge for four days.

Van Gennep (1960) gives a variety of interesting examples of initiation rites among various Indian tribes of North America, as well as among the Australian aborigines and some African groups. In each of these examples, the character of the separation from the old group, the transition period itself, and the induction into the new group are marked by special aspects of the appropriate ceremonies. Suffice it to say here, no such clear-cut transition, with its public display and universally recognized social consequences, is provided for the child in the United States or Western Europe.

In studies of New Guinea and Samoa, Margaret Mead (1935, 1949, 1953) found that adolescents in various societies are treated with varying degrees of severity at puberty and that in some societies the onset of puberty goes unnoticed. Among the Arapesh of New Guinea, a large group initiation for boys is held every few years, and girls go through ceremonies at menarche. But for both sexes these ceremonies have little psychological significance since they do not change the adolescent's social status. The Manus of New Guinea celebrate the puberty of males and females with feasting and painless ceremonies, but again there are no new economic duties and responsibilities and thus no sudden change in status. In the Samoan culture, the onset of puberty has even less social or sexual significance. No formal ceremonies mark the puberty of Samoan girls, and menarche goes unnoticed by society. No traumatic initiation rite is associated with maturity. Instead, there is a slow, continuous transition from childhood to adulthood, with the girls gradually taking on more adult obligations and responsibilities. Social and sexual status do not change abruptly. The society's nonpunitive attitude toward sexual exploration among children continues into

Margaret Mead

Courtesy of the American Museum
of Natural History

adolescence. Consequently, adolescence is a relatively peaceful and pleasant period of Samoan life.

The significance of Mead's work can be seen by contrasting the treatment of adolescents in New Guinea and Samoa with that of adolescents in the United States. Its significance lies in its emphasis on cultural differences and on their importance in determining whether adolescence will be a period of storm and stress or of an untroubled existence.

SOME NATIONAL DIFFERENCES IN ADOLESCENT DEVELOPMENT

The period of adolescence differs in a number of Western countries, both in the behavior of the youth themselves and in the society's attitude and reaction to them. Although the differences are not as marked as those among the preliterate peoples we just discussed, still it is clear that the youth of Holland, France, the United States, Russia, and Japan experience somewhat different transitions into adulthood. This, too, though in a less major way, is an example of the cultural relativism to which Benedict referred.

These five countries have been selected because they provide examples of contrasting methods of dealing with the issue of identity. The student will notice, for example, that in Russia from early childhood an adherence to the standards of adult authority and an emphasis on association within the peer group provide a basis for the transition into an adult identity in which allegiance to the nation is stressed and in which the rule is conformity rather than rebellion. Dutch youth, by contrast, maintain a continuing identity within the family in both childhood and adulthood. In addition, their occupational identity is aided by an educational system which "tracks" its students according to ability levels from the primary years and therefore provides a sense of continuity and a knowledge of expectations and limits in the occupational area. Similarly, French youth must deal with preset limits, which seem strict in contrast to American practices, yet because of their clarity and openness provide youngsters with a straightforward preparation for the novel experiences and impulses of puberty and adolescence. The identity problems of Japanese youth are influenced by the break with a traditional past which the culture itself has experienced.

In studying these national groups as examples of varying practices which aid or hinder the development of identity, the reader will undoubtedly think of other points of comparison and contrast with other national groups.

Soviet youth

One major study on the socialization of young people in Soviet Russia is Bronfenbrenner's (1970) *Two Worlds of Childhood*. Based on observations that Bronfenbrenner made during a series of visits to Russia, the study compares child-rearing practices in Russia and the United States and the effects of these practices on the behavior of the children in the two countries. One main difference cited by Bronfenbrenner is the importance of the children's collective in the socialization of Russian children—that is, the upbringing of Russian children is the responsibility not only of the family, as in the United States, but also of the children themselves.

In addition, however, there are major differences in the role of the family itself in Russia and the United States. Although the upbringing and education of children is considered the right and responsibility of American parents, Russian parents are in a sense granted that privilege by the state and are expected to love their children not only as a parental duty but as a state-imposed obligation. Russian parents are instructed on the seriousness of their responsibilities toward their children if they are going to have children at all. The parents' child-rearing practices are not merely guided but are explicitly directed by the authorities.

A similar situation occurs in the school. Not only is the training of children a function under control of the state, but it is exercised in such a way that children are actually educated for the state. One main difference between the education of children in Russia and the United States is, as mentioned before, the importance placed in Russia on peer interactions, on group conformity among children. Children are expected to participate in group activities, to do things in common. Independent and individual efforts are discouraged, and group efforts are praised and rewarded. Children are taught to praise and punish the members of their own groups. There is a good deal of intergroup rivalry and intragroup cooperation among the various children's groups.

One might ask in what ways Russian boys and girls differ from American boys and girls by the time they become adolescents and what differences there are in the ways the cultures induct young people into their adult roles. Sherman (1965), like Bronfenbrenner, has observed that conformity to group standards is encouraged in the Soviet Union and deviation discouraged: "The line between innocent innovation and criminal delinquency is hard to draw in the Soviet Union. Any action not officially inspired and controlled is potentially dangerous to the regimented society. A kind of Victorian puritanism, inflexible and humorless, dominates the scene. Established authority makes full use of it to stamp hard on all overt signs of nonconformity" (p. 316). It would appear that nonconformity and rebellion which serve as major ways in which adolescents in the United States define their own position and arrive at some self-clarification are simply not tolerated in the Soviet Union. Sherman reports what seems to be an almost fearful distaste among some adult Russians for the fashions and tastes of the young. "Letters and articles in the Moscow press complain that roving bands of 'Komsomol police' have hunted down and molested vacationing young men in bright shirts and young women in slacks on the streets of fashionable Sochi. Stylish girls have had their hair chopped off with 'sheer violence' " (pp. 316–317). In any culture in which children must break away from home in order to assert their independence, there will always be a certain amount of resentment or hostility toward the emergent fashions of the young. Sherman, however, believes that something far deeper than this underlies the Soviet adult's rejection of youthful nonconformity. "It reflects a much deeper social conflict in the Soviet Union: the conflict between stifling paternalism and rebellious youth, characterized in less regimented societies as the 'conflict between generations.' According to Communist mythology, this conflict cannot exist in socialist society. All generations are supposed to be helpmates along the predetermined road to a new heaven on earth" (p. 319).

Sherman argues that for young Russians the revolution is over. That is, Soviet society is established, and the young now see relaxation as a desirable value. Their parents, however, remembering the collective and its values, the importance that was attached to hard work and conformity, are finding it difficult to pass on these values to their children. Indeed, some become delinquent. Sherman points out that the young who have seen their parents work very hard are tempted by the prospect of easy money. Such youngsters want to break out of their old surroundings; they have lived in working-class slums and are now, though sometimes outside the law, able to achieve more luxurious lifestyles for themselves. Sherman points out, however, that besides being outside the law these individual delinquents are unable to acquire any respectability and that in Soviet society respectability is a very important value. And so, truly marginal persons, the delinquent adolescents are neither children nor adults and in addition experience neither the impoverishment of parents who have lived in working-class slums nor the respectability of those who have long been better off. Sherman makes it quite clear, however, that these maladjusted young people are not characteristic of youth in the Soviet Union. He simply cites them as examples of a difficulty which arises because of the insistence on conformity and obedience to the law by parents and because of the need for rebellion by some of the youth. On the other hand, what is more characteristic of Soviet youth, and what many observers would maintain also characterizes American youth, is that they are more conforming than rebellious. Sherman says that this is particularly true of young workers and of most institute and university students. In addition, Sherman maintains that some strange inconsistencies have resulted from a system of child rearing which has made a virtue of hard manual labor. He claims that the upper classes feel degraded if they are reduced to hard work and that they separate themselves from laborers. Therefore, although Soviet society ostensibly places a premium on collective work and classless common effort, one still finds such status symbols as ballet schools, military schools, and prestigious secondary schools.

In this connection, Sherman cites difficulties arising from "tracking" (homogeneous grouping) in the educational system: "These educational gaps have conflicted sharply with the egalitarian features built into the overall educational system from the revolutionary past. An upward mobility of workers and peasants has been encouraged in the name of that revolution. Everyone, regardless of social position or sex, has access to a free secondary school education" (pp. 325–326). Since teacher-student relations have become rather informal, and since the primary schools have placed an almost overbearing emphasis on collectivism, some negative consequences have been felt. Sherman believes that these have led in general to a certain leveling. He says that "this egalitarianism puts an unbearable strain on the higher educational establishments which, by design of the economic plan, cannot absorb all secondary school graduates" (p. 326). He points out that it was Khrushchev who attempted to change the school system by relating it more closely to life. Khrushchev noted when he was premier that only 30 to 40 percent of the students in the higher educational institutions of Moscow had come from peasant or working-class families. His response to this was the development of more technical education. Changes in the educational system since that time have been most appropriate for those who are regarded as thoroughly reliable and are handpicked by the Communist party to go on for higher full-time education.

Part of the reason for these reforms was clearly the unrest among college youth as well as among the Russian people in general in 1956 and 1957. The intellectuals among the Soviet youth tended to side with the dissidents and to oppose the establishment. For example, young Soviet intellectuals were in sympathy with the Hungarian rebellion of 1956. Sherman believes that such dissident intellectuals are far less willing than their conformist peers to accept what seems to be simply a change in tactics on the part of the government (that is, instead of being brutal, the government attempts to distract them). Sherman quotes a young dissident who confided in him, "We have found out that when you beat your head against a stone wall, you break your head, not the wall." Another confided, more in sorrow than in anger, "The secret police have changed their tactics, they are more polite. Whether they call it arrest or education, however, their power amounts to the same thing. They are the stick, and the leadership of the Party wields it" (p. 329). Thus, the rebellion of Soviet youth seems to be confined to a group of intellectuals among the students. Most of the students, 90 percent in Sherman's view, belong to the Komsomol, and among them a small group are highly active. These activists are the somewhat cynical students who have learned the mechanics of political power and are making progress for themselves by learning how to use that power. If, like the United States, the Soviet Union has its dissidents and its activists, its delinquents and its conformists, these categories pertain more to a stance with respect to a dominant political philosophy than they do in this country. This is only reasonable since the Soviet government, as compared to that of the United States, plays such a large role in society.

Youth in Holland

In many respects it is rather difficult to compare the youth in European countries to those of the United States, simply because the European educational system is vastly different from that of the United States. For example, in Holland there is no such thing as a bachelor's degree or an undergraduate college. A youngster who has been privileged to go through one of the superior high schools can enter the university, which is roughly equivalent to the last two years of college plus graduate school in the United States. The first degree is a doctorandus, which is something between the master's and the Ph.D. degree in the United States. Thus, while college may serve in the United States as a moratorium on the requirement of making occupational and vocational decisions, there is no such educational mechanism in Holland. By and large, however, Dutch boys and girls do not go on to universities; in fact, probably not more than 7 or 8 percent actually attend a university. A far larger percentage go to technical schools and institutes which train them for specific occupations. The basis for routing students into the various tracks of higher education is the sort of high school from which the students came. The basis, in turn, for determining the sort of high school which the students attend is their success in passing a set of exams. Although this educational system has been breaking down rather rapidly since 1968, when a major educational law was enacted, there is still quite a bit of class distinction based on education. Traditionally, only students who have gone through the gymnasium or the atheneum (the superior high schools) can enter a university. Those who have attended the lower or middle high school either go to work after high school or enter one of the technical schools or institutes. Such fields as journalism, nursing, social work, and education are taught in the institutes. This is another major difference between universities in the United States and universities in the Netherlands. Much of what is taught at universities in the United States is taught in separate institutes which are often not affiliated with a university in Holland.

The status of the adolescent in Holland is defined by two very important institutions, namely, the family and the school. The family exerts far greater influence on individuals of any age in Holland than it does in the United States. In Holland most individuals, roughly 90 percent, live in families. The Dutch have the special word *gezin* to signify the nuclear family in which they live. The *gezin* is the *familie* in which the individual is living at the moment. Thus, a boy leaves his parental gezin to begin his own marital gezin. The importance of family life in Holland is illustrated in a variety of ways. First, a rich language surrounds the various aspects of homemaking and housekeeping. Second, although many women have been educated and trained for roles outside the home, the main function of a large majority of the women still lies within the home. Dutch society places a much higher value on domestic activities than does that of the United States. The word *gezellig* is used to describe a gezin which is characterized by a certain warmth, friendliness, and love of companions. Attachment to one's family persists throughout life. Birthdays, anniversaries, and so on are celebrated by parents and children, brothers and sisters. The importance of the family is seen even in industry and business. For example, on evenings when stores stay open late, such as before holidays, the stores close during the supper hour so that the managers can eat with their families. It would be unthinkable not to be home with one's family at that time.

One also sees the importance of the Dutch family in its recreational pursuits. It is quite common in Holland for a family to spend an afternoon at the park together, or to skate together on the canals, or to visit or be visited by another family as a family (that is, including the children). This is very different from the situation which Bronfenbrenner describes as characterizing the U.S. family, in which many activities, especially leisure, are age-segregated. The effect of this family orientation on Dutch adolescents is seen in the fact that by and large they continue along the same sort of educational track as that of their parents (McKinney, 1970). In addition, adolescents as well as young children spend much more of their free time at home with their parents than is true in the United States.

The age categories in Dutch society are much the same as those in the

United States, with one or two notable exceptions. Goudsblom (1967) has followed the categorization of Ponsioen (1963), who divided the population into five age groups: *"children,* up to the age of 14; *youth,* from 15 to 24; *younger adults,* from 25 to 39; *adults,* from 40 to 64; and the *aged,* 65 and older."* (p. 43) According to Goudsblom, the age group that we are talking about here would be what the Dutch consider youth. The category which seems to differ from the age groupings in the United States is that of younger adults (*jongeren*). These are persons who have finished their education and enjoy full adult status in some social senses but occupy a somewhat subordinate position until they are promoted to higher occupational ranks. The term is generally used more in the middle and upper-middle classes (Goudsblom, 1967) than in the lower classes, and it is interesting to us here only because it indicates that the importance which Keniston (1968) attaches to youth as the period after adolescence and before full adulthood is already an established fact in Holland (Ponsioen, 1963). The term is well established in the language, at least among the middle classes. But the main adolescent group in Holland consists of the youngsters in high schools who are still close to the *familie* and are heavily engaged in their primary activity, which is education. The educational training of these youngsters follows more rigid tracks than does that of the United States, although this is changing rapidly. One reason for tracking is the economic reason; namely, individuals are trained for roles which they are capable of handling and for which positions may be available.

In one study comparing the vocational aspirations of Dutch and American youth it was found that the values underlying vocational choice were somewhat different (McKinney, 1970). The main value underlying the choice of vocation among Dutch youth was the satisfaction they hoped to find in the vocation chosen, and the second most important value was the preparation and ability which they thought they might have for that vocation. Although data were gathered on both boys and girls, the most striking differences are between American and Dutch boys. For American boys, the two most important values were the interest they thought the job vocation would have for them and the satisfaction that they might get from it. The consideration of preparation and ability was 6.5 in their ranking of values. Much more important than that, for example, was salary, which was ranked third. This value ranked fifth among the Dutch boys. The difference between the development of Dutch and American adolescents may be summarized very simply by saying that there is a closeness to one's family among Dutch youth which continues into adulthood. Second, compared to American youth, among Dutch youth there is a greater tracking of education and less flexibility in choice of occupation. For the interested student there is an excellent chapter on Dutch youth in Ishwaran's (1959) *Family Life in the Netherlands.*

Youth in France

Many of the characteristics which distinguish American adolescents from their Dutch counterparts also distinguish them from French adolescents. An excellent source for a study of adolescents in France is a paper by Wylie (1965).

Wylie cautions the student interested in the study of national differences by noting that though there are differences in national groups and in the rearing of children in different nations, these are not so obvious nor so extensive as the differences among, let us say, widely separated primitive cultures. On the other hand, the differences are real, and the differences in adolescent behavior can be attributed to these real cultural differences. Although, as Wylie indicates, many differences can be found within a single nation, the differences among nations seem to transcend them. He observes, for example, that a boy going through a New England prep school may be more different from a youngster in New York's Harlem area than from a Parisian boy attending the *lycée*. However, he goes on to say that nevertheless "there is something about the adolescent experience of a French boy which makes it different from the normal adolescent experience of an American. The basic differences which exist between French and American adolescents transcend social class and are evidence of contrasts between the cultures themselves" (p. 291).

The most important differences, according to Wylie, are concerned with the treatment of limits. Wylie contends that in France society imposes distinct limits on adolescents, and that the adolescents' task of growing into adulthood has much to do with coping with the limits which are set for them. On the other hand, in the United States there is a semblance of greater freedom for adolescents, and their developmental task may be to discover, without the help of adults, just what their behavioral limits are. In some respects, this is similar to the situation of the Dutch youth, who know full well what occupational choices are open to them and the rather confining limits within which they must make a choice. This is in contrast to American adolescents, who seemingly have a wide range of possibilities open to them. The limits are physical as well as social. To a much greater extent than American children, French children know how far from home they can wander and are also taught to live within the established guidelines of social class distinctions.

Wylie believes that this difference in the setting of limits influences how youth handle the physical aspects of puberty. He says, for example, that the young in France are more likely to be upset by the sudden awakening of sexual desires because in a rational and compartmentalized world such newly encountered feelings seem not to fit with their earlier knowledge and beliefs and with their familiar world. The response to these feelings, however, is much helped by the new set of rules which they learn for the handling of such impulses. Wylie says, "He may be more upset than the American child by the feelings that accompany puberty, but he is better equipped to handle those feelings. From early childhood he has been taught the necessity of controlling his impulses, of not expressing them freely. With puberty, he is confronted with the most violent urge of all. The urge may frighten him, but he is a least used to exerting self-control" (pp. 295–296). To American children the feelings do not come as powerfully simply because, according to Wylie, they are not as used to compartmentalizing their lives in rational components. On the other hand, American children are given less preparation in dealing with powerful impulses, and the notion that they now have to restrain themselves and control those impulses is a difficult one for them to master. In addition, children in the United

States must cope with the differences between accepted practices and behaviors and expressed attitudes and values. It is true that a double standard also exists in France, but the double standard is clear in France, whereas in the United States, according to Wylie, there tends to be a greater need for children to piece together for themselves what acceptable behavior really is. What they have learned at home, at school and in church may be at variance with what they see in the movies, the magazines, the locker room, and so on.

Wylie believes that sexual initiation of the young male in France is undoubtedly carried out by the woman. He points out that this is the way in which the situation has been described in novels and films, but admits that whether or not these actually reflect reality is unclear. But he believes that in many cases the fictional description is an accurate analysis of what actually takes place. In the United States, on the other hand, sexual initiation is often handled poorly and informally by a youngster and his peers. The unwillingness of Americans to set limits makes this problem more difficult for the American child than for the French child—what is expected is not as clear-cut. Wylie gives the graphic example of Jimmy, the youngster in the James Dean movie *Rebel without a Cause,* who asks repeatedly for guidelines or rules. His father is unable to cope with the situation and suggests that the important thing is simply to understand.

The notion of limits that Wylie uses in describing the psychosexual development of French youth extends also to vocational aspirations. The French boy knows about the political, religious and moral traditions of his family and how they fit into a social and professional life. He is guided by these traditions in his own choice of an occupation or a profession. While such limitations and expectations may seem to restrict one's freedom, it is also true that the experience of freedom gives rise to a sense of identity diffusion in the American child. Wylie believes that the French child's retaliation against the confinement he may feel is expressed in rather personal, artistic ways. "Even though one of the most common feelings may be hatred for *les autres,* the people around him who force him to conform superficially, so long as the adolescent's retaliation is confined to his feelings or even to verbal or artistic expression, society imposes no sanction" (p. 299).

The use of limits as guides pertains as much to family life as it does to sexual behavior and occupational and educational decision making. Wylie points out that in the French family the father's rule is the law until adolescents leave home. He describes the French father as a benevolent despot whose regulations are sometimes softened by the mother's individual behavior to the children. However, he mentions another very important difference between the French and the American family, namely, that, just as was seen with respect to sexual development, the French father's restrictions on the child have to do with behavior and not with opinions, feelings, and ideas. Wylie ends his comparison of French and American youth by pointing out that in France, as in the United States, adults are showing a growing concern that the young are marrying too early. As a result, the youngsters are beginning to feel the constraints of their parents. They are beginning to rebel more openly against the father's authority. Conversely, American youth may be asking that limits again be set on their behavior. Indeed, their parents also seem to feel a greater need for setting limits on their children's behavior. In other words, a shift in both cultures may reduce the differences which we have described here.

Youth in Japan

The problems of leaving the world of childhood and entering into the world of the adult are also evident among the youth of Japan. However, as with the other countries we have discussed, the form which these developmental tasks take and the intensity with which they are experienced are in many respects peculiar to that country. Thus, though youth in Japan, like youth in France, Holland, and the United States, experience the general problem of identity, the identity problem in Japan is based on a cultural discontinuity resulting from that country's defeat in World War II, as well as its industrialization and historical change in its perspective concerning such things as social and religious tradition. Thus, the peculiar problems of the adolescent are set in a cultural context by the problems of the culture as a whole. The way in which the adolescent experiences an identity struggle is bound to be related to the way in which the society is changing. In a paper on youth in postwar Japan, Lifton (1965) suggests that three bases must be considered in studying the development of Japanese youth. These are the psychological and social components of Japan's cultural tradition, the psychobiological tendencies which are common to all mankind, and the current forces of historical change which are specific to Japan. In other words, Lifton points to one set of characteristics common to children of all countries and to two sets of characteristics which are specific to Japan, namely, historical traditions and current social situations.

Among the cultural and historical factors which influence the identity problems of Japanese youth is the break with the traditional past which the Japanese have experienced. Lifton notes that the youth of Japan regard their traditional past and its rituals as irrelevant and antiquated. They consider many of Japan's inherited social customs as feudalistic. On the other hand, they also reject as "monopoly capitalism" what seems to be modern or even the postmodern society of the large cities. In effect, this makes it difficult for youth to identify either with the past or the present. On the basis of a series of intensive interviews with Japanese youth, Lifton has concluded that individual Japanese adolescents resolve this disconnection in a variety of ways. One is by simply being a bystander, that is, an alienated individual standing on the sidelines and hoping for the recovery of some symbols of the past while at the same time condemning those very symbols. Another is excessive experimentation, that is, exposing oneself or being exposed to a variety of circumstances, which, according to Erik Erikson, would be characteristic of a person undergoing serious identity diffusion. An excellent and graphic example of identity diffusion is provided by Lifton's description of the life of a young Japanese student. Lifton asks the reader to "consider the confusing array of identity fragments . . . experienced by one rather sophisticated Tokyo-born young man, whom we shall call Kondo—all before the age of 25." He goes on to relate how the shifting aspects of Kondo's identity were influenced by the changes taking place in postwar Japan. Kondo was socialized into the Japanese middle-class way of life by his professional family. However, as a result of being evacuated from Tokyo to the countryside during World War II, he was exposed to the life of the farmer and the fisherman. Thus he developed a taste for the "common" life. Kondo accepted without question the divine descent of the Japanese emperor and the sacredness of Japan's cause, and he "hated the Americans." He was shocked and confused when Japan surrendered to the Allies, but he was curious rather than hostile when he first met an American soldier. It took only a short time for Kondo to become "an eager young exponent of democracy" when the "democracy boom" swept Japan, but he became equally devoted to aspects of the traditional Japan, especially its poetry, novels, and drama and its art of flower arrangement.

Kondo's activities in junior high school and high school included student government, athletics, and social activities, and in addition he excelled in his studies. Drawing ideas from Marxist doctrines then current in Japanese intellectual circles, he began to criticize society. At the same time, he criticized fellow students for focusing all their interest only on preparation for getting into the best universities so that they would get the best jobs and ultimately lead stuffy, conventional lives. Favorably impressed by the affluence and seemingly relaxed manner of Americans he had met, Kondo's interest in America grew. At this point he began to lose interest in everything he was doing and developed what he called a "kind of neurosis." Seeking a change of scene, he applied and was accepted for admission to a program of study at an American high school.

Kondo became increasingly enthusiastic about American life. His American "father" was a Protestant minister who so moved Kondo that he converted to Christianity on a sudden, emotional decision. After a year the time came for him to return to Japan. He did so reluctantly, only to find that he was looked upon as "something of an oddity." He was criticized for having become fat, crude, and insensitive, and was told that he "smelled like butter." Wanting to be accepted again, he developed an awareness of his "Japaneseness" and engaged in the traditional Japanese customs of drinking tea, eating on floor mats, and "sharing with friends a quiet and somewhat melancholic mood."

Later aspects of Kondo's identity diffusion were influenced by his failure to pass the university entrance examination on his first attempt, his lack of interest in university studies once he was accepted, and his later participation in demonstrations with student activists advocating "pure communism." But he eventually "drifted into a life of dissipation" centered on drinking, Mah-jongg games, and bar girls. This was followed by employment in a huge business organization where he again found a "central focus." He conformed to the conventions of being a proper businessman but at the same time felt much self-contempt for becoming a "machine for capitalism." Lifton says that the example of Kondo is not common among Japanese youth. Still, the way in which this one individual looked for an identity of his own helps us to realize the particular character of identity seeking among Japenese youth.

In writing about the family life of the Japanese, Lifton suggests that the students tend to be very close to their families even into late adolescence. Although there may be differences of opinion about political or social problems, "the son's emotional state is less one of 'rebellion' than of continuous inner search" (p. 268).

The Japanese have come to look to the West with a good deal of ambivalence. They reject attempts to over-Westernize the Japanese, yet at the same time they have incorporated much of the industrial culture of the Western world. In addition, the defeat in World War II has been a humiliation for the Japanese youth since it was a defeat not only for their country but also for a mystical ideological concept of *kokutai,* which Lifton describes as national polity or national essence. Moreover, the rapid industrial expansion which has occurred since World War II has not been an unmixed blessing. Students have seen the dehumanizing effects of such rapid industrial development in the Western world and, indeed, in their own country. Lifton says that they now look to the West but see that there is a good deal of ethical, political, and social uncertainty in the Western countries. On the other hand, they see communism as a dominant, powerful force, but they also see the cruelty with which it has been exercised in some of their neighboring countries. As marginal men in a variety of ways, they are torn between their identification with the Asian world and their own more rapid westernization. In a sense, they are not completely Asian since they have already passed through much of the revolutionary stage which the rest of Asia is currently experiencing. But neither are they completely Western, and indeed they still tend to reject as odious much of what they see in Western capitalism. The questions of identity and marginality pertain to adolescent development in Japan as elsewhere, but here they take on peculiar characteristics associated with the cultural situation in that particular country.

Lifton points out that over and above the historical and cultural factors there is an ideological gap of generations which is found in varying degrees in all cultures. One way in which youth have attempted to overcome the dislocation they feel with the past is by emphasizing the self—the development of the individual. Egocentrism has become a popular topic of discussion and study. Western films depicting this phenomenon have become exceedingly popular. Despite this emphasis on selfhood and individuality, importance is also attached to the renewal of a meaningful group life so that, as Lifton says, "one feels this tension between the ideal of individualism and the need for the group in the concern of young people with that much discussed, elusive, sometimes near-mystical, but always highly desirable entity known as *shutaisei*" (p. 274). Lifton translates this word to mean "subjecthood," that is, the idea of man as an active agent. Just as there is a rejection of the past and still a longing for some of the order and beauty of the past, and just as there is a rejection of the Western world at the same time as there is incorporation of some of its industrial values, so too there is another paradox. Emphasis on individuality and subjecthood are occurring at the same time as the importance of a renewal of group life is stressed. Lifton, however, does not see this as a contradiction. He says, "Yet the very groups to which youth are drawn may themselves become arenas for the struggle for selfhood. In this group life there is always a delicate balance between competition (often fierce, though usually suppressed), mutual support and encouragement, and (perhaps most important) constant comparison with other members as a means of self-definition'' (p. 274). Thus, for Lifton, to be an individual and to be a member of the group are two sides of the same coin. Perhaps this is akin to the balance between being both subject and object simultaneously which Rollo May (1967) describes as the human dilemma.

In summary, it would appear from Lifton's observations that the youth of postwar Japan do engage in a struggle for the development of their own identity. It is a struggle which is intensified by cultural and historical conditions and which, as is true among Dutch but not American youth, is undoubtedly abetted by their close relations with their families.

Black youth in the United States

Now that we have discussed the youth of a number of other countries, it may be appropriate to examine the variety of ways in which the youth of subgroups in our own country develop, and how this development may be related to their specific cultural heritages. As examples of differing cultural experiences, we will consider black American youth and youth living in Appalachia, as well as Native American youth.

In characterizing any group, one needs to be constantly aware of individual differences and subgroup differences within the group. A failure to do so could be seen as supportive of prejudice. Within the black community, for example, social class differences account for a good deal of behavioral variability. While few black families are found in the upper class or among the corporate rich, an increasing number are members of the middle class. The socialization of the adolescents in these families is necessarily different from the socialization of the street-wise ghetto youth (Wilkinson, 1975). In addition, changes in the black community during the past 20 years make many observations almost instantly anachronistic. Wilkinson (1975) suggests that black youth are at a new juncture: "With each slight change in their parents' economic and occupational statures and with increasing educational opportunities for themselves, their conceptions of what roles they should play as adults and their accompanying political consciousness have been altered" (Wilkinson, 1975, p. 302).

The developmental task of a black teenager in American culture is one of resolving a compounded identity problem. If the identity problem is characteristic of youth as a whole in this country, it is particularly characteristic of black youth. Besides being required to resolve the issue of their identity as adults and their sex identity, black youth must also resolve the question of racial identity. In the powerful literary example of this struggle depicted in James Baldwin's (1953) novel *Go Tell It on the Mountain*, the main character is faced with examining the implications of being black while holding some interests and values that are more generally ascribed to whites; of being in many ways a child, yet with the growing body of a man; and of being a religious person like his father, yet resenting the apparent inevitability of that fact. Although the novel is somewhat dated, this character still appears to be an appropriate exemplar of the struggle of black youth for meaningful selfhood. If, as Lewin says, the adolescent is a marginal man, the black adolescent is doubly so.

However, any characterization of a minority group suffers in a number of ways, not the least of which is its tendency to quick obsolescence in a rapidly changing society. Lewis Jones (1965) describes the changing world view of the black during the 1960s. "Population changes, expansion of the Negro middle class, emergence of a new leadership among Negroes, adoption of direct action once their prerogatives were legally clarified, and new policies of the federal government in the protection of civil rights—together, these have effected some improvement in Negro status in the South" (p. 74).

It was not until 1960 that young blacks discovered and began to use social action measures that meant taking a strong initiative. They rejected the rewards of subservience and the acceptable means of obtaining them. Rejected too was the slow pressure against limits and boundaries. Their hope of being the individuals who escaped as "first" or "only" was gone. The new tactics and strategy adopted by black youths themselves began the revolution to change the black's world.

"The hopes of Negro youth today about their tomorrow are in striking contrast to the hopes their fathers held. . . . This generation of children lives in a climate of change and they will increasingly influence its course" (Jones, pp. 74–75). Jones goes on to describe the features of a new self-image of black youth. First, the new self-image includes the awareness that the blacks must rely on themselves for support in the revolution for equality. Second, Jones maintains that this new vision of black youth includes seeing themselves as leaders among people rather than as simply being prepared to be leaders. Third, their image of blacks as a helpless minority is fading. Jones believes that the black youth now "sees himself as belonging to the majority that includes the federal government, Negroes who have advanced outside the South, and white people of powerful influence outside of the South" (p. 78). Finally, Jones belives that this new self-image includes the belief among blacks that they hold tenaciously to the important human values.

Over and above this world view and changing self-image, Jones sees a variety of orientations into which black youths divide themselves. First there are *accommodators,* who are willing to accept with gratitude the changes that have already occurred and to play the traditional black professional and occupational roles. Second, there are the *transcenders,* who are serious about their studies, strive for new occupational opportunities, and have little time for political activism or student demonstrations. Third, there are the *social activists,* such as the members of the Student Non-violent Coordinating Committee, the followers of Martin Luther King, and the campaigners for civil rights. Fourth, there are the *apartheids,* who include the Black Muslims. Finally, there are the *black worlders,* whom Jones describes as being to the right of the Black Muslims and as having a "black internationalist view, seeing the world they want brought into being by darker peoples becoming an effective majority that will reduce the Caucasian minority to its fitting minority status" (p. 82). Jones goes on to note that the variety of positions held by black youth makes it clear that there is no one black world view among the youth and that the black adolescent presents a rather complicated picture. Clearly, the various orientations provide identifications for black adolescents. The description given above of the black adolescent as a marginal man becomes less appropriate as a variety of legal, political, and educational institutions assume responsibility for changing the black man's status.

In a paper on identity in black youth, Erik Erikson (1964b) comments similarly that in the last few years "Negro youth finds itself involved in action which would have seemed unimaginable only a very few years ago" (p. 29). The identity of black youths is confusing in part because of the number of identifications open to them. In Jones's view, for example,

> "By 1960, the Negro was relatively poorer than he had ever been before at any historical point in his presence in America. During slavery each Negro knew his worth: he had a price determined by age, weight, sex, and the intermeshing of skills-fecundity, appearance, and occupation. He was a commodity, and as such, he was valued and protected. In freedom, his economic worth went through changes because his world had changed" (p. 71).

One needs to ask how one who had known the degradation of being a "commodity," an object, can begin to integrate an identity as an agent of change in his environment and in his own destiny. The answers that social scientists and others have given to this question have included economic power, political position, adequate education, and family stability.

The early attempt to change the negative view of being black (and by cruel association, dirty, dumb, "nigger") involved an identification with the dominant white values. This process is examined in the psychoanalytic framework by Erikson: "The result, especially in those Negroes who left the poor haven of their Southern homes, was often a violently sudden and cruel cleanliness training, as attested to in the autobiographies of Negro writers. It is as if by cleansing, a whiter identity could be achieved" (p. 30).

Erickson makes clear that identity is not merely identification with others but a sameness or integrated continuity that makes the individual able to "recognize himself and feel recognized." He suggests that some black youth turn toward a negative identity which has been most clearly delineated.

Native American youth

If it is dangerous to compare national groups and assume that differences among them are all cultural, it is equally dangerous to lump all North American Indian groups together and assume a common culture. Indeed, Thompson (1950) long ago described personality differences, not only between, for example, Hopi Indians and such other groups as their neighbors, the Navaho, but even between Hopi groups living in different communities on the same reservation. Still, some commonality, in social and political situations if not in personality, is suggested by the very existence of the American Indian Movement. Surely the commonality extends to victimization by the white person, systematic attempts to educate children in government schools, the deprivation of usual means of self-sufficiency, and relegation to reserves, and other governmental policies designed to rob the Indian of his or her Indian identity. For example, Ojibway children on the Cape Croker reserve in Ontario were once paddled for speaking their native language on the playground or in the schools. Today the children have few adults who can teach them Ojibway in the schools, so the government has instituted a special program for native language instruction. As one Ojibway woman observed, "First they (the government) take it away from us, now they pay to give it back."

The various steps into Indian society have been documented both by anthropologists (e.g., Benedict, Thompson) as well as by Native Americans. For example, Helen Sekaquaptewa, a Hopi, has described the Kachinvakis or whipping of the children by the Kachinas, as an initiatory step into the Hopi society (Udall, 1969). In the same work, Ms. Sekaquaptewa also recalls that during her youth Indian youngsters were forcefully taken from their homes and villages and forced to attend government schools.

It is not surprising that under such circumstances, the maintenance of one's identity as an Indian has become a major issue. The observations of Ruth Benedict and the anthropological data of Margaret Mead, described earlier, attest to the fact that there were among Indian tribes a number of continuities in development which make adolescence less problematic. Still, initiation rites prevailed as a way of signaling the end of childhood and the beginning of adulthood, again a way of ameliorating adolescent conflict.

This is not to say that there was no concern with adolescent identity versus role diffusion over and above the identity crisis brought on by the white person's demands for conformity. The Indian concern with the issue of identity is beautifully illustrated in an Ojibway myth, recounted by Johnston (1976):

Pitchi-Robin
Ten years elapsed before Menominee (Rice) and his wife, Nadowaequae, (Iroquois Woman) became parents of a boy. Having been disappointed to despair by years of hoping, the couple were overjoyed. They both aspired for their son from the very first. In fact, they became so inordinately pleased, not only with their son, but also with themselves that they harboured all manners of hopes for their son. While the mother doted upon her infant son, the father nurtured ambitions.

By the time the boy was seven, Menominee had determined what his son would be and what he would do to attain his end. More than anything else, Menominee wanted his son to excel over all other young men in the village in hunting, fishing, fighting, racing, shooting, and in all physical skills. Menominee's son would be the first man.

In the years that followed, the training Menominee imposed upon his son was intense. But in one respect, Menominee failed. Although the boy developed remarkably and amazed the village, the boy did not foster a mean disposition, an essential part of the character of warriors.

And although swimming, wrestling, and shooting contests pleased the boy, he much preferred to listen to the songs of birds and to hear the chants of singers and to dance to the beat of drums. Secretly, he aspired to chant and to make people happy, through music and dance. Still he tried to please his father.

When the time for contests arrived, the boy did not, even though he excelled, triumph or win in every instance. It was true he was victorious in most matches, but he lost a few times.

To come first or to be victorious in the majority of encounters was not good enough for Menominee. He drove and urged his son to greater efforts, and try as he might, the boy could not overcome his lack of strength. He was born of average size and docile disposition.

When the boy triumphed, there was joy; when he failed, desolation. On occasions of defeat, Menominee would reproach his son bitterly and refuse to speak to him sometimes for days. For the boy, the only solace was in listening to the songs of birds. There was no gratification in triumph; dread in losing.

Eventually, Menominee realized that his son would never, as he had hoped, be the foremost man in the community. But mediocrity in the physical order, Menominee reasoned, did not preclude excellence in the moral order. The father, therefore, determined that his son would excel through vision.

With a change in ambition, came change in father's attitude. He now encouraged his son to seek vision.

The boy was glad, his time was near in any event. At his father's direction, the boy went out to the Place of Vision. The first vigil was abortive, there was no vision. Nor did the second vigil produce vision. Five years came, lingered, went; nothing.

At first, Menominee said nothing about the failures; but as time passed, Menominee's solicitude turned to contempt and bitterness and he began to consider his son to be somewhat unworthy, while the boy began to despond.

Nevertheless, father and son persevered. In the spring of the sixth year of quest, Menominee said to his son as they were setting out for the Place of Vision, "I don't know why you have not yet had your vision. Most young men your age have received theirs." The lodge was set up and the father withdrew.

Four days later bringing meat and corn to feed his son, Menominee returned to the Place of Visions. As he approached the lodge whose entrance was open, Menominee sensed that something was wrong. There was no sound, no sign of life. He looked into the lodge which was stark and empty. Anxious, Menominee looked around before calling out. But there was no reply to his shout except the echo of his voice resounding throughout the forest. All that day, he searched and shouted.

Exhausted, despondent, and sensing the worst, Menominee abandoned his search late that evening. On his tearful way home, a little bird, black of head, orange of breast, and a dark grey, followed the dejected man. Flitting from tree to tree the strange little bird accompanied Menominee home, singing all the while.

Near Menominee's lodge, the little bird made his nest and chanted daily afterward, morning and evening.

Next day and for weeks after, Menominee went back to the Place of Vision to resume his search for his son. His only and ever constant companion was the little bird who went with him every time he returned to the Place of Vision.

Eventually, Menominee despaired of ever seeing his son again. Still, over the years, the man returned to the Place of Vision almost daily, often to sit in gloom. And as often as he went, the little bird accompanied him. Eventually, too, Menominee found solace in the little bird who was his companion.

And even though time passed, Menominee's sense of loss did not diminish. He, very old and frail, continued to go frequently to the Place.

One day, tired from the walk and weary, Menominee fell asleep upon the grasses at the Place of Visions. He dreamed. And in his dream, he saw his son descend from another sphere, and stand beside him. Holding up his hand as in greeting, the boy, youthful and happy, spoke.

"Father, I'm glad that you have come. I have waited for a long time to see you here. Only here, where our paths once parted a long time ago could we meet. I am glad that we met because now I can tell you that I love you. Since that day when I received my vision, I have been sad for you. When I was a boy I loved you and tried to make you happy, but I could not. You too loved me; tried to make me happy but could not. In my quest, I asked for the ability to please you, at the same time, bring happiness to our people and peace to myself.

"During my quest, I was suddenly enveloped by a brilliant orange light as blinding as the sun. The light itself was circumscribed by dark grey and crowned by black. At the same time I was suffused by song and music which touched and moved my innermost soul-spirit. When I opened my eyes, I was soaring in the skies; tired, I rested upon a tree and sang the state of my soul-spirit which was filled with happiness. I learned then that song is the utterance of the soul-spirit. I knew then that I could move you, touch men, women, and children and by so doing, bring gladness to myself in form proper to my being and aspirations.

"On the day of my vision and transformation I saw you come; I heard you call; I followed you in your quest for me. I met you but you did not see me. I answered your call but you did not hear.

"I saw and felt your sorrow. In time your grief diminished; and you found, as I did, solace in music. I was glad. At last I could bring you some happiness. Now, father, as a bird, I shall continue to live near you and the Anishnabeg; as 'pitchi,' robin, I shall make you glad. I leave you now."

Menominee woke up. And with his awakening vanished the anguish that had burdened him over the years. He saw himself.

What the old man learned from his bitter experience he now imparted to his fellow Anishnabeg.

Never interfere with the vision quest of another.

Never allow another to interfere in your quest.

Love your children for what they are; not for what they can do.

Do not aspire beyond your scope and your own being.

When the old man died, he was met by his son in the Land of Souls; Pitchi's son and daughters continued to sing to the Anishnabeg.

A variant of this legend was told to me by Mrs. Irene Akiwenzie, an Ojibway Indian of the Cape Croker band, who said the same basic story has many variations, this being only one:

> You know that the partridge has many sinews going down from its legs into his feet? I'll tell you how they got there. When a certain Indian boy became 12 years old, his parents thought it was time for him to have his vision, so they took him to that place in the woods where it could happen. They left him there alone with food and water, but after several days and weeks he still didn't have his vision. His parents grew tired of waiting. Winter came, and the boy grew thin and frail. He was weak from not eating. Still he had no vision. His parents needed someone to pull their sled which was heaving with their provisions, so they went out to the boy and harnessed him to the sled. As he struggled with his weak body to pull the heavy sled, he suddenly turned into a partridge and flew off. The ropes and leather thongs which attached the boy to the sled became the sinews down the legs of the partridge. (I. Akinwenzie, personal communication)

Both of these legends seem to speak to the difficulty of parent-child separation at adolescence and the difficulty some adolescents have in taking hold of some separate identity or "vision" of their own.

An Appalachian adolescence

Another subgroup among American youth are the boys and girls who grow up in the mountains of Tennessee, West Virginia, and Kentucky. According to a sociological analysis by Manning (1975), youngsters growing up in a rural area are likely to be influenced by such demographic and environmental facts as low population density, generally lower income than in urban areas, greater out-migration, a more fundamentalist Protestant religious orientation, limited cultural opportunities, and lower educational and occupational attainment. Besides their rural character, however, the youth of Appalachia command our attention for other reasons. In a moving documentary of life in the hollows of Tennessee and Kentucky, Coles and Brenner (1968) have spelled out the idiosyncrasies of family life among a people who are both isolated and integrated. Coles, a child psychiatrist who had formerly worked with more affluent youth of the Northeast, gives us a picture of youths who learn the importance of family and of shared leisure and work in their mountain communities. Although these youths are timid, almost fearful, they do not appear to suffer the neurotic malady common to large numbers of their city counterparts, namely a constant striving and a constant questioning of identity. Coming of age in these isolated regions appears to be unique in a number of ways. First, the family unit is the extended family of cousins, aunts, uncles, and grandparents rather than the more insular nuclear family known to the majority of American youth. Second, mountain youth neither rebel against the family unit nor want to leave it. The question of dispersal mentioned in Chapter 1 takes on a new dimension here. Is there less conflict between parent and child in the Appalachian family? If so, why? Does urban affluence provide the impetus for intensified territoriality struggles? Do material possessions in a densely populated urban area involve a sense of constraint or a sense of the importance of work as a necessary means to an end? Do ample space and living close to the earth give mountain youth a greater sense of freedom? Coles believes that "the intensity between parents and children can be attenuated when there are many children and many 'parents'—grandparents, great-aunts and uncles, aunts and uncles, older cousins who in fact are parents themselves" (p. 42).

The family situation of the Appalachians is dissimilar from that of black Americans, whose attachment to the children is influenced by a history of having to give up children into slavery.

> An example: a colicky infant recently fed but still crying loud and strong will be held and held by his Negro mother; he will be held then put down by his Southern white mother, who nevertheless will be made fretful and irritable; he will be alternately held and put down by his middle-class suburban mother while, you can be sure, a doctor will be called, a book read, perhaps some medicine or a pacifier given. In the case of the Appalachian mother, the child's cry will be heard but somehow accepted as (so I've heard several women say) "the way it goes for a while." Of course we do not mean to be rigid about these distinctions. They merely represent certain general trends, the product, no doubt, of complicated historical, social, cultural, and psychological influences which, in given locations among certain people, sort themselves out into particular patterns. Just as it is not at all irrelevant to remember that Negro mothers once (not so long ago) had to surrender their children to the demands of slave markets—and thus have good historic reason to keep close to their children now—so it may well be that a mother herself born and reared in a region whose fate seems unshakable will find the vicissitudes of the growing baby to be yet another reflection of just that fate. (p. 37)

Sex is learned naturally and without inhibitions by those who live close to nature. No pornographic jokes there. From Coles and Brenner's observations, it would seem that the struggle for sexual identity is not as great for Appalachian youth as for youth in other parts of the United States.

Although one might be tempted to accuse Coles and Brenner of romanticizing what is assuredly a miserably impoverished life, it is probably closer to fairness to acknowledge that 20th century progress has been a mixed blessing, especially for the youngster who is coming of age. Identity crises are more likely to be experienced by a changing individual in a rapidly changing environment than by an individual growing up in a community marked by inevitable sameness and historical and family continuity, however harsh the elements of sameness and continuity may be.

SUMMARY AND CONCLUSIONS

The idea that storm and stress is a universal component of adolescence was seriously reevaluated in light of the field research of cultural anthropologists in the 1920s. The work of Margaret Mead and Ruth Benedict was foremost among this research.

In an important theoretical paper Benedict drew the distinction between continuities and discontinuities in cultural learning. Continuous behaviors are appropriate throughout life, from infancy through adulthood, whereas discontinuous behaviors are appropriate at one stage and inappropriate at later stages. Likewise, the training for social behaviors may be continuous or discontinuous. Three areas of discontinuity in conditioning between childhood and adulthood in our culture are the responsibility of the adult versus the nonresponsibility of the child (in one sense, work versus play), the sexual behavior of the adult versus the asexual life of the child, and adult dominance versus the submission of children.

The problem of adolescents is to unlearn some of their childhood conditioning and to learn a set of new behaviors appropriate to their adult status. The age at which this adult status is achieved, however, is unclear in our society. Some cultures clarify the distinction between child and adult by elaborate ceremonies or puberty rites. None of the rituals of adolescence in our culture seem to provide the same clarification of status. Graduations, "coming out" parties, and so on do not enjoy the universal adult acceptance that is accorded to puberty rites in some other cultures.

There are also distinct differences in the way different national groups handle the transition from childhood to adulthood. We have seen that though the problem of establishing adult identity is common to youngsters in Russia, Japan, France, Holland, and the United States, national differences in childhood training provide a variety of aids or hindrances to the solution of that problem. Moreover, among subgroups within the United States, itself, there are vastly differing styles of coming of age.

SUGGESTED ADDITIONAL READING

Benedict, R. Continuities and discontinuities in cultural conditioning. *Psychiatry*, 1938, *1*, 161–167.

Mead, M. *Coming of Age in Samoa.* New York: Mentor Books, 1949.

BOX 7–1
Study questions

What factors does Bandura cite as contributions to the growth of a mythology of adolescence?

What criticisms can be made of these factors?

What processes does social learning theory introduce in addition to operant conditioning for learning behaviors?

How do the studies by Meissner, Hess, and Goldblatt, and Offer, Sabshin, and Marcus on adolescents' views of their parents support social learning theory?

What are three ways in which adolescents' perception of their parents influence identification?

How does the quality of adolescent-parent interaction relate to peer group involvement in adolescent males?

What kind of parental attitudes towards their children lead to low levels of self-esteem in adolescents?

Describe some findings of the studies on resource control by parents.

In Brittain's study, what factor seemed to determine whether an adolescent would appeal to parent or peers for help in decision making?

If, as Mead says, we are moving toward to prefigurative culture in the United States, what implications does this hold for parents?

Name some of the issues that need to be dealt with in children and adolescents affected by a parental separation or divorce.

CHAPTER 7

ADOLESCENTS IN THE FAMILY

In the last chapter we saw that the view of adolescence as a turbulent, stressful period could not be universally supported. Although such stress and turbulence may have characterized adolescence in Freud's Vienna or Hall's America, the research of cultural anthropologists in the 1920s made it clear that they were not a necessary part of growing up. Indeed, in some areas of the world adolescence was found to be no more stressful than any other period of life.

REBELLION VERSUS CONFORMITY

More recently, some observers have questioned whether even in the United States the life of an adolescent is as stressful as Hall proclaimed it to be. Although Hall's theory has been a favorite for years, some theorists and researchers have begun to argue that it does not properly represent the majority of American adolescents.

Interview data about family relations

Douvan and Adelson (1966), for example, interviewed a national sample of over 3,000 boys and girls in grades 6 through 12 on a wide variety of subjects, including such things as their social clubs; their educational, vocational, and occupational aspirations; and their relations with their parents, teachers, and friends. As mentioned in Chapter 1, it is always possible to question the validity of the interview technique and the generalizability of the findings that are gleaned therefrom. However, when researchers are as cautious about making inferences and interpretations as Douvan and Adelson have been, it is extremely useful to have the sort of data which they provide about the development of normal adolescents. One of their most revealing chapters deals with adolescents and their families. Douvan and Adelson found that, far from being completely rebellious and disturbed, most adolescents lead a rather conventional and conforming life. The middle-class members of their adolescent sample were often concerned with the very issues of status, popularity, and social success that commanded the attention of their parents.

Whether adolescent boys and girls are rebellious or conforming need not be an "all-or-none" or an "either-or" question. Indeed, it may be that conformity and rebellion are two sides of the same coin, namely, the coin of establishing identity. As mentioned earlier, Erik Erikson views the major task of adolescence as the stabilization of a personal identity. Some individuals accomplish this by incorporating the values of their environment and behaving accordingly. Others find a "negative" identity in rejecting their environment and pursuing what appears to be a more independent course. The whole issue of conformity in adolescence will be dealt with in a later chapter. Our purpose here is simply to point out that not all observers see adolescence as a stressful period during which rebellion is necessary or universal.

The "myth" of adolescent rebellion

Perhaps the most vigorous opponent of the view of adolescence as a turbulent period is Albert Bandura (1964). His interviews revealed that adolescents and their parents hold rather positive attitudes toward one another. For example, the following interview between the researcher and the parents of a 17-year-old boy is given by Bandura as "typical" of his findings.

M. (mother): I don't have to do anything like that anymore. I think he's getting so mature now, he's sort of happy medium. I don't have to do much with him.

I. (Interviewer): What are some of the restrictions you have for him? How about going out at night?

F. (Father): We trust the boy, we never question him.

I: Are there any things you forbid him from doing when he is with his friends?

F: At his age I hate to keep telling him that he mustn't do this or he mustn't do that. I have very little trouble with him in that regard. Forbidding I don't think creeps into it because he ought to know at 17, right from wrong.

I. Are there any friends with whom you have discouraged him from associating?

F: No, not up to now. They are very lovely boys.

I: How about using bad language?

F: Only once have I; of course, I'm a little hard of hearing in one ear and sometimes he gets around the wrong side and takes advantage of that. (pp. 224–225).

Bandura suggests that this interchange was typical of his data and also that the accounts given by the teenagers themselves largely corroborate this somewhat idyllic picture of adolescents and their relations with their parents. The adolescents themselves were nearly as positive, as can be seen in the following interview.

I: What sort of things does your mother forbid you to do around the house?

B: Forbid me to do? Gee, I don't think there's ever anything. The house is as much mine as theirs. . . . Oh, can't whistle, can't throw paper up in the air, and can't play the radio and phonograph too loud. Rules of the house; anybody, I mean, it's not just me. . . .

I: Are you expected to stay away from certain places or people?

B: She knows I do. I'm not expected; I mean, she figures I'm old enough to take care of myself now. They never tell me who to stay away from or where. Well, I mean, they don't expect me to sleep down on Skid Row or something like that. (p. 225)

Bandura found that the same pleasant interactions governed the growing independence of most adolescents. He states that "emancipation from parents had been more or less completed rather than initiated at adolescence." Why, then, given this rather pleasant picture, does adolescence have such a bad name? Bandura cites a number of factors which may have contributed to the growth of a "mythology" about adolescence.

First, he mentions the "overinterpretation of superficial signs of nonconformity" and suggests that adults, too, have their fads. Bandura gives some rather anecdotal examples of such things as the sometimes bizarre apparel and comportment of adults at cocktail parties and the like.

Second, Bandura believes that another source of the mythologizing about adolescents is the mass media, which have capitalized on the limited view of adolescents as nonconforming and have blown it out of proportion. Third, he belives that the generalizations about adolescence have too often been made from deviant samples. Too often, he argues, a picture of the so-called typical adolescent has been derived from delinquents or from disturbed young people. Bandura considers the behavior of such youngsters to be symptomatic of their individual problems rather than of their status as adolescents.

The natural question to ask here would be whether certain problems are more characteristic of adolescents than of other age groups. Clearly, it is always a mistake to overgeneralize from deviant samples to the general population. Yet the major tasks which adolescents face may, indeed, be part and parcel of their being adolescents. However, youngsters will handle these problems in varying ways, just as their parents vary in dealing with the developmental tasks of adulthood. In addition, the same behavioral problem may express itself in quite different and characteristic ways among individuals of different ages. For example, it is Erikson's theoretical notion that identity versus identity diffusion is the main conflict to be resolved during the adolescent period. One would expect that the way in which adolescents might handle a problem of, say, aggression, would reflect their typical concern with identity. They might use aggression to establish who they are and who they are not. A two-year-old, by contrast, might use aggression in a typical two-year-old fashion—to establish a sense of autonomy from the parents. The aggression of a young adult or a senescent individual would also be expected to reflect the developmental concerns of their age groups.

Finally, Bandura mentions the problem of inappropriate generalization from cross-cultural data. He belives that too often data of diverse cultures which have little to do with coming of age in the United States have been used to explain

FIGURE 7–1   Group identifications are an important part of adolescence.

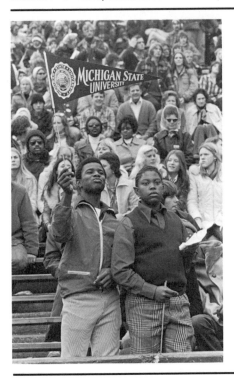

Photograph courtesy of Dan Hughson

the development of American youngsters. He does not reject all anthropological findings, however; in support of his theory, he states: "Cross-cultural studies have been valuable in demonstrating that stresses and conflicts are not inevitable concomitants of pubescence, but rather products of cultural conditioning. Indeed, in some societies, adolescence is one of the pleasant periods of social development" (Bandura, 1964, p. 229).

In general, then, Bandura perceives the behavior of adolescent youngsters as being less discontinuous from their previous experience and less disruptive than did earlier theorists who emphasized a more strictly biological interpretation of adolescence. Social learning theorists, such as Bandura, consider adolescent behavior to be a product of a certain continuity with earlier conditioning rather than a sudden biological reawakening.

SOCIAL LEARNING THEORY

In the last chapter we observed that the cultural anthropologists consider adolescence to be a consequence of certain discontinuities in the cultural conditioning of youngsters. In this chapter we can go one step beyond that position by examining the ways in which the social conditioning of boys and girls actu-

Albert Bandura

Courtesy of Albert Bandura

ally takes place. It would be more appropriate to say social learning rather than social conditioning since the social learning theorists contend that a good deal of learning takes place through simple observational procedures and without reinforcement. In line with Bandura's conviction that adolescence is not a stormy period and that the disruption of adolescence is a myth, he and other social learning theorists would take the position that there is a certain continuity in the social learning of the adolescent stage of development. This provides an excellent framework for the study of the family since the main socializing agents, in infancy and to some extent into adolescence, are the parents.

An overview of the theory

The following brief summary will give an overview of social learning theory, which has been described more fully in the earlier volumes of this series. Basically, the theory differs from other learning theories by extending the range of behaviors which can be easily accounted for by learning. This is done through the introduction of such concepts as modeling and imitation. Thus, according to social learning theory, children can learn to do something by observing other people do it, as well as by being rewarded for doing it right or punished for doing it wrong. For a child, the reinforcing agent is most often a parent or someone else who is seen as having a certain status or power. Where traditional operant conditioning theory postulates the necessity of a sequence of shaping up behaviors, social learning theory can account for the observation and imitation of a complex sequence of novel behaviors, no part of which was previously in the child's repertoire.

Bandura and Walters (1963) have shown that this transmission of novel responses can account for the development of such behaviors as aggression, dependency, and self-control. These social learning theorists, then, explicitly reject interpretations of behaviors which are based solely on biological stages. They view the behavior of an adolescent as a product of the sort of social learning that has occurred in his or her life since childhood. Comparing their own view to that of maturational stage theories, Bandura and Walters (1963) state: "In contrast, social learning theories would predict marked changes in the behavior of an individual of a given age only as a result of abrupt alterations in social-training and other relevant biological or environmental variables, which rarely occur in the social-learning histories of most individuals during pre-adult years" (p. 26).

Consistency of adolescents' views of adults

In support of Bandura and Walters' position, it should be noted that little research has demonstrated the kind of disruptive experience that is postulated by some of the stage theorists. For example, in a study by Meissner (1965) over 12,000 teenage high school boys were questioned concerning their views about their parents. In general, the boys' views were positive. Only 15 percent felt that their parents were overly strict, and 74 percent said that they were proud of their parents. Meissner found that the older adolescent boys tended to resist the authority of their parents, but he interpreted this as gradual disengagement from authority rather than rebelliousness. Most of the boys in Meissner's sample claimed to be happy with their home life, with 84 percent of them saying that they spent more than half of their leisure time at home.

The study by Hess and Goldblatt (1957), cited in an earlier chapter, came to much the same conclusion. The 32 teenage boys and girls and their parents who were questioned in that study expressed positive views of one another, despite the fact that each group expected deprecation by the other group. As stated earlier, the problem here seems to be more one of communicating a positive view rather than a problem of adults holding a negative view of adolescents. Similar results were obtained in a study by Maxwell, Connor, and Walters (1961).

In another study (Offer, Sabshin, & Marcus, 1965), 84 boys between the ages of 14 and 16 also reported favorable attitudes toward adults. These adolescents reported few intense conflicts, and in a later study Offer (1967) found that the same positive attitudes were sustained among the 73 boys whom he was able to interview 3 years later.

College students, too, predict that there is a greater gap between their views and their parents' views than there actually is (Lerner et al., 1975). Conversely, parents predict that their views are closer to the views of their college-age children than is actually the case. In other words, when we talk about a generation gap we should specify; do we mean adolescents' perception of the gap? Lerner and his associates would say that this gap is considerable. Or do we mean the parents' perception of a generation gap? The researchers concluded that that one was negligible. Or do we mean an actual difference in views. That actual generation gap was somewhere in between the other two—not as dramatic as the students thought but stronger than the parents believed.

Identification and imitation

Not only is the social learning position of adolescent development supported in a negative sort of way by research which fails to demonstrate a sudden disruption in parent-child relations during adolescence, but it is also supported more directly and positively by the growing volume of data on identification and imitation. It has been shown that the likelihood that children will act like their parents depends, at least in part, on their perception of the parents as rewarding and affectionate (Bandura & Walters, 1959). In addition, they are most likely to imitate the behaviors of persons whom they perceive as powerful (Bandura, Ross, & Ross, 1961). In this sense, however, perceiving one's parent as powerful refers to the fact that the child sees the parent as the controller of important resources and not necessarily as domineering and punitive.

In summary, then, we can see that the social learning interpretation of adolescence is supported by these questionnaire and interview data, or at least that these data provide little support for the view that adolescence is necessarily disruptive and ridden with parent-child conflicts. The importance attached to the family and especially to the parents by the social learning theorist is obvious, since these are the primary agents of socialization throughout childhood. It is therefore important to examine some of the child-rearing practices which give rise to the differential behavior of youngsters during their adolescent years.

PARENTS AS CONTROLLERS OF RESOURCES

One change which occurs in the parent-child relationship during adolescence is the conflict over the control of resources that the child wants or regards as his or her due. With increasing autonomy and independence, it becomes increasingly difficult for the child to submit to the authority of the parents. Still, in many material ways the parents control resources which adolescents find necessary for their psychological, social, and physical well-being. Such things as spending money, the use of the family car, having food available whenever one is hungry, and the right to come and go as one pleases come under this heading. Even into late adolescence and young adulthood, many children feel that their parents are overcontrolling and require reasons for every exercise of parental authority. One of the authors of this work has taught adolescent psychology for the past 20 years, and he has noticed that it is sometimes difficult for college students to isolate their own feelings and separate themselves sufficiently from the situation of adolescence to be objective in their study of this topic. This difficulty arises more frequently with the area of parent-child relations than with any other topic. The complaints of the college students, much like the complaints of their younger high school counterparts, focus on the desire to be treated like adults and to be given reasons for their parents' decisions.

Sex differences in the perceptions of control

Which parent calls the shots for most adolescents? In a study of the effects of parental resource control, Grinder and Spector (1965) tested 19 girls and 19 boys from each of the 9th, 10th, and 12th grades of a public high school. They asked their subjects to respond to 28 questions concerning which parent held control over a wide variety of situations and circumstances. These included such things as giving the youngsters permission to go out in the evening, helping them to choose a career, giving them consolation and comfort if they were unhappy, and planning the use of family leisure time.

The authors predicted and indeed found that there was some sex role differentiation in the selection of the parent who was perceived as controlling the resources. Although in general children may go to their mothers for nurturance and may expect authority from their fathers, Grinder and Spector found that girls perceived their mothers as having more resource control whereas boys perceived their fathers in that role. The authors present only the statistical data derived from the subjects' total scores across all 28 items. It would be interesting to know whether there is a set of items for which both boys and girls are more likely to see mothers as having control and another set of items which reflects the father's control. One logical division of authority and resource control in the traditional family, for example, might center on the distinction between at home versus away from home interactions. Thus, it would seem logical to expect mothers to exercise more control over behaviors and social interactions which involve the immediate family and the time spent at home. Fathers, on the other hand, might be expected to exercise more control over things which take the family out of the home and into settings which, in the traditional family, might be more a part of the father's day-to-day existence and would therefore be more familiar to him than to the mother.

In interpreting these data, it is important to keep in mind that the control exercised by either parent was always considered relative to that of the other parent; that is, the subjects were merely asked which parent would be more likely to exercise control in each situation. As important as these data are, they do not give us information about the absolute control of the parent or about the amount of control that the parent has over the decisions of the youngster relative to the amount of informal control that the youngster's peers might exercise.

Parent versus peer influence

A traditional view of adolescence is that youngsters at this stage turn from their parents as a frame of reference and tend to adopt the standards of their peers. That view went untested for many years. Finally, however, one study (Brittain, 1963) focused on this issue of the relative influence of parents and peers on the adolescent's choices. Although the study did not refer directly to the control of resources, it did examine less formal influences which these two reference groups exercise. Brittain used a rather interesting technique to ascertain whether a youngster would conform to parental or peer pressures in decision making. He asked a large number of high school girls to respond to 12 situations by choosing between two alternatives as a hypothetical youngster might choose. Brittain gives the following example to illustrate his procedure:

> A large glass in the front door of the high school was broken. Jim broke the glass. But both he and Bill were seen at the school the afternoon the glass was broken and both are suspected. Bill and Jim are friends and they agree to deny that they know anything about the broken glass. As a result, the principal pins the blame of both of them. Nell is the only other person who knows who broke the glass. She was working in the typing room that afternoon. She didn't actually see the glass broken, but she heard the noise and saw Jim walking away from the door a few moments later. Nell is very much undecided what to do. The three girls she goes around with most of the time don't think Nell should tell the principal. These girls hate to see an innocent person punished. But they point out to Nell that this is a matter between Jim and Bill and between Jim and his conscience. Nell talks the matter over with her mother and father. They felt that Jim is unfairly using Bill in order to lighten his own punishment. Her parents think Nell should tell the principal who broke the glass. Can you guess what Nell did when the principal asked her if she saw who broke the glass?
> —She told him that she didn't see it broken.
> —She told him who broke the glass (p. 385)

The twist in Brittain's technique was that he developed two different versions of the same instrument. The 12 stories were identical in both versions, with one exception—the opinions and preferences attributed to the parents in version A were the opinions and preferences attributed to the peers in version B, and vice versa. Brittain then administered the instrument on two separate occasions. He gave version A to half of the experimental group, then two weeks later presented that half with version B. The other half of the experimental group was given version B first, and then about two weeks later it was given version A. In addition, he used a control group, of which half were given version A and half were given version B on both occasions. What Brittain wanted to see was how often the girls would change their opinions in order to maintain conformity with whatever was presented as the parents' or the peers' view. Since there might be a certain amount of change in either direction simply as the result of chance, or for some other extraneous reason, Brittain used a control group.

As can be seen in Table 7–1, the data show that there was significantly more shifting by the experimental subjects than by the control subjects. That is, the control subjects, who were given the same version on both occasions, were more consistent in their responses than were the experimental subjects, who were given the versions with reversed reference groups. Thus, the shifts must have been due to the change in reference group. The data which Brittain presents do not support the traditional view that youngsters of high school age shift from parent-conforming behavior to peer-conforming behavior. Nor do they completely reinforce the view that adolescents will rely on their parents for all advice. Rather, Brittain reports somewhat unsurprisingly that what person ado-

TABLE 7–1
Proportion of control group and experimental group shifting responses

Item	Experimental group N = 280	Control group N = 58	Difference $p^E - p^C$	Chi square*
1. Which course to take in school	.52	.23	.29	15.60**
2. Which boy to go steady with	.50	.28	.22	12.71**
3. How to get selected for a school honor	.33	.28	.05	.94
4. Whether to report boy who damaged school property	.35	.14	.21	13.57***
5. Whether to enter beauty contest or be cheerleader	.44	.16	.28	22.52***
6. How to dress for football game and party	.51	.19	.32	26.42***
7. Whether to be beauty contestant or appear on TV program	.39	.14	.25	18.56***
8. Which dress to buy	.58	.19	.39	39.39***
9. Which one of two boys to date	.49	.16	.33	29.00***
10. Which part-time job to take	.34	.16	.18	10.66**
11. Whether to report adult who damaged public property	.38	.19	.19	10.23**
12. How to let boy know she is willing to date him	.36	.21	.15	6.66**

* Chi square computed from frequencies, df = 1.**p < .1.***p < .001.
Source: C. V. Brittain, "Adolescent choices and parent-peer cross-pressures," *American Sociological Review*, 1963, *28*, 385–391. By permission of the author and American Sociological Association.

lescents will ask for advice will depend upon the kind of advice that they want (see Table 7–2). For example, when it came to some of the less important decisions they had to make, the girls were more likely to request this advice from their friends. These might include such matters, for example, as how to dress for a football game or party, or which dress to buy. On the other hand, for more important decisions, such as taking a part-time job, or reporting an adult who had damaged property, they were more likely to turn to their parents for advice. It is important to note that Brittain's subjects were all ninth-grade girls. It would be valuable to obtain comparable data for males and for older and younger subjects. Once again, it should be remembered in considering these data that the conformity they disclose is relative; that is, the subjects were given the opportunity to respond in such a way that their answers reflected conformity either to their parents or to their peers. But one cannot learn from these data how absolutely conforming the youngsters are. They may be deciding without advice from either parents or peers. It would also be instructive to know about the developmental

TABLE 7–2
Frequency of shifts in choice of content alternatives from one form to the other

Item	Not shifting content alternatives (NS)	Shifting content alternatives			Chi square*
		Total (S)	Alternative selected		
			Parent (P)	Peer (F)	
1. Which course to take in school	135	145	48	97	16.56****
2. Which boy to go steady with	141	139	70	69	.01
3. How to get selected for a school honor	187	93	63	30	11.70****
4. Whether to report boy who damaged school property	182	98	58	40	3.30
5. Whether to enter beauty contest or be cheerleader	156	124	93	31	28.26****
6. How to dress for football game and party	138	142	47	95	16.22****
7. Whether to be beauty contestant or appear on TV program	170	110	83	27	31.00****
8. Which dress to buy	118	162	59	103	11.92****
9. Which one of two boys to date	143	137	81	56	4.56**
10. Which part-time job to take	184	96	69	27	18.37****
11. Whether to report adult who damaged public property	174	106	73	33	15.09****
12. How to let boy know she is willing to date him	180	100	64	36	(7.84)***
Column totals	1,908	1,452	808	644	—

* Chi square for differences between columns P and F computed on the basis of 50/50 assumption, df = 1; **$p < .05$; ***$p < 01$; ****$p < .001$.

Source: C. V. Brittain, "Adolescent choices and parent-peer cross pressures," *American Sociological Review*, 1963, 28, 385–391. By permission of the author and American Sociological Association.

changes in the amount of self-reliance in making decisions. There is some evidence which bears on that topic.

A study by Gardner and Thompson (1963) showed that as adolescents got older they tended to base their decisions on values which were characteristically their own, rather than by referring to the values of parents, teachers, friends, or adages. In other words, it is apparently a mark of greater maturity to make one's own values the referent for decisions rather than the values of others, whether parents or friends. In light of these data it would be interesting to repeat the Brittain study in a way that would allow the experimenter to make some inferences about the amount of conformity. One might, for example, use an open-ended procedure, such as asking the subjects "What would you do?" in each instance. The data could then be analyzed into categories which include not only peer conformity and parent conformity but also independent decisions.

An extension of the Brittain study (Emmerich, 1978) included both boys and girls and two grade levels. Using items similar to those used by Brittain, Emmerich found that 12th grade boys were higher on peer conformity than 9th graders, while 9th grade boys were higher on parent conformity than 12th graders. Among girls there were no significant differences between the 9th and 12th grades on parent and peer conformity. In other words, 9th grade boys are more influenced by their parents than both 9th grade girls and 12th grade boys and girls.

When a very different sort of method is used to assess parent and peer influence, such as when subjects are asked directly on a questionnaire to what extent they value advice from parents and peers, the results are not widely different. Curtis (1975), using such a questionnaire, found that females depend more on peer opinions than males do, and generally prefer their mothers' opinion over their fathers'. Furthermore, the reliance on parent opinions was found to decrease gradually from grade 7 to grade 12.

Not surprisingly, the relative influence exerted by parents and peers is related to the adolescents' perception of the major source of need satisfaction (Floyd & South, 1972). In those areas where peers are seen to provide the predominant need satisfaction, conformity to peers is higher; where parents are perceived to provide the need satisfaction, they are more influencial.

If needs are not being satisfied by parents, do adolescents spend more time interacting with their peers? Iacovetta (1975) posed this question in a study of 674 male seniors in high school. He related the quality of adolescent-adult interaction, to peer group involvement. Adolescent-adult interaction was assessed with six questionnaire items, such as "do your parents understand your problems?" The respondent could answer from among the following: "always, most of the time, sometimes, very seldom, or never." Peer group involvement, the other variable, included three dimensions: first, how often the respondent got together with peers; secondly, how dependent the respondent felt on his peers for help in facing his problems; and third, how autonomous the respondent felt in his activity with his peers, that is how free it was of adult supervision. Iacovetta's results are summarized in Table 7–3. The data are compelling. The quality of adolescent-adult interaction is significantly correlated to peer-group involvement on all three counts; frequency, dependence, and autonomy. Once again, however, it is important to remember that this study was done on males only.

CHILD-REARING PRACTICES

Authoritative versus authoritarian control

The sort of control parents exert, if they exert any at all, has been found to relate significantly to the adolescent's personality development and social growth.

TABLE 7–3
Frequency of peer interaction by quality of adolescent-adult interaction

Frequency of peer interaction	Quality of adolescent-adult interaction		
	Low	High	Percent
Low	39.3%	58.2%	49.0%
High	60.7	41.8	51.0
Total	100%	100%	100%
Number	(267)	(287)	(554)

Gamma = −.3645
Chi-square = 18.94
P < .001

Peer dependence by quality of adolescent-adult interaction

Peer dependence	Quality of adolescent-adult interaction		
	Low	High	Percent
Low	33.7%	63.9%	50.7%
High	66.3	36.1	49.3
Total	100%	100%	100%
Number	(270)	(288)	(558)

Gamma = −.5535
Chi-square = 49.59
P < .001

Peer autonomy by quality of adolescent-adult interaction

Peer autonomy	Quality of adolescent-adult interaction		
	Low	High	Percent
Low	27.6%	65.2%	48.9%
High	72.4	34.8	51.1
Total	100%	100%	100%
Number	(250)	(296)	(546)

Gamma = −.6177
Chi-square = 63.79
P < .001

Source: R. G. Iacovetta, Adolescent-adult interaction and peer group involvement. *Adolescence*, 1975, *10*, 327–336.

Baumrind (1967) argues cogently and convincingly for a distinction between permissive, authoritarian, and authoritative parental control. The permissive parent uses little power and shows little interest in controlling behavior. The authoritarian parent asserts power as a way of controlling and curbing self-will. Reason and verbal give-and-take are not part of such a parent's disciplinary repertoire. The authoritative parent, as described by Baumrind, is also interested in directing the child's activity, but is not interested in obedience as a virtue or for its own sake. The parent's rights and the child's rights are both of concern to the authoritative parent. Baumrind's distinction appears similar to that made some years ago between laissez-faire, authoritarian, and democratic social climates (Lewin, Lippitt, & White, 1939). In those studies the researchers found that when a group leader created a democratic social climate by acting as an interested facilitator rather than a dictator, children were more productive, shared a greater group cohesion, and tended to be more creative.

Baumrind argues once again for democratic child-rearing practices and emphasizes the value of legitimate authoritative control, as distinct from the passivity and lack of interest in so-called permissive or laissez-faire child rearing. She examines the arguments against parental control and offers counterevidence in support of authoritative control. For example, the use of punishment has been rejected by many as ineffective and liable to damaging side effects. Baumrind contends that too often punishment has been confused with the punitive and rejecting attitudes associated with it. Furthermore, punishment may reduce guilt feelings and result in the child's imitating the assertiveness of the parent in prosocial ways. Baumrind marshals evidence from research on delinquents and nondelinquents which demonstrates that delinquency arises in a familial context of lax, not firm, demands (Bandura & Walters, 1968; Glueck & Glueck, 1950; McCord & Howard, 1961) and that hostility in children is related to parental rigidity, not firm control (Finney, 1961).

One can find strong support for Baumrind's thesis in some earlier work (Elder, 1963) which showed that where parents asserted legitimate (democratic) power over their adolescent children and provided frequent explanations for their requests, the children were more likely to model their parents' behavior, to be independent and self-confident (to trust their own opinions), to associate with parent-approved peers, and to have a strong academic motivation. Elder defined parental power in terms of the adolescent's answer to the question: "In general, how are most decisions made between you and your (mother/father)?" Typical responses taken from Elder (p. 55) were:

Autocratic: My (mother/father) just tells me what to do.

Democratic: I have considerable opportunity to make my own decisions, but my (mother/father) has the final word.

Permissive: My (mother/father) doesn't care what I do.

Power legitimation was defined in terms of the adolescent's response (on a five-point scale) to the question: "When you don't know why your (mother/father) makes a particular decision or has certain rules for you to follow, will (he/she) explain the reason?" Power legitimation was found to be most beneficial when parents exercised a moderate, that is, democratic, level of power.

Parental influences on adolescent self-esteem

An important effect of the way in which children and adolescents are reared is the image those children develop of themselves. It is a truism, but no less important for that fact, that children who are loved will be themselves capable of loving and also capable of loving themselves. Children who are rejected tend to be rejecting—of themselves as well as of other people. However, it is not only rejecting parents whose adolescents care little for themselves. Rosenberg (1963, 1965) found that extreme parental disinterest also leads to low self-esteem. By assessing three diverse areas of parent-adolescent interaction in high school juniors and seniors, Rosenberg was able to arrive at some general conclusions about parental interest without the fear that his results were limited merely to a specific situation. Furthermore, by selecting situations that were recurrent in an adolescent's interaction with his or her parents, he assured himself that he was getting a general statement about the amount of parental involvement. Finally, he picked items that would be answered objectively and which could be stated in a relatively neutral way, so that a social desirability response bias would not influence his results. If one is going to use a questionnaire in the study of adolescent personality, he could do well to emulate Rosenberg's care in selecting items.

The behavioral items Rosenberg chose reflected three areas: (1) relationships with friends ("during this period—age 10 or 11—did your mother know who most of your friends were?") (2) Reaction to the child's academic performance ("when you were in the 5th and 6th grades in school, what did your *mother* usually do when you brought home a report card with good grades?" The same question was asked about low grades and about the father's reactions). (3) Responsiveness to the child at the dinner table ("How often do you participate actively in mealtime conversation? As far as you can tell, how interested are other family members in what you have to say on such occasions?"). Rosenberg then correlated the answers of 1,684 high school juniors and seniors to these questions with their scores on a questionnaire measure of self-esteem. The following results emerged. With respect to *relationships with friends,* the high self-esteem subjects were more likely to say their mother had known *all* their friends (47 percent) while low self-esteem subjects said their mother had known none, or almost none (55 percent), of their friends. See Table 7–4. These results were not substantially altered when the investigator controlled for the effects of the adolescent's level of identification with the mother, his willingness to confide in her, or her behavior toward his friends. When the same question was asked about the fathers, the results were essentially the same. Whether parents are perceived as having known all, most, or some of the adolescent's friends doesn't

TABLE 7–4
Reports of mother's knowledge of child's friends and subject's self-esteem

Respondent's self-esteem	During this period (age 10 or 11) did your mother know who most of your friends were?				
	All of them	Most of them	Some of them	None, or almost none	Don't know or can't remember
High	47%	45%	33%	30%	27%
Medium	28	24	27	15	38
Low	30	31	41	55	35
Total percent	100	100	101	100	100
Number	848	559	113	20	26
$\chi^2 = 19.0$; $d.f. = 8$; $P < .02$.					

Source: M. Rosenberg. Parental interest and children's self-conception. Sociometry, 1963, 26, 35–49.

seem to matter in terms of self-esteem. It is when the parents are seen as not having known any of the youngster's friends that self-esteem is affected.

The same pattern of results emerged with respect to the parents' reaction to the child's school marks. See Table 7–5. The interesting thing here is that the adolescents' self-esteem is affected not so much by a punitive response as by indifference.

TABLE 7– 5
Report of parental reaction to low marks and subject's self-esteem

Respondent's self-esteem	Mother's reaction			
	Supportive and punitive	Supportive only	Punitive only	Indifferent
High	49%	44%	34%	26%
Medium	25	25	25	13
Low	26	30	41	61
Total percent	100	99	100	100
Number	178	533	228	23

$\chi^2 = 22.2$; d.f. = 6; $P < .01$.
Indifferent versus all other: $\chi^2 = 8.4$; d.f. = 2; $P < .02$.

Respondent's self-esteem	Father's reaction			
	Supportive and punitive	Supportive only	Punitive only	Indifferent
High	47%	46%	36%	34%
Medium	28	25	24	19
Low	25	30	40	47
Total percent	100	101	100	100
Number	139	413	241	85

$\chi^2 = 19.8$; d.f. = 6; $P < .01$.
Indifferent versus all others: $\chi^2 = 8.0$; d.f. = 2; $P < .02$.

Source: M. Rosenberg, Parental interest and children's self-conception. Sociometry, 1963, 26, 35–49.

Finally, the amount of an adolescent's participation in mealtime conversation and the adolescent's estimate of others' interest in his or her opinions are directly related to self-esteem. (See Tables 7–6 and 7–7.) The conclusions are obvious. To the extent that parents care enough to show an interest in their adolescent, that adolescent will experience a positive self-regard. Unfortunately, many parents don't know how to take an interest in their children often because nobody has shown an interest in them or served as a role model of caring. Still other parents would gladly show an interest in their children if only they had the time. For example, to participate in mealtime conversations presupposes that the family eats together. What of Jerry, a child whose dad goes to work before Jerry gets home from school and is sleeping when Jerry leaves for school the next morning? Or Francis, whose dad is in the Army and whose mother works two jobs to feed her six children? Or 16-year-old Sally, who, after losing her mother at 11 and raising her two younger brothers, moved out of the house when dad's girlfriend moved in? Surely self-esteem is related to many variables (see Rosen-

TABLE 7–6
Frequency of respondent's participation in mealtime conversation, and self-esteem

Respondent's self-esteem	(If your family usually or always eats together) how often do you participate actively in the mealtime conversation?			
	Always	Usually	Sometimes	Rarely or never
High	52%	45%	33%	33%
Medium	23	27	25	16
Low	25	28	42	52
Total percent	100	100	100	101
Number	698	446	173	89

$\chi^2 = 48.2; d.f. = 6; P < .001.$

Source: M. Rosenberg. Parental interest and children's self-conceptions. Sociometry, 1963, 26, 35–49.

TABLE 7–7
Subject's estimate of family's interest in his opinions, and self-esteem

Respondent's self-esteem	As far as you can tell, how interested are the other family members in what you have to say on such occasions?			
	Very interested	Fairly interested	Not interested	Don't know
High	56%	43%	19%	37%
Medium	23	26	20	17
Low	21	30	61	46
Total percent	100	99	100	100
Number	432	833	80	108

$\chi^2 = 77.7; d.f. = 6; P < .001.$

Source: M. Rosenberg, Parental interest and children's self-conceptions. Sociometry, 1963, 26, 35–49.

berg, 1965), and parental interest is one of them. However, what may look at first like a lack of interest may on closer inspection, be found to be an incapacity for caring or an inability because of environmental circumstances. Most parents do try, even against great odds.

Implications of the theory and data on parent-child relations or child-rearing practices

What implications can be drawn from these data? First of all, it should be obvious that the time-honored theory that adolescents universally and necessarily reject their parents' values and enter into conflict with their parents simply cannot be supported. On the other hand, it is quite obvious that with increasing maturity, high school boys and girls will tend to become more self-reliant and therefore to expect more autonomy. Needless to say, the roles in the family shift as a result.

In a rather interesting account of the changes in the family relationship over changing historical periods, Margaret Mead (1970) has mentioned three kinds of family styles—the postfigurative, the cofigurative, and the prefigurative—which also describe three sorts of cultural styles. By postfigurative, Mead means the traditional culture of our ancestors and of many of our parents in which the purpose of education was to pass on the values and the knowledge of the dominant culture to the children.

The cofigurative culture refers to what is perhaps the dominant culture in the United States today. This is the culture in which children learn as much from their peers as from their parents and in which one finds a great deal of segregation by age. Surely, children in our day spend most of their time with their age-mates, just as adults do. (In a number of places, Urie Bronfenbrenner has commented on this trend and its dangers.) It is the unusual situation which brings people of different ages together, as was more customary in the past. For example, frequent family parties, picnics, and so on formerly involved all members of the family, regardless of their age. Moreover, when the family was the major recreational and economic unit in society, in addition to performing its rather restricted present functions, its members were an integral part of an extended family much larger than our current nuclear family. Aunts, uncles, cousins, brothers, sisters, mothers, fathers, children, and grandchildren lived, played, and worked together.

In the co-figurative culture, the values of the home and the values of the peer culture may be of two different sorts, and the child may be learning as much from the peer culture as at home. The situation in immigrant families exemplifies the cofigurative culture. The younger members of such families need to learn the language, the traditions, and the customs of their new country in order to progress at school and in society, but they must also retain to some extent the culture of their parents.

By prefigurative culture, Mead refers to the situation in which parents learn from their children, that is, to the situation in which change proceeds at an ever-accelerating rate and the children are more exposed to change than are their parents. Mead feels that we are rapidly moving into this cultural situation.

If Mead is correct, one implication is clear—parents need to be both ready for change and stable in their own convictions. Being able to balance on that fine line between authoritarianism and laissez-faire passivity—being flexible and fair, yet adhering to principle—is probably the earmark of an excellent parent. If youngsters are selectively to reject and accept the values of a rapidly changing environment, it is important that some aspects of that environment be relatively stable. If in the prefigurative culture the home environment were so unstable that the free movement of the younger generation could not be delineated against a relatively unchanging background, the value of that free movement would be lost.

A number of pediatricians and psychiatrists have written remarkably fair and perceptive works for parents and teachers of adolescents and younger children (Gesell et al., 1956; Ginott, 1969). One major theme of these works has been mutual respect—that it is as important for the parent to respect the rights and feelings of the child as it is to expect that the child will respect the parent's rights and feelings. In so doing, the parent is teaching the child not only to respect its own feelings but also the feelings of others since the respect learned by the child at home will generalize outside the home.

Haim Ginott's book *Between Parent and Teenager* (1969) is an important popular source for parents. Ginott's theme is not new, but it seems to bear repeating. He stresses the point that in any personal situation one must respond to the behavior; that is, one should praise or punish the behavior, not the person. To tell a youngster who has just painted a beautiful picture that he is an excellent artist is perhaps to immobilize him into artistic inactivity for fear of being unable to live up to that high praise. Ginott would rather have us tell the child that he painted an excellent picture. The meaning of that praise is clear; it is the kind of reward that has no strings attached.

In discussing conflict, which is inevitable in any human relationship, Ginott points out adolescents often interpret attention as attack. Adolescents view parental concern as an indication that the parents distrust their ability to make their own decisions. In this guise, Ginott believes that adolescents will resent and reject the guidance that is offered to them. He says that if identity is the issue, parental choice making is really not growth producing. He points out that accepting a child is not the same thing as approving everything the child does, that being tolerant of the child is not the same thing as sanctioning everything that the child wants to do. Ginott therefore cautions the parent not to be too understanding and too quick to agree with the adolescent, and suggests that adults not emulate the language and the conduct of adolescents, but rather make themselves increasingly dispensable. If adolescents are choosing their own language and habits as a way of solidifying their own identity within a peer group, the adoption of those patterns of speech and conduct by adults would only make it necessary for the adolescents to seek new badges of their own identity. Ginott's work also tells the parent how to express anger without being attacking and insulting, and how to handle, in a growth-producing way, those potentially conflictual issues which inevitably arise between parents and teenagers.

Just as it is important for parents to be neither too understanding nor too rigid and inflexible in dealing with adolescent children, so too it is important for psychologists to refrain from taking a strong position which states either the universality of adolescent rebellion or the complete absence of conflict between parents and their adolescent children. If parents can be prepared for the naturally increasing autonomy of their youngsters and for the continued changes in lifestyle that that will entail, and if they can be prepared for conflict without fearing catastrophe, perhaps some of the studies cited will have served not only theoretical and research purposes but practical purposes as well.

The adolescent with divorcing parents

A special problem arising in the lives of more and more children and adolescents is that of separated and divorced parents. Recent estimates suggest that almost half of the marriages in the United States end up in divorce. Many of these marriages have produced children, and some of the children are adolescents when the divorce occurs. It is impossible to say how divorce will affect children as a general rule. Some children suffer terribly, while others seem less affected. In some instances, the children seem to do better after parents have finally divorced. Often the children have known for years that their parents would separate and appear relieved when the deed is finally done. Some would prefer the actual separation and divorce to the bickering, or emotional aloofness, or sense of hostility which may have permeated the family atmosphere before the divorce (Despert, 1953; Sorosky, 1977).

Although it is not possible to make a blanket statement about the effects of divorce on adolescents, Sorosky (1977) suggests that the following factors should be considered: (a) "The psychodynamics of the family prior to the divorce, including the severity of marital discord; (b) the nature of the marital breakup; (c) the postdivorce relationship of the parents; (d) the age or stage of development of the youngster at the time of the divorce, and (e) the personality strengths and coping skills of the adolescent" (p. 123).

An initial response of many children (and even some adolescents) to their parents' divorce is a sense of guilt. In younger children, this may be coupled with a feeling of abandonment, as if abandonment were justifiable punishment for whatever wrong the child did which produced the divorce. Such magical thinking needs to be dealt with. If parents are themselves too guilt ridden, confused, or angry, then it is best to have a family therapist, school counselor, or other trained professional encourage the child to express not only his or her feelings, but also any fantasies about why the divorce occurred so that erroneous fantasies can be replaced with factual explanations. Westman (1972) observes that adolescents are often more concerned about the welfare of their younger siblings or their parents in a divorce than about their own needs. They may also tend to be highly moralistic in judging their parents' behavior, holding up standards of morality they don't hold even for themselves. "One 17-year-old girl opposed her parents' divorce on moral grounds but could see nothing wrong with her own premarital sexual activity and depreciation of the importance of marriage" (Westman, 1972, p. 50). Another reason why professional or paraprofessional help can be important to the adolescent whose parents are divorcing is that these youngsters often live with a fear of their own marital inability. Nor does the recent trend toward "good" divorces or "friendly" divorces leave the adolescent any less confused. Good references on this subject include Despert's (1953) *Children of Divorce* and Anthony's (1974) paper "Children at Risk from Divorce: A Review." When parents are well informed about the potential impact of their divorce on the adolescent children, damaging effects can be greatly reduced.

SUMMARY AND CONCLUSIONS

The view of adolescence as a necessarily turbulent and stressful period is further challenged in this chapter by the findings of several researchers. Bandura suggests that some factors which may underlie the myth of adolescence as a stressful period are: the overinterpretation of superficial signs of nonconformity, the emphasis of the mass media on adolescent nonconformity, generalizations based on deviant samples, and inappropriate generalization from cross-cultural data. Thus, Bandura, like other advocates of the social learning theory of human development, sees adolescence more as the product of past development and conditioning than as a sudden biologically based upheaval. One sort of support for the social learning position, in contrast to the upheaval hypothesis, is provided by the interview and questionnaire data which reveal that the majority of adolescents maintain a consistently positive attitude toward adults.

Although adolescents of both sexes grow toward greater autonomy and require more explanations for parental control, there is evidence that boys and girls differ in their perception of parents as controllers of important resources. Boys tend to see the father, and girls the mother, as the more important controller. Although adolescents turn increasingly toward peers as referents in decision making, it has been demonstrated that the content of the decision is an important element in determining whether parents or peers are more likely to be consulted. Furthermore, adolescents are most likely to value the opinions of those whom they perceive as satisfying their needs in the area in which the opinion is sought.

Parents can exercise authoritative, authoritarian, or permissive control over their children. A number of studies were cited which demonstrate that adolescents are more independent, more achievement-motivated, and less hostile when parents exercise legitimate authority of a democratic sort, and when parents respond with appropriate explanations to their children's questioning of their decisions. The practical implications of these data are clear. Parental concern for adolescence is best marked not only by acceptance and honesty but also by an increasing willingness to be a sounding board for the child's decisions, rather than a decision maker for the child. While the parent's role necessarily changes with the developing adolescent, the development of a positive self-image in adolescents is directly correlated with the degree of interest the parents take in their offspring.

Although the picture of the adolescent's family presented in this chapter may' seem idyllic and unrealistic to some, it should be recalled that we are discussing the average, based on group data. To be sure, individual adolescents rebel, and many adolescents leave home. Problems occur in adolescence which were unknown in childhood, and often these revolve around the issue of identity formation. A number of writers have observed that for many adolescents rebellion and the rejection of home-based values are a necessary part of establishing an individual identity. Although we have not stressed this in the present chapter, we recognize that the family is the battlefield on which many identity struggles are fought. Such issues and the available pertinent data will be discussed in Chapter 10, where we deal more specifically with the psychological problems of adolescence.

A special problem in the lives of more and more adolescents is that of separated and divorced parents. It is impossible to make a blanket statement about the effects of divorce on adolescents. Several factors may act to influence the adolescent, such as the severity of mental discord prior to divorce, the nature of the marital breakup, and the age or stage of development of the adolescent at the time of divorce. Adolescent reactions to marital breakup vary widely and may include highly moralistic judging of their parents' behavior. Adolescents are often more concerned about the welfare of their younger siblings or parents than about their own needs. For this reason and others, professional or paraprofessional help can be important to the adolescent facing these problems.

SUGGESTED ADDITIONAL READING

Bandura, A. *Adolescent aggression.* New York: Ronald Press, 1959.

Despert, J. L. *Children of divorce.* Garden City: Doubleday, 1953.

Douvan, E. & Adelson, J. *The adolescent experience.* New York: John Wiley & Sons, 1966.

Ginott, H. *Between parent and teenager.* New York: Macmillan, 1969.

CHAPTER 8

THE DEVELOPMENT OF PEER RELATIONS DURING ADOLESCENCE

In the last chapter we described the changing family relations of the adolescent and pointed out that it is difficult to find evidence that adolescents reject their families in an abrupt or dramatic way. It is equally difficult, if not impossible, to find substantial support for the notion that adolescence is filled with conflicts between parents and children. Though the separation may not be sudden, however, and the conflicts may not be intense, we also know that sometime during adolescence or afterward, individuals do leave their families of origin and set about establishing their own families. As we noted in Chapter 1, this is as true for the human species as for a variety of other species. In the process of leaving their families of origin, however gradual that process may be, individuals tend to turn their attention to others of their own age and to spend more time in the peer group.

A number of psychological studies have addressed themselves to peer relations during adolescence. Some of these studies deal with the effects that peers have on an adolescent's choice-making behavior, activities, and self-image. Others focus on the establishment and maintenance of friendships, and on the effect of socioeconomic status on the formation of friendships and peer groups. A very special sort of peer relation that takes on importance in adolescence is the heterosexual friendship, which includes cross-sex friend selection, dating, going steady, courtship, and ultimately, marriage. In this chapter we will discuss peer influences on adolescent behavior, and we will deal specifically with self-acceptance and its relation to acceptance by others and with friendship formation and stability. In addition, we will examine heterosexual relations, specifically dating, courtship, and finally, marriage. The chapter will also examine some of the current peer relation styles which have been investigated in research studies.

SULLIVAN'S INTERPERSONAL THEORY

Before beginning an examination of these data, however, it may be helpful to examine in detail one theory which addresses itself to peer relations in adolescence. Once again, it should be noted that in selecting one theory for examination we do not mean to suggest that it is the only theory which deals with this subject, nor do we mean to suggest that the theory we have selected deals only with peer relations. It is true, however, that among all the theories of adolescent development the psychoanalytic theory of Harry Stack Sullivan speaks most clearly about the importance of the shift from a predominance of group activities during middle childhood (when playmates are important) to the more selective pairing off that takes place during adolescence. Sullivan's essentially developmental theory can be found in his book *The Interpersonal Theory of Psychiatry* (1953), which deals with the "developmental epochs" and psychological dynamics that characterize each stage of development from infancy through late adolescence. More similar to ego psychology (that is, Erikson's view) than to classical psychoanalysis, Sullivan's theory places its main emphasis on interpersonal relations, in normal as well as in pathological development.

The importance of "significant others"

Sullivan, who was born in 1892 and died in 1949, was an American physician and neuropsychiatrist. His basic premise is that personality is "the relatively enduring pattern of recurrent personal situations which characterize the human life" (Sullivan, 1953, p. 110). In other words, Sullivan considers personality to consist chiefly in interpersonal behavior. He emphasizes that the individual cannot exist apart from his or her relations with other people. One's definition of self, in Sullivan's terms, is bound up with a set of relations; that is, one may be a father, brother, and cousin as well as a friend, lover, and student, or a sister, daughter, and niece and also a confidante, neighbor, and roommate. Each of these reciprocal relationships implies a "significant other" in one's self-definition and self-understanding. In one sense, this position sounds very much like the view of some modern existential philosophers, such as Martin Buber and Gabriel Marcel. In his book *I and Thou* (1958), Buber argues that *I* is not a single term and *thou* is not a single term, but that *I-thou* is a single term. The point of Buber's philosophical view is that the fundamental requirement, the sine qua non, of being a human is a relationship. The notion of "participation" in the theory of Gabriel Marcel (1960) is similar to Buber's idea. These views should not be at all foreign to the student of developmental psychology who has noticed the importance of other persons in the lives of children from their very infancy. The psychotic development of infants who are severely deprived of mothering is a well-documented fact. Suffice it to say that, in Sullivan's theory, the term *personality* is a hypothetical construct used to refer to human development as a product of social interaction.

Harry Stack Sullivan

*Courtesy of the William Alanson White
Psychiatric Foundation, Inc.*

The concept of dynamism

In the area of interpersonal relations, Sullivan made significant contributions to the field of developmental psychology. He stresses, as does Freud, the importance of early experience, but he also conceptualizes the nature of this experience. One of his main concepts is that of *dynamism,* which he describes as the relatively stable pattern of energy transformations which characterizes interpersonal relations. These are the relations which make the human being distinctly human. As in physics or biology, then, dynamism here refers to an energy change. In interpersonal theory, energy transformation could apply to a wide variety of social relations, attitudes, and behaviors, whether crippling, like anxiety or fear, or facilitating, like leadership or curiosity.

Sullivan identifies two kinds of dynamisms of tension: *conjunctive* dynamisms (for example, the need for intimacy), which lead to a union or the overcoming of separateness and which result in the integration of a situation and the reduction of tension; and *disjunctive* dynamisms (for example, anxiety), which lead to psychosocial disintegration.

The stages of adolescent development

Preadolescence   Sullivan has divided the period of adolescence into three major units: preadolescence, early adolescence, and late adolescence. He describes preadolescents as characterized by a need for interpersonal intimacy. Just as the earlier "juvenile" period was marked by a need for peers (that is, for a group of playmates), the need now is for a particular individual of the same sex. Now occurs what Sullivan (1953) calls "full-blown, psychiatrically defined, *love*" (p. 245).

FIGURE 8–1 Affiliation serves a variety of needs.

Photograph courtesy of Dan Hughson

This relationship, according to Sullivan, is very often "isophilic," that is, between members of the same sex. What he is describing is similar in some respects to what Freudian psychoanalytic theory has labeled the "homosexual" phase, which supposedly follows a brief reenactment of oedipal striving in preadolescence. Perhaps by using the term *isophilic* in preference to the term *homosexual,* we can emphasize the fact that this experience is considered to be relatively universal and is in no way considered pathological. This relationship is completely different from what has gone on before, both in the kind of relationship that is involved and in the intensity of the relationship. That is, it is a relationship of an exclusive sort between two members of the same sex, and one which appears to elicit more personal involvement than did the relationship between playmates that occurred during the juvenile period. This is the time when a young boy has a special friend, or buddy, and a young girl her confidante, to whom innermost secrets, concerns, and hopes can be revealed without fear of rejection.

Sullivan's theory, and especially his notion of intimacy, comes mainly from his observations of boys. However, there is no reason to doubt that the same process occurs in the development of girls as well.

Isophilic attachments during early adolescence seem to be well documented in the autobiographical and fictional literature of this period and to be observed by parents, teachers, and clinicians dealing with preadolescent youngsters. Nor is research data to support Sullivan's position entirely lacking. A study by Harris and Tseng (1957) demonstrated that negative attitudes toward the opposite sex increased during preadolescence. This was truer of girls' attitudes toward boys and was at its peak for girls at about the sixth grade, whereas boys' negative attitudes toward girls peaked about two years later. The study disclosed no corollary tendency, however, toward an increase in positive feelings toward one's own sex.

Edgar Friedenberg (1959) describes the changing peer relations and the introduction of love into interpersonal relations in much the same way as Sullivan. He suggests that intense "love" begins in adolescence, and that this first love is merely someone *other* than oneself (often same sex). It is only later that the quality of "*different* from oneself—as different as man is from woman" (p. 49), comes into play. Friedenberg believes that a strong homophilic love at this stage paves the way for the possibility of strong heterosexual attachments later.

Perhaps the value of such isophilic relations can best be described, not in terms of Sullivan's or Friedenberg's theories, but in Erikson's terms. It may well be that the close attachment to one like oneself is a defense against identity diffusion at a time when bodily changes and beginning sexual urges challenge the stability of one's identity and self-image. Undoubtedly, young adolescents help one another face these changes by the intimate exchange of experiences. Surely the continued love for one another which Sullivan and Friedenberg describe would validate self-worth for the adolescent who might otherwise be uncertain of such worth. That parents do not fulfill this function might simply be because a peer is experiencing similar changes, whereas parents are not. The same reasoning would explain why these early relations are isophilic rather than heterophilic.

The intimacy which Sullivan is describing is not necessarily physical closeness but rather an interpersonal relationship in which one can validate his or her own personal worth. That is, a youngster at this age knows that his friend loves him just as surely as he knows that he loves his friend. He also knows that this love is not based on superficial or accidental characteristics but on a genuine concern for the welfare of another person. Unlike the juvenile period, during which playmates may have worked together on a common goal, preadolescents not only cooperate in that manner but also collaborate; that is, they adjust their behavior to the needs of a specific individual. *Intimacy* in Sullivan's theory is psychological closeness and does not imply genitality, though genital play among preadolescents is not uncommon.

The reader should bear in mind that this use of the term *intimacy* is somewhat different from Erikson's use of that term. Erikson refers to intimacy as the antithesis of isolation, thus defining the core conflict of late adolescence. This conflict follows the earlier conflict of identity versus identity diffusion. The counterpart in Erikson's theory to the sort of intimacy which Sullivan describes as occurring during the preadolescent period would be the transition between the stage of industry versus inferiority and the stage of identity versus identity diffusion. In Erikson's theory, the psychosocial moratorium known as adolescence helps children to bridge the gap between what they were as children and what they are about to become as adults, between their own conception of themselves and what they perceive as the expectations of the world for them. The formation of an internally consistent identity is aided by having friends and particularly by having one close friend. It is not surprising that a child just beginning to sense the uniqueness of his or her own personality turns to another special person for support. Comparison with a person like oneself may be an aid to establishing one's own sexual identity before contrasting that with one who is different. Becoming a man means both not being a boy and not being a woman, and becoming a woman means both not being a girl and not being a man. The disentangling of the two connected questions of identity is aided by the psychological and physical presence of a confidant who is going through the same developmental stage at about the same time.

According to Sullivan, the timing of puberty is important for the development of isophilic relationships. It should be noted that, in general, Sullivan sees isophilic attachment in preadolescence as healthy and integrating, not as pathological and debilitating. However, he points out that when adolescence is delayed for a single individual and is not correspondingly delayed for his or her age-mates, the preadolescent "chumships" break up and the physiologically delayed individual may shift from one close association to another or have a progression of generally younger buddies.

The corollary of the need for intimacy or a close chum during the preadolescent period is the real experience, or at least the possibility, of loneliness. What might have been rejection and the need to be liked by one's peers during the juvenile period becomes the fear of loss of one's own worth through the deprivation of companions during preadolescence. This is simply to say that the coin of interpersonal relations has two sides—fulfillment in intimacy and deprivation in loneliness.

Early adolescence   With the development of puberty and the first appearance of the lust dynamism, the period of adolescence itself occurs. Sullivan considers lust to be the last of the integrating dynamisms. It is important to note his definition of the term *lust* is psychological and carries no moral overtones. By lust he means the sexual feelings associated with genital satisfaction. Whereas the preadolescent period was characterized by the need for interpersonal intimacy, the early adolescent phase is characterized by the eruption of the need for lust. Sullivan argues that these two integrating dynamisms are quite distinct, that in some people the need for intimacy may be strong and the dynamism of lust weak, and that in other people the opposite may be true. The important thing here is that intimacy characterizes an earlier stage of development than does lust.

The shift from the intimacy need of the preadolescent period may lead to certain need collisions. However, the eruption of genital interests and the shift from an isophilic interest to a heterophilic one (that is, from an interest in a person who is like oneself to an interest in a person who is very different from oneself) is generally aided by the fact that the other member of the isophilic two-member group is also going through the same transition. Once again, the timing of puberty is important. Often, a whole gang of youngsters will be shifting from two-person isophilic intimacies to an interest in the opposite sex at about the same time.

There is strong empirical evidence to support Sullivan's theory of a shift from isophilic to heterophilic attraction at the adolescent stage. Although he was not attempting to test Sullivan's hypothesis, Dunphy (1963) conducted a careful observational study of informal adolescent groups in Australia. By developing rapport with his subjects, Dunphy was able to study the structure and functioning of several adolescent groups for some months. We will return to an examination of his careful methods in a later section. Here we wish to draw attention to one finding, namely, that the cliques characteristic of younger adolescents are by and large unisexual (see Figure 8–2), whereas the cliques and crowds of older adolescents are heterosexual. Dunphy is careful not to indicate an average age for this shift, suggesting that there is a great variability in the development of individuals and groups. He merely points to the stages in the development of adolescent groups.

According to Sullivan, the need collisions that could occur at this time include a collision between the need for lust and the need for security. Sullivan points out that one's sense of personal worth and one's self-esteem may come in for a hard time in the face of the development of the need for lust, especially if

FIGURE 8–2 Stages of group development in adolescence.

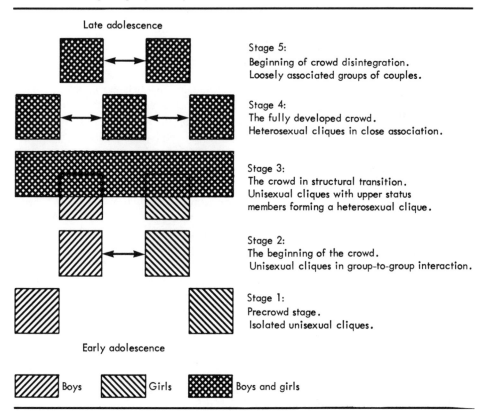

Late adolescence

Stage 5:
Beginning of crowd disintegration.
Loosely associated groups of couples.

Stage 4:
The fully developed crowd.
Heterosexual cliques in close association.

Stage 3:
The crowd in structural transition.
Unisexual cliques with upper status
members forming a heterosexual clique.

Stage 2:
The beginning of the crowd.
Unisexual cliques in group-to-group interaction.

Stage 1:
Precrowd stage.
Isolated unisexual cliques.

Early adolescence

Boys   Girls   Boys and girls

Source: D. C. Dunphy, "The social structure of urban adolescent peer groups," *Sociometry*, 1963, 26, 230–246. By permission of the author and the American Sociological Association.

genital interests are considered immoral. The awakening of these interests may leave the adolescent feeling puzzled, embarrassed, and/or guilty. Second, the need for intimacy and the need for lust may themselves collide. Thus, a certain awkwardness may occur when an individual relates to the opposite sex in a new way. For example, the girl next door, who may have gone unnoticed for years except as a bothersome troublemaker, may suddenly become sexually interesting to the adolescent boy. A new skill is involved when one tries to be both intimate and sexually appropriate. Diffidence, embarrassment, excessive precaution, and overboldness are reactions which Sullivan describes as potential results of this collision. Another way in which some adolescents learn to deal with this phenomenon is to separate persons who satisfy their need for lust from persons who satisfy their need for intimacy—the whore versus the good girl, for example. Although this phenomenon cuts across social classes, it can be seen quite explicitly in Whyte's (1943) description of the slum sex code. Among some youth there has been a tendency to segregate girls with whom they satisfy sexual desires and urges from girls whom they consider potential mates. Such segregation of dynamisms does not lead to maximal psychological development. The separation of lust from intimacy could result in crippling pseudosibling relationships which do not allow an adolescent to develop a repertoire of interpersonal behaviors that permit both the expression of one's own needs and the awareness of the needs of others.

Late adolescence   After the adolescent has firmly made heterosexuality his or her preferred mode of relating to others sexually, the specific patterning of this activity goes on during late adolescence. This is the period of dating, of establishing a fully mature repertoire of interpersonal behaviors, and of looking forward to and profiting from new interpersonal relations. It is the period which Erikson would call a psychosocial moratorium in the sense that the choices made are not necessarily permanent. That is, one is not necessarily committed for life to a single individual simply by having a date with him, nor is one committed for life to a specific occupation simply by showing an interest in it. One may take a variety of courses in school just as one may date a large number of individuals without being committed completely. Both Sullivan and Erikson stress the importance of freedom of movement during this period, of allowing the individual to choose and to develop a set of values around his or her choices. Internal restrictions might occur; one might, for example, isolate oneself from others because of inferiority feelings or failures in social relations. One's freedom might also be sharply restricted by external rules. Rules formulated at home, in school, or in the community can help adolescents if they allow them a certain freedom of movement and if they provide them with opportunities to participate in the rule setting or the rule changing; but they can be crippling if they provide little freedom of choice and are handed down in an autocratic and authoritarian way.

FRIENDS AND FRIENDSHIPS IN ADOLESCENCE

Having looked at one theory of social interaction during adolescence in some detail, it may be useful to turn to the data on peer relations in adolescence.

The making and maintaining of friendships

It would be difficult to overestimate the importance of having friends at any age, or the special importance which attaches to friends and friendships during the adolescent period. Conformity, as we shall see, tends to increase in early adolescence. This may relate to the desire to be liked and not to be rejected. Perhaps conformity during adolescence is an attempt not to appear different. It has been found, for example, that children's fear of failure, of rejection, and of seeming different increases with age up to adolescence, whereas their fear of objects, of animals, of loud noises, and so on tends to decrease after early child- hood.

Some of the functions served by friends during adolescence should be clear. Friends may be important in helping one to decide on his or her own identity. At a time when identity formation versus identity diffusion is a major issue, a per- son of the same sex who has a similar developmental task may serve as an aid in this developmental process. A friend in this sense is a person with whom one can be honest about fears without an additional fear of rejection, a person whose love is not contingent on conformity. The confidante or special buddy relationship, described by Sullivan as beginning during the preadolescent years, serves important adolescent needs.

There is some research data to support the notion that a friend is one who is similar rather than different in personality characteristics (Izard, 1960; Davitz, 1955; Hilkevitch, 1960). Although the old saw "Birds of a feather flock to- gether" is contradicted by another—"Opposites attract"—in the literature on friendship there seems to be more support for the former proverb than for the latter. A number of similarities provide the basis for friendships. Age is certainly one, and sex is another. Living in the same neighborhood or the same apartment complex provides a basis for friendship in a surprisingly high percentage of cases. However, the data on this issue of whether friendships are based on similarities or on complementarity is far from clear. The student interested in the issue should see the excellent review on friendship formation in the article by Hartup (1970) in *Carmichael's Manual of Child Psychology*. Hartup suggests that there is more evidence for the similarity position than for the complementarity position. For example, he cites a study by Izard (1960), who found that for 30 friendship pairs of high school and college students the scores on the Edwards Personal Preference Schedule were more similar than were the scores for a con- trol group of 30 pairs of similar students who were randomly selected.

One issue which may be important in distinguishing between the similarity and the complementarity position is that of the intimacy involved in friendship. Douvan and Adelson (1966) emphasized that there is a real difference between intimacy in friendships and the superficial cordiality which characterizes some acquaintanceships. Aside from being shallow, this pseudofriendliness may in some instances be compulsive.

Whatever the psychological bases of friendship formation, it has been demonstrated that the stability of friendships increases with age. This relation- ship holds true for rural children (Horrocks & Thompson, 1946), urban children (Thompson & Horrocks, 1947), preadolescents (Horrocks & Buker, 1951), and college students (Skorepa, Horrocks, & Thompson, 1963). The increased stability of friendships with age has also been shown to relate to mental level in a study (Kay & McKinney, 1967) which compared friendships among retarded children with those of normal children. This pattern of increasing stability is undoubtedly an example of the increasing stability of children's choices in general. This was shown in a study by McKinney (1968) in which boys and girls in grades 2, 4, 6, 8, 10, and 12 were asked to name their favorite television programs, desserts, animals, games, and so on, as well as their favorite friend. Two weeks later the same children were asked the same questions, and it was found that with respect to all of the choices the older children demonstrated greater stability. In other words, friendship stability is probably a specific case of a more general tendency for choice stability to increase with age.

The measurement of sociometric status

A number of techniques have been used to assess the individual adolescent's social standing in his or her peer group. Apart from teacher ratings, "Guess Who" tests, and observations, perhaps the most common is the well-known sociogram (Moreno, 1951). The typical sociometric technique involves asking the individuals in a group to list in rank order those group members with whom they would most prefer to associate in some group activity or situation. For example, the individuals might be asked to name the three persons with whom they would most prefer to play or whom they would most prefer to have as seating partners. Such sociometric results can be tabulated and depicted graphically in a number of ways. The most common graphic depiction is the sociogram, an example of which is shown in Figure 8–3. That sociogram depicts the seating choices of the 16 members of a hypothetical fifth-grade class. With such a presentation it is easy to spot the isolates (those who are chosen by nobody) and the stars (those who have many friends). Sociograms can also be used to depict classroom cliques (the mutual choices of small clusters of people).

FIGURE 8–3 Sociogram depicting preferences for table partners in a hypothetical fifth-grade class.

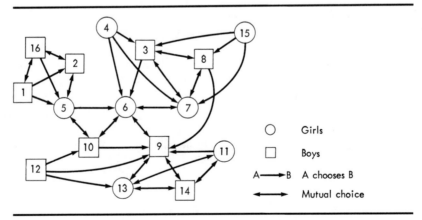

A variety of adaptations of the sociometric technique have appeared. One of these, the Syracuse Scales of Social Relations (Gardner & Thompson, 1958), is used at the elementary school, junior high school, and high school levels. In administering the Syracuse Scales, the respondent is asked to rate all of his or her classmates on a five-point scale from most to least in terms of how the individual being rated compares with key individuals who are used in the scale itself. An interesting feature of the Syracuse Scales is that each respondent is asked initially to establish his own scale against which he will then rate each member of his class. Moreover, classmates are rated on scales relating to specific needs of the respondent. The directions have been very carefully standardized. The child is asked to consider all the people he has ever known and to select the five who would be most representative of the five points on the scale. For example, in regard to the need for succor, he would be asked to select from among all the people he has ever known the one person to whom he would be most likely to go for help, then the person to whom he would be least likely to go for help. Finally, he is asked to fill in the other three points of the scale, that is, to name a person who would represent a midpoint or neutral position on the scale and two persons who would represent positions between the midpoint and the two extremes.

The advantage of the Syracuse Scales compared to the typical sociometric technique is apparent immediately. First, each respondent is rating his or her colleagues according to his or her own norms. Thus, one respondent may find that, relative to all the people he has ever known, none of his classmates receive a very high rating as interactants with respect to his need for succor. Another respondent may give all of his classmates a relatively high rating. In the more typical sociometric technique each classmate is ranked rather than rated, and the individual ranked highest by respondent A is given the same weight as the individual ranked highest by respondent B. Second, the Syracuse Scales allow each classmate to be rated by and to rate all the members of the class, thus yielding two scores. The first is the average rating that the individual *gives* to his classmates (for example, a score representing the individual's need for succor relative to his classmates); the second is the average rating that he *receives* from his classmates (for example, a score representing his press for succor).

Other techniques for assessing the individual's status in the group include the "Guess Who" test (Thompson, 1960), self-reports, teachers' ratings, and observations during group situational tasks. The advantages of the sociometric technique, however, include the ease with which it can be administered, its relative flexibility, and its adaptability to a variety of situations and need states.

A somewhat different approach to the study of the structure of adolescent peer groups has been taken in Dunphy's (1963) field research. In this research, Dunphy used a wide variety of techniques to study the peer associations of over 300 boys and girls between the ages of 13 and 21 years in Sydney, Australia. Aside from his nonparticipant observations, Dunphy used questionnaires, interviews, and diaries of the participants. By means of these wide-ranging techniques, he was able to gather large amounts of information while leaving the groups themselves relatively undisturbed throughout the process of examination. (The disturbing effect of experimentation or observation on the behavior of the organism under study has long been the bugbear of social developmental psychology.)

Dunphy found two distinct organizational structures among the adolescents. The larger group, the "crowd," was composed of a number of smaller "cliques." The crowd and clique differed in function, the clique centering on talking and the crowd centering on more organized social activities. Moreover, a developmental trend was associated with the likelihood of belonging to these structures. This trend is best illustrated in Figure 8–2.

From the preadolescent unisexual cliques (Stage 1) youngsters begin to associate with similar cliques of the opposite sex (Stage 2), but always within the security of the group before they form heterosexual cliques (Stages 3 and 4). As couples begin to go steady and become engaged, the crowds, composed of interacting cliques, begin to disintegrate. The adolescent crowd has by then served its very important function of providing each of its members with the "opportunity for establishing a heterosexual role."

Within the cliques, Dunphy discovered two distinct, but interdependent, main roles: the leader and the sociocenter. The leader, who was expected to carry out the administrative and executive functions, played an essentially instrumental function. He or she was generally more advanced heterosexually than other members of the clique and was therefore expected to set a heterosexual style that the clique members could follow. The sociocenter, on the other hand, played a more expressive role, being, as Dunphy described him, "a specialist in humor." Curiously enough, because of his popularity the sociocenter is often perceived by adults as the group leader, and the group's activities are perceived as primarily frivolous. What is often unrecognized is that the sociocenter serves to reduce the tension caused by the press for achievement which comes from the "crowd" leadership.

Further research will be needed to ascertain how well these observations of Sydney youth fit the large majority of adolescents in other areas. The great value of Dunphy's work is that it demonstrates the effectiveness of both the field study and the study of naturally occurring groups of adolescents.

The contribution of youth sports to the development of peer relations

An important activity for many adolescents, and one which can consume a significant proportion of their time, is an involvement in sports. Coleman (1961), for example, found that being an athletic star ranked as one of the highest values for high school boys. At that time, girls preferred to be known as a leader in school activities. More recent research, however, has demonstrated that girls too place a high value on athletic activities. Feltz (1978) argued that since the late 1950s, when Coleman did his research, many events together have produced a greater pro-sports attitude among females. The government's passage of Title IX, greater television coverage of women's sports and the greater exposure of athletic models for females are some of these events. Indeed Feltz found, by 1976 many high school girls, when asked specifically, would like to be remembered as a star athlete. Over 20 percent of her sample gave that response in preference to "brilliant student," "most popular," or "leader in activities."

Both boys and girls value sports and use it as a status marker. This should come as no surprise, since, as an extracurricular activity, sports is an activity that adolescents can engage in freely. It is play rather than work, by and large. It is an activity that teaches cooperation as well as competition. Most sports require a significant ability to role play. The first baseman must obviously be able to consider the game from the point of view of the pitcher and the batter. Since ability to role play is such a crucial element in most sports, it makes sense that the elements of moral judgment can be learned best in this arena. In studying the moral judgment of children, Piaget (1965) focused on their ability to formulate and adhere to the rules of a game of marbles. Among adolescents, one could easily focus on sports to learn about the participant's understanding of the formulation of rules, rule following, cooperation, limit setting, division of roles, and territoriality.

While the adolescent can profit from sports participation and can learn crucially important social skills, he or she can also learn less desirable traits and behavior. Anxiety can be increased in situations that are intensely competitive and that don't provide "fun" for the player (Scanlan & Passer, 1978). Violence can be learned, especially in sports where professionals model violent behavior. Hockey, for example, seems particularly susceptible to that charge. Canadians, who love the game and play it vigorously and well, almost as a national winter pastime, also abhor its potential for violence. In a careful study of 740 Toronto adolescents, aged 12 to 21, Smith (1978) demonstrated that more players of hockey than nonplayers condone the violence of the game and players consume more professional hockey via radio, newspaper, books, and TV than nonplayers. Following Bandura's social learning theory of the acquisition of aggression, Smith concludes "I have argued that the mass media portrayals of violence in professional hockey have contributed to the spread of a social climate in youth hockey conducive to violence" (Smith, 1978, p. 105). Parents and coaches may unwittingly contribute to that climate. An excellent pamphlet "You and Your Child in Hockey" has been published jointly by the Ontario Ministry of Culture and Recreation and the Ontario Hockey Council. It would be highly appropriate reading for parents, not only of hockey players, but of players in all sports that have the potential for excessive competition and violence. It should be required reading for their coaches. An anonymous letter is quoted in that booklet:

Dear Mom and Dad:

I hope that you won't get mad at me for writing this letter, but you always told me never to keep anything back that ought to be brought out into the open. So here goes.

Remember the other morning when my team was playing and both of you were sitting and watching. Well, I hope that you won't get mad at me, but you kind of embarrassed me. Remember when I went after the puck in front of the net trying to score and fell? I could hear you yelling at the goalie for getting in my way and tripping me. It wasn't his fault, that is what he is supposed to do. Then do you remember yelling at me to get on the other side of the blue line. The coach told me to cover my man, and I couldn't if I listened to you, and while I tried to decide they scored against us. Then you yelled at me for being in the wrong place. You shouldn't have jumped all over the coach for pulling me off the ice. He is a pretty good coach, and a good guy, and he knows what he is doing. Besides he is just a volunteer coming down at all hours of the day helping us kids, just because he loves sports. And, then neither of you spoke to me the whole way home, I guess you were pretty sore at me for not getting a goal. I tried awfully hard, but I guess I am a crummy hockey player. But, *I love the game*, it is lots of fun being with the other kids and learning to compete. It is a good sport, but how can I learn if you don't show me a good example. And, anyhow I thought I was *playing hockey for fun*, to have a good time, and to learn good sportsmanship. I didn't know that you were going to get so upset, because I couldn't become a star.

Love

Your son

Within the past several years, some psychologists have specialized in youth sports and several recent volumes attest to the quality of research and writing being done in that area (Smoll & Smith, 1978; Thomas, 1977; Martens & Seefeldt, 1979; Magill, Ash, & Smoll, 1978). The National Association for Sport and Physical Education has published a set of *Guidelines for Children's Sports* (Martens & Seefeldt, 1979) which includes a bill of rights of young athletes:

1. Right to participate in sports.
2. Right to participate at a level commensurate with each child's maturity and ability.
3. Right to have qualified adult leadership.
4. Right to play as a child and not as an adult.
5. Right of children to share in the leadership and decisionmaking of their sport participation.
6. Right to participate in safe and healthy environments.
7. Right to proper preparation for participation in sports.
8. Right to an equal opportunity to strive for success.
9. Right to be treated with dignity.
10. Right to have fun in sports. (Martens & Seefeldt, 1978, p. 15)

Heterosexual social development

One type of peer association which is highly important to the adolescent is the heterosexual friendship, for which there is a rich language of description. From the casual encounter, or date, with an opposite-sex peer to the frequent culmination of the friendship through courtship and marriage, the typical adolescent passes through a series of heterosexual social developmental stages, each with its own nomenclature, symbols, understandings, and commitments. From the casual date and playing the field, a pair may begin to go steadily, which somehow denotes regular and exclusive dating. Going steady suggests a further level of commitment—the expectation that the relationship, though not necessarily permanent, is at least for the moment an exclusive one which does not permit dates with anyone but each other. More serious intentions are sometimes signaled by the exchange of school rings or fraternity or sorority pins. Engagement and marriage are the hoped-for culmination of these stages. One of us, having the temerity to describe these stages to a group of college students, was recently reminded that he had forgotten to include the important stage of living together, which may occur before marriage, before engagement, or even before going steady. We will examine the data on this important topic later. Undoubtedly, the stages of heterosexual involvement vary widely among communities. It is also safe to say that the advent of an emphasis on women's rights is changing traditional mores, just as it is changing the traditional sex roles in marriage.

Dating

One encounter that does not seem to be losing favor, however, is the time-honored American custom of dating, or going out. The date, a casual encounter between a boy and a girl with no further commitment than that they will engage in some mutually enjoyable social activity in each other's company for a day or an evening, is almost universal among American high school students. According to the data of Douvan and Adelson (1966), most American girls begin dating between the ages of 14 and 15, with boys beginning to date a little later. Although there is very little cross-national data on the age at which adolescents begin to date, it is our opinion (based on our associations with European and Oriental students both in the United States and abroad) that Douvan and Adelson are correct in their observation that Americans tend to date much earlier than do youngsters of many other countries. In light of the importance that Sullivan attaches to establishing isophilic relations before heterosexual relations are established, one wonders whether early dating may hinder the important development which would otherwise occur during this early adolescent period.

A number of criticisms can be leveled against dating as we know it in the United States, and social critics, sociologists, and psychologists never seem to tire of listing the advantages and/or the disadvantages of the practice. On the negative side, the sorts of things that usually get cited are that our dating practices seem to be undemocratic; that they encourage a certain superficiality in heterosexual relations; that they prevent the youngster from getting an accurate picture of the behavior and interests of the opposite sex; that they tend to overemphasize the importance of the sexual element in interpersonal relations to the detriment of other aspects of social interaction; and that they somehow tend to encourage the too early exclusive dating known as going steady. Some have argued that dating promotes sexual intimacy without sexual release, and others have found that dating tends to be a sexist and degrading form of interaction in which the girl is required to make herself available but to show little initiative. Along these lines, it has been suggested that the most familiar dating habits force youngsters into rigid sex-role patterns which may prove to be crippling in marriage and which do not allow for full development of personality.

On the positive side, observers have noted that our dating practices provide situations in which youngsters can learn certain social amenities; give youngsters an entrée into the valued group activities of their age-mates; and enable youngsters to experiment with a variety of sexual and nonsexual roles without having to make firm commitments to one another. Unlike courtship and engagement, dating provides the individual with a graceful out if he or she does not wish to maintain an unsatisfying relationship. Although breaking off an engagement is still seen as a rather serious matter, not being called again for a date or not initiating further dates can go all but unnoticed.

The reader will notice that the exaggeration of some supposed advantages of dating can convert them into disadvantages. For example, the social roles learned in dating might be stretched to become the rigid adoption of sex roles which are inappropriate or at least insufficient for full personality development. The measure of one's success at having learned social graces can easily become excessive concern with superficial mannerisms. The development of ease in casual interpersonal relations could lead to using superficial relations as a defense against intimacy and commitment. The pseudointimacy of the cocktail party as a substitute for genuine involvement in human relations is an often-cited aspect of American social life. To borrow a phrase from Kozol, it appears to be something of a "death at an early age" when one observes the somewhat sudden change from the spontaneity and euphoria of childhood to the artificial mannerisms of bridge-club adulthood which are sometimes adopted by even young adolescents. Obviously such criticisms cannot be made of all, or perhaps even most, of the adolescents who are dating. Still, aspects of the dating procedure that have been cited as advantages can easily be carried too far and become disadvantages.

When youngsters themselves have been asked why they date (McDaniel, 1969), they have cited the following reasons: (1) mate selection, (2) recreation, (3) anticipatory socialization, and (4) adult role clarification. McDaniel defined three stages of courtship: random dating, going steady, and being pinned or engaged. He found that the females in his samples went through each of these stages in a rather systematic progression in the order given. He also found that they cited somewhat different reasons for dating during each of the three stages. During random dating the girls tended to be more assertive and to date for recreational reasons, whereas in the last stage, that is, when they were pinned or engaged, their basis for dating was the anticipated socialization that would be involved, and they tended to be more receptive. When girls were going steady—the second stage in the sequence—the main reason they cited for dating was mate selection. Table 8–1 gives a summary of McDaniel's results.

Douvan and Adelson (1966) found that especially in the early stages of dating the negotiation of contracts between the partners was a way of dealing with the anxiety aroused by heterosexuality. The commitments of the partners to each other could be stated explicitly. This might well be one reason for the explicitness of the stages which was mentioned, each having its own outward symbol; these stages and their symbols may provide the adolescent with some security in

TABLE 8–1

Socialization sequence: Stages of courtship	Relationship between role behavior— Reasons for dating	Reference-group orientation	Degree of comple-mentarity	Degree of commit-ment	Degree of satisfaction with dating role
1. Random dating	Assertive— recreation	Original family, peer group	Comple-mentary plus	Low/ medium	Satisfied
2. Going steady	Assertive receptive—mate selection	Original family, peer group	Comple-mentary plus	Medium	Satisfied/ dissatisfied
3. Pinned/ engaged	Receptive— anticipatory socialization	Self and boyfriend	Comple-mentary plus	Medium/ high	Dissatisfied

Source: C. O. McDaniel, Jr., "Dating roles and reasons for dating," *Journal of Marriage and the Family*, February 1969, *31*(1), 97–107. Copyright 1969 by the National Council on Family Relations. Reprinted by permission.

a relatively insecure situation. Douvan and Adelson also found clear stages in the development of dating and also noted that girls' conceptions of dating change with these stages. Initially, girls' notion of dating is a rather intellectual one, involving little emotional commitment. By early adolescence, however, girls are involved in the beginning stages of dating but are still defensive in their reactions to boys. Not until late adolescence, when they have gradually overcome their initial anxieties about dating, can girls engage in dating more comfortably and take a more positive stance toward their dating partners, a stance that, according to Douvan and Adelson, includes understanding and sympathy.

Perhaps one of the least desirable aspects of the so-called dating game is that it causes both boys and girls to view themselves as objects of assessment by the other sex. Just as they have been evaluated in school for their cognitive performance, they now perceive themselves as being evaluated by their peers for their social performance. A performance ethic develops which, carried to its cruelest extreme, demands that the girl continuously present herself as an appealing commodity according to the latest marketing standards. The boy's performance is measured in terms of all sorts of masculine achievement, including athletic prowess, sexual accomplishments, and later, vocational success.

The tragedy in this emphasis on the product rather than the process was brought home to one of us recently in the counseling of a young man. He complained about an inability to perform in the sexual aspects of his marriage, and as counseling progressed it became painfully evident that his worries about performance extended to his other social relations and to his work as well. He had already been out of graduate school for a year and had not published. He had lived in the community for six months and had not made many friends. And to top it off, he had been married for three years and was not "making it in bed."

To be able to see ourselves as others see us is an important ability provided that it does not become an obsessive and one-sided preoccupation. The self-consciousness of adolescence can only be augmented by an excessive concern with one's acceptability to others, by attempts to measure up to externally defined performance standards, and by validating one's own worth against the standards of others.

Intimacy: The psychological task of late adolescence

In an earlier chapter we outlined Erikson's eight psychosocial stages and noted the emphasis he placed on interpersonal intimacy during late adolescence or early adulthood. Once identity is achieved, it is possible for the young man or woman to establish an intimate relationship with a member of the opposite sex. What is meant by intimate relationship is not an easy question to answer. Erikson was referring to an emotional commitment without a fusion or blurring of ego boundaries for either partner. That is, one doesn't need to give up one's own individuality in order to enter into an intimate relationship. On the other hand, it is essential for one already to have achieved a certain level of identity. The components of intimacy are not absolute, but Whitebourne and Weinstock (1979) have suggested a number of distinguishing characteristics: "a sense of mutuality, sensitivity to the partner's needs, physical closeness, willingness to share, and openness or lack of defensiveness with the partner" (p. 152). Persons do not have to be married or engaged to be intimate. It is possible to have several intimate relationships simultaneously. While persons obviously differ in their capacity for intimacy, a level of trust and a willingness to share are essential. When adult partners enter into a relationship characterized by these qualities and by an emotional commitment to one another, they express intimacy, whether they are of the same or opposite sex, the same or a very different age, and regardless of their marital status. While not all late adolescents develop an equal capacity for entering into such relationships, this is clearly the interpersonal task of their developmental period.

Cohabitation

Although a fair amount of research has been devoted to dating practices, less data are available on the meaning and incidence of premarital cohabitation, since it represents, at least in the United States, a relatively new lifestyle in terms of general acceptance. For some, cohabitation represents a trial marriage, while for others it is an alternative to a traditional married life. Cohabitation could also refer to communal arrangements, with or without sexual involvement, or to college students' private living arrangements, on campus or off.

Data on the attitudes of college students (Yankelovich, 1973) reveal an increasing (at least between 1968 and 1971) disaffection with traditional ideas of marriage. In 1971, approximately 34 percent of the 1,244 students sampled by Yankelovich said that they believed marriage to be obsolete. This was a substantial increase over the 24 percent who held the same view in 1969. Although

Yankelovich is cautious about these figures, some observers (for example, Dreyer, 1975) interpret such data as evidence of a rapid change in mores. Our own view is somewhat cautious. A majority (at least 70 percent) of the students sampled expressed faith in marriage, but a growing number questioned its value and were looking for alternatives. However, all institutions were under scrutiny, if not attack, during the years covered by Yankelovich's survey. It would be desirable to repeat the survey in order to ascertain the extent to which its data represent a relatively permanent change in attitude toward marriage and the extent to which they reflect a temporary disaffection with establishment values and institutions. In any event a good number of American adolescents— probably a third—are in favor of exploring alternative lifestyles to marriage.

Many college campuses offer a wide variety of living arrangements, including coed dorms and floors, if not rooms. One study (Luckey & Nass, 1969) found that such arrangements were favored by over 35 percent of U.S. male college students and over 26 percent of female students. The percentages were about the same among Canadian students but were much higher in Germany (males, 65 percent; females 54 percent) and England (males, 66.9 percent; females 62.4 percent). Segregation by sex has given way to a variety of options. In general, the traditional view of courtship and marriage is changing under the pressure for greater flexibility of role definitions for both men and women.

CONFORMITY

Because of the popular assumption that adolescents are more peer-oriented than parent-oriented in their values, the topic of conformity at this age deserves special attention. As Dunphy (1963) demonstrated, the structure of the social group changes throughout adolescence. It is in this context of a changing social peer structure that conformity becomes an important issue for the adolescent boy or girl.

In the last chapter we cited Brittain's study of adolescent choices under parent-peer cross pressures. Brittain was examining the hypothesis that in choice making adolescents turn for counsel to their peers rather than to their parents. He found that adolescent girls responded to hypothetical dilemmas involving conflicting parent-peer expectations in a way which supported the hypothesis that their choices would depend upon the content of the alternatives presented to them. In other words, though it is true that adolescents have established relations with peers which were unknown in childhood and may go to their peers for advice in some circumstances, it is also true that those circumstances will include the content of the advice being sought.

Age differences in conformity

To what extent, then, do adolescents conform to the behavior and the expectations of their peers? One study (Costanzo & Shaw, 1966) demonstrated that boys and girls tended to conform more at puberty than either before or after puberty. The authors investigated the level of conformity as a function of age by

178

asking the subjects to participate in an experiment in which they were required
to judge the length of lines. This design, first described by Asch (1958), is a
rather standard procedure in the study of conformity. The subjects, tested in
groups of four, are each presented with a panel of lights which represent the
supposed responses given by each of the other subjects. However, the experimenter can control these actually fictitious responses of the other subjects. In the
Costanzo and Shaw study, for example, the experimenter presented each subject
with erroneous data about the other subjects' responses on 16 of the 24 trials.
The measure of conformity, then, was the number of times that the subject conformed to these obviously incorrect responses. The authors used this technique
to test a large number of subjects in four age groups—7 to 9, 11 to 13, 15 to 17,
and 19 to 21. The data are presented in Figure 8–4.

FIGURE 8–4   Mean conformity as a function of age.

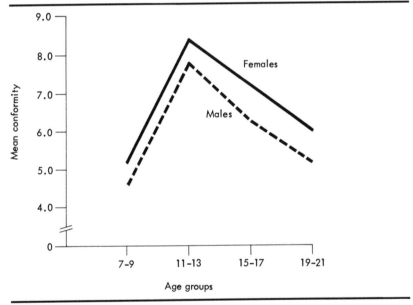

Source: P. R. Costanzo and M. E. Shaw, "Conformity as a function of age level," *Child
Development,* 1966, *37,* 967–975. By permission of the Society for Research in Child
Development.

It can be seen from the graph that the 11- to 13-year-olds were the most
conforming. The results on conformity as a function of age are highly significant
both for boys and girls. According to Costanzo and Shaw, these findings suggest
that conformity behavior follows the developmental trend of socialization in
general. That is to say, younger children are unaware of the pressures by their
peers to conform, whereas older adolescents or adults, who have developed
greater social skills and greater reliance on their own judgment, have come to
learn that they are expected to conform in some situations and are quite free to
be independent in other situations. The pubescent child, on the other hand, is

aware of the reactions of other persons and of the need to conform to their expectations.

This interpretation fits very nicely with David Elkind's (1967) observations about the egocentrism of adolescence. Elkind's view is that at each stage of cognitive development the child at first goes through a period of egocentrism. Adolescence begins the new stage of cognitive development known as formal operational logic in Piaget's terminology. Elkind believes that the egocentrism which is characteristic of this period involves two aspects: the notion of an imaginary audience and the idea of the personal fable. By imaginary audience, Elkind means that adolescents at this age are self-consciously aware of the effect that their behavior has on others and behave as though they were constantly being watched. In a sense, it is as though they were objects of the perceptions of others rather than agents of their own activities. This might help explain why Costanzo and Shaw found that boys and girls in their 11- to 13-year-old age group were more conforming than boys and girls in either the younger or older age groups. That is to say, it is at precisely this age that Elkind, following Piaget, would predict that boys and girls would be most egocentric. If, indeed, they are more egocentric at this age and perceive others to be observing them, it makes sense that they would be more likely to conform to the behavior of others and to their perception of others' expectations for them.

Although the data of Costanzo and Shaw were very much in line with earlier data, particularly with studies which had used an Asch-type conformity situation (for example, Berenda, 1950), the findings on conformity in general at both childhood and adolescent ages reveal that children tend to conform more often in ambiguous or difficult situations than on clear or easy problems. It has also been found (Patel & Gordon, 1960) that the decline in conformity from early to late adolescence is less marked when the adolescent is conforming to norms of higher prestige. In other words, high school students are more likely to conform to the norms set by students slightly older than themselves than they are to conform to the norms of their own age group. A fairly common example of this phenomenon is the rather marked extent to which the coeds in small college towns often set the style of dress for the younger high school girls. The popular thing to wear in high school is very often the style of apparel which was seen on campus the year before.

Social class and conformity

A study by Tuma and Livson (1960) demonstrates the effect of social class on conformity behavior in adolescents. The authors studied 19 boys and 29 girls at ages 14, 15, and 16. These youngsters were participants in the Guidance Study group at the Institute of Human Development at the University of California at Berkeley (MacFarlane, 1938). The Guidance Study was a longitudinal study of children born between 1928 and 1929. They were first studied at the age of 18 months and periodically thereafter until they were 18 years old. The data from the present study were taken, as mentioned above, from 48 of these children when they were 14 and then again when they were 15 and 16. The study investigated conformity through clinical evaluation at each age level. These evaluations were based on interviews with the subjects and their mothers, on teachers' ratings, and on sociometric evaluations. A combined overall index of conformity comprised a five-point scale ranging from "hectic drive to conform" (5), to "extremely resistant to rules, regulations, and authority, extreme individualism and nonconformity" (1). The index was applied to each subject's attitude toward authority in three settings: at home, at school, and with peers.

The results disclosed a slight tendency for girls to appear more conforming than boys. In addition, girls' conformity increased from ages 14 to 16, whereas boys showed no consistent age trend. These data are similar to the data reported by Costanzo and Shaw which showed girls to be more conforming, though not significantly. From the Costanzo and Shaw data, however, one would expect the subjects' conformity to decrease rather than increase from ages 14 to 16.

In the Tuma and Livson study, for both boys and girls, high correlations were found for conformity across all three settings—at home, at school, and with friends. For boys there was generally a negative correlation between conformity and socioeconomic status. In other words, at each of the three ages and in all three settings, boys from families of higher socioeconomic status tended to conform less than did boys from families lower in socioeconomic status. This was shown to be mainly the result of the level of education of the parents, with the economic standing of the family having little effect. It should be noted that the sample was confined largely to the upper middle-class range.

The Tuma and Livson data on the relationship between conformity and socioeconomic status square nicely with Kohn's (1959) conclusion that middle-class parents tend to encourage their children to adhere more to internal standards of conduct (for example, self-control and dependability) than to external standards (obedience and neatness).

SUMMARY AND CONCLUSIONS

During adolescence peer relations come to assume an increasingly important role in an individual's life. If the human personality is defined in terms of interpersonal relations, it would be safe to say that whereas the infant is a "family person," the child and the adolescent turn away from the family for a good deal of their social involvement. The theorist who wrote most convincingly about the interpersonal aspect of personality—who, in fact, defined personality in interpersonal terms—was Harry Stack Sullivan.

A theoretical concept which Sullivan used frequently in describing interpersonal relations was that of dynamism. This idea referred to the changing energy patterns, whether positive or negative, which characterize human social interaction. Sullivan noted that different dynamisms seem to characterize different stages of human development.

In Sullivan's theory, preadolescence is characterized by a need for intimacy, especially intimacy of an isophilic sort. This dynamism is accompanied during early adolescence by the dynamism of lust, or the sexual feelings associated with genital development. The shift to a lust dynamism is associated with an increased interest in heterophilic rather than isophilic relations.

During late adolescence the specific patterning of the lust dynamism continues to develop. Friendship choices stabilize, and for many adolescents dating becomes more selective, regular, and intense. Late adolescence is still a time for experimenting with a variety of social roles, however, or, in Erikson's words, a psychosocial moratorium from permanent choices.

Heterosexual social development has a well-developed nomenclature to distinguish each succeeding stage of involvement. This language and the external symbols of courtship and engagement help to clarify the meaning of each successive commitment. Although these practices are undergoing change, dating continues as a common social practice among high school students. Early dating provides a field for important social learning and experimenting, but it has been criticized for its capacity to become a setting for conformity and sex stereotyping. Conformity increases during early adolescence, then declines again among young adults. In males at least, conformity appears to be negatively related to the socioeconomic level of the parents.

Erikson noted the importance of intimacy as a developmental task of late adolescence. In order to establish an intimate relationship it is essential for one to have already achieved a certain level of identity. A willingness to share and a certain level of trust are also essential components of one's capacity for intimacy. While not all late adolescents develop an equal capacity for entering into such relationships, this is clearly the interpersonal task of their developmental period.

SUGGESTED ADDITIONAL READING

Hartup, W. Peer interaction and social organization. In P. H. Mussen (Ed.), *Carmichael's manual of child psychology*, 3d ed. New York: John Wiley & Sons, 1970.

Sullivan, H. S. *The interpersonal theory of psychiatry* (chaps. 16, 17, and 18). New York: W. W. Norton, 1953.

CHAPTER 9

VALUES: THEIR DEVELOPMENT AND INFLUENCE ON ADOLESCENT BEHAVIOR

The development of values is perhaps one of the most important topics in the whole area of adolescent psychology. The term *value* has been used in a wide variety of ways, and a number of authors (for example, Kluckhohn, 1951; Rokeach, 1968, 1973) have attempted to reduce the resulting conceptual confusion by distinguishing value from such related concepts as attitude, need, interest, norm, and trait. For our purposes, value refers to "matters of importance" as distinguished from "matters of fact." In other words, by values we refer to what ought to be rather than to what is. In this sense, values serve as guides in the direction of behavior. These same guides also provide the basis for evaluating behavior after it has occurred.

When one defines values in this way, it is easy to see their importance as a topic of psychology in general. Indeed, with adolescent development occurring in an environment of ever-increasing complexity, the need for values becomes readily apparent as greater skill is required in making appropriate choices.

In this chapter we will begin by examining three theories of values: the psychoanalytic position, the learning theory position, and a perceptual interpretation. We will then consider the related topic of moral development and the moral judgment of the adolescent, with particular attention to the work of Piaget and the American cognitive-developmental psychologist Lawrence Kohlberg. The remaining sections will deal with the effects of the school and the "youth culture" on the development of values and with the political values and the political socialization of adolescents.

THEORIES OF VALUE DEVELOPMENT

A number of theories of values have been articulated. Among the most prominent are the psychoanalytic and the learning theory positions.

The psychoanalytic position

We have already examined Freud's theory in some detail in Chapter 3. Here we want to review that theory as it bears on the development of values. The main agent of socialization in Freud's theory, as we have seen, is the superego. This aspect of personality refers to the internalized authority of the parents (Freud, 1953). For the very young child, the parents represent the only authority with power to reward and punish. Gradually, however, the superego—an internal rewarder and punisher—develops. This occurs as the result of the child's identification with his or her parents, that is, with the child's intense desire to be like the parents. The child adopts the parents' manners as well as their style of rewarding and punishing. If, for example, the father has been stern and inflexible, the superego gradually takes on that role. The child then feels guilty and expects punishment for wrongdoing. Freud held that in some neurotic disorders the maintenance of symptoms and their resistance to treatment represented just such an unconscious wish to be punished. In Freud's theory this punitive component of the superego is called conscience.

However, to the extent that the child's desire to be like the parents is aided by positive and rewarding guidance, the ego ideal—an ideal of what the child would like to be—develops.

Both of these components of the superego—conscience and the ego ideal—develop as the result of parental identification, and both serve to guide one's behavior once the submission to parental authority begins to lessen. The child has gradually developed his or her own set of values, and now the child's behavior is no longer directed exclusively by the fear of parental punishment or the anticipation of parental approval.

The learning theory explanation

According to learning theory, values are acquired through experience and reinforcement. A clear statement of this position has been given by Hill (1960). He argued that the psychoanalytic terms in this area are confusing because of their too frequent lack of operational definition. Instead, he substituted more empirically definable terms from learning psychology.

Since values are learned, generally through verbal instruction, the same principles, according to Hill, should apply to values as are useful in explaining any type of learning. For example, the principle of reinforcement is exemplified in a child's learning of a generalized tendency to imitate other people. If the child is rewarded for imitating particular behaviors, he or she will soon learn not only to repeat those behaviors but to imitate in general. In the same way the child could learn to conform to verbal instructions in general by being rewarded for obeying verbal instructions in specific instances. The principle of stimulus generalization is invoked here. That is, to the extent that situations are similar, the child will again conform. In light of this principle it is not surprising that though the referent may change from parent to peer, youngsters who have learned to conform during childhood in order to gain a reward (for example, the assurance of somebody's admiration) will continue to conform during adolescence.

The additional notion of "vicarious" reinforcement gives this explanation added mileage by suggesting that a person can be reinforced indirectly by observing the reinforcement contingent on another person's behavior. Such reinforcement operates, according to Hill, so as to inhibit punished behavior (that is, to use the psychoanalytic language, in the development of conscience) as well as to facilitate the production of rewarded behavior (that is, in the development of the ego ideal).

A perceptual interpretation

The relationship between perception and values has been explored in both theory (Köhler, 1959) and research (Bruner & Goodman, 1947). Recent research by McKinney (1973, 1975) extends this relationship and suggests an alternative explanation for the development of values. One advantage which McKinney sees in the perceptual model is that it places strong emphasis on the action (that is, self-produced movement) of the individual whose values are developing. In other words, the perceptual model sees the adolescent as an active agent whose values develop as a function of feedback from his or her self-initiated behavior rather than as a passive recipient of the values of the environment. Once again, the view of the child as an active organism to whom the environment is simultaneously responding (that is, as both subject and object) seems to fit the developmental data best.

Basically, the perceptual interpretation states that values develop as schemata or templates which are built up through experience and are then used in guiding future behavior. The analogy here is to those central nervous system representations of active motor behavior which have been identified as the body schema.

The analogy relates to ease of movement. Some people develop a good deal of coordination in their movements, and this has been attributed to a good body image (Schilder, 1950; Head, 1920), that is, to a central nervous system representation or a postural model of their body which provides them with immediate feedback of the location of each body part or of each felt movement in space.

Such a body image develops by experience, especially experience in a relatively stable environment which provides a certain amount of reafferent feedback. Thus, for example, in studies of adaptation to prism-induced visual distortion (Held & Bossom, 1961), it has been shown that active self-produced body movement is essential for individuals to overcome the distortion produced by prism lenses. For subjects wearing prism lenses, objects appear to be several degrees to the left or right of where they "really" are. In pointing to an object, such subjects will be that many degrees off center. They will continue to be off until they have a chance to move about and to associate such self-directed motor activity with the visual stimulation which changes as a result of their movements. Such changes in their visual environment are called reafferent stimulation.

Translating this theory of body image and visual perception into the social psychology of values, McKinney suggests that individuals develop values when they are allowed to choose freely (self-produced movement) and when they see stimulus changes as contingent on their own behavior (reafference). He argues that what would be analogous to the self-produced quality of one's movement would be the generalized expectancy that one is responsible for his or her own behavior; that is, an internal locus of control.

A number of studies dealing with adolescents would seem to support such a view of the development of values. For example, one sociologist (Caro, 1966) studied the values which middle- and working-class youngsters attach to various occupations. Lower-class adolescents rated less prestigious occupations as more desirable than did middle-class boys and girls. The same working-class subjects rated more prestigious occupations as lower in value than did middle-class adolescents. The middle-class youngsters seemed to "stretch" their values in the sense that they perceived more prestigious occupations as more desirable and less prestigious occupations as less desirable than did the working-class youngsters.

One interpretation of these data (McKinney, 1975) was that the middle-class adolescents had a greater internal locus of control and a greater sense of personal freedom with respect to the choice of occupation. Such freedom would be analogous to the self-production of behavior in the development of body image, and thus it would make sense that the middle-class youngsters develop a stronger set of both positive and negative values with respect to occupational choice.

Another study that might be interpreted as lending support to this perceptual view of the development of values was conducted by Gardner and Thompson (1963). These authors compared delinquent and nondelinquent children on a measure of "telenomic trends," that is, the values which were perceived as characteristic of a happy-successful or an unhappy-unsuccessful person. Gardner and Thompson found that in 10 of the 13 categories they tested their nondelinquent subjects gave ratings which were significantly higher for the positive values and significantly lower for the negative values than did the delinquents. It appeared that the nondelinquent boys and girls had a stronger sense of what it meant to be either a happy-successful person or an unhappy-unsuccessful person. Again, these results may be interpreted to mean that nondelinquent subjects are more likely to have an internal locus of control and thus to have made choices dealing with their own happiness and unhappiness. The fact that the nondelinquents had been able to choose more freely than had the delinquents may explain why such values were more highly developed in the nondelinquents.

Both of the above studies were interpreted in a post hoc fashion as support for the perceptual theory of values. Other research has been done as a direct test of this hypothesis (McKinney, 1973, 1975). In two studies using undergraduates as subjects, McKinney found that individuals with an internal locus of control, as measured by Rotter's (1966) test of that dimension, had stronger values than did individuals with an external locus of control. In other words, adolescents who perceive the relationship between their own behavior and the results of the behavior have a more strongly developed set of values than do externally controlled subjects who do not perceive that relationship.

MORALITY AND MORAL JUDGMENT

The structure of adolescent values has been shown (McKinney, 1973) to be fairly well differentiated, at least by the early college years. One important factor in adolescent values concerns achievement and the symbols of success, such as money, prestige, and academic grades. Another well-differentiated adolescent value factor is the more general issue of competence, with its emphasis on the quality of behavior rather than on either its outcome or validating symbols of achievement. A third factor in the adolescent value structure concerns interpersonal relations and emphasizes the moral or ethical quality inherent in or attributed to such proscribed behaviors as lying, cheating, and hurting others and such prescribed behaviors as helping others, sharing, and keeping promises. Let us examine this factor more carefully.

Piaget's study of moral judgment

Although first published in 1932, Piaget's classic work *The Moral Judgment of the Child* (1965) provides the theoretical backdrop against which much of the recent cognitive-developmental research and theory can be viewed. According to Piaget, a child's moral judgment develops in stages which parallel the stages of cognitive development. By interviewing young children and by watching them play a simple marble game, Piaget discovered that the morality of the young child is guided by what he called realism. At that stage, an act is considered wrong in terms of its consequences and not in terms of the actor's intention. Only later does the child develop a more autonomous morality, that is, realize that rules are mutually agreed upon and not immutable. Then intention becomes a more salient factor in determining morality. Values have become internalized so that the child can take the point of view of another person and consider what that person's intention may have been. Obviously this would require that the child be able to decenter cognitively; this is not possible for the young child in the egocentric stage of cognitive development. However, since adolescents, or even preadolescents, can generally decenter, they are able to make relativistic moral judgments.

Kohlberg's elaboration of Piaget's theory

Kohlberg (1958, 1963a) has extended Piaget's statement of moral development by amplifying the stages and suggesting ways to measure them. He has outlined the stages given in Table 9–1.

TABLE 9–1
Relations between Piaget logical stages and Kohlberg moral stages (relations are that attainment of the logical stages is necessary, but not sufficient, for attainment of the moral stage)

Logical stage	Moral stage
Symbolic, intuitive thought	Stage 0: The good is what I want and like
Concrete operations, substage 1 Categorical classification	Stage 1: Punishment-obedience orientation
Concrete operations, substage 2 Reversible concrete thought	Stage 2: Instrumental hedonism and concrete reciprocity
Formal operations, substage 1 Relations involving the inverse of the reciprocal	Stage 3: Orientation to interpersonal relations of mutuality
Formal operations, substage 2	Stage 4: Maintenance of social order, fixed rules, and authority
Formal operations, substage 3	Stage 5A: Social contract, utilitarian law-making perspective
	Stage 5B: Higher-law and conscience orientation
	Stage 6: Universal ethical principle orientation

Source: Reprinted from *Twelve to Sixteen: Early Adolescence,* edited by Jerome Kagan and Robert Coles. By permission of W. W. Norton & Company. Copyright © 1972, 1971 by The American Academy of Arts and Sciences.

Kohlberg divides these six stages of moral thought into three major levels: the preconventional level, which incorporates the first two stages; the conventional level, which incorporates stages 3 and 4; and the postconventional, or autonomous, level, which comprises the last two stages, 5 and 6, including the subdivisions of stage 5. Table 9–1 shows how these stages of moral development are related to Piaget's stages of thought.

For Kohlberg, as for Piaget, moral judgment is a specific case of cognitive development. It is directional, that is, it is sequential, and develops by a series of stages which always occur in the same order. Kohlberg demonstrated this quality of the invariance of the sequence by testing a number of boys and girls at different stages with a set of moral dilemmas. Their responses to these stories fell into one of the six categories of moral judgment which Kohlberg derived.

It appeared (see Figure 9–1) that the higher stages of moral judgment increase with age, whereas the lower stages decrease with age. Two cognitive processes are held accountable for this change. First of all, there is the person's increasing ability to role play, that is, to take the point of view of another, which is a social kind of decentering. Secondly, a cognitive disequilibrium results when a person confronts moral reasoning one stage higher than one's own. After a time, in the process of resolving that tension-producing disequilibrium, the individual attempts to understand solutions based on a higher level of moral reasoning.

While the theory appears sound, Kohlberg's research has come under damaging criticism (Kurtines & Greif, 1974; Simpson, 1974; Hoffman, 1980). The reliability of the measure and validity of the research results, the inaccessibility of the measure and the difficulty of scoring and interpretation have all

FIGURE 9–1   Use of six types of moral judgments at four ages.

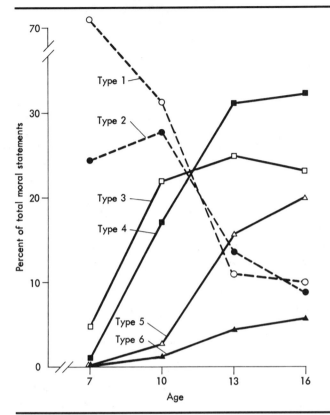

Source: L. Kohlberg, "The development of children's orientations toward a moral order. 1. Sequence in the development of moral thought." *Vita Humana,* 1963, 6, 11–33. By permission of the author and S. Karger AG.

been subject to question. A more recent adaptation of Kohlberg's theory (Rest, 1976; Rest, Davison, & Robbins, 1978) provides an alternative method of assessing the moral judgment stages and perhaps an answer to some of the criticism. Rest and his colleagues have developed a measure, called the Defining Issues Test, which, while still using moral dilemmas, involves an objective method of scoring a respondent's rating and ranking of the important issues in each dilemma. With the Defining Issues Test, it was demonstrated that as children and adolescents advance in age and educational level, they also advance in the moral judgment stages. Among adults, those with the highest educational attainment are those who reach the highest stages of moral judgment.

As important as these studies are in demonstrating the development of one sort of social cognition, they do not deal, nor do they pretend to, with the issue of moral behavior. There is still a long way between knowing what is right and doing it, or between being able to dissect philosophically the issues in a moral dilemma and being able to follow one's conscience, however it is formed. The issue of motivation for right-doing is undoubtedly the link between cognition and behavior in the moral sphere.

VALUE DEVELOPMENT AND THE HIGH SCHOOL

For the vast majority of adolescents the school is a highly important institution. A good part of the waking hours of an adolescent are spent in schoolrooms. Although that time is divided between academic pursuits and such cocurricular activities as social functions and athletic development and contests, it is fair to say that most of it is spent in learning, that is, in preparing. The development of the adolescent's instrumental values and future orientation is almost guaranteed by that fact. What the adolescent is doing in high school is not an end in itself so much as a means to an end.

While in school, the adolescent is under the authority of persons other than the parents, but this is not a new situation. In addition, he or she is in the company of a large number of peers, but this is not particularly new either. What is new about the association with peers lies in the importance which that association takes on during adolescence. Peers become important as agents of socialization and as a background against which the young adolescent can hew out his or her identity. Along with parents, peers become important referents for value formation.

Because adolescents spend as much time as they do in the classroom, we tend to blame the schools for a variety of social ills, particulary those related to the values of youth. Delinquency, political corruption, lack of achievement, periodic second place in the space race, and cultural decadence have all been blamed at one time or another on an educational system which seems uniquely designed to be blamed.

Friedenberg's socioeducational position

For a theoretical perspective on the school life of adolescents, we can turn to social critics and educational sociologists, such as Paul Goodman, Edgar Friedenberg, and John Holt. Because Friedenberg has written extensively on adolescent development and its relationship to the educational system, we will examine his work in some detail. In this context, his most important publications are probably *The Vanishing Adolescent* (1959), *Coming of Age in America* (1963), and a collection called *The Dignity of Youth and Other Atavisms* (1965). Friedenberg's main theme is the self-definition of the adolescent and the role of social institutions, such as the school, in facilitating or hindering that process. His view of adolescent self-definition, or self-clarification, is strikingly similar to Erikson's notions of identity. To some it appears that Friedenberg tends to idealize adolescents and to put down too many of those who work with them. He sees adults as very often fearful of the developing independence of adolescents and the democratization of the school. He argues that this fear underlies repressive measures which hinder the self-clarification of the adolescent.

Friedenberg defines adolescence in terms of its major trends, that is, self-clarification, conflict, and emotional development. This definition is perhaps best spelled out in *The Vanishing Adolescent*. There he points out that adolescent self-clarification seems to arouse anxiety in adults, and criticizes the language that adults use in talking about young people. The terms used to denote them are condescending, like the term *teenager,* or pedantic, like the term *adolescent,* or lacking in conviction, like the term *young person.* On the other hand, it might be fair to say that persons of all ages tend to reject labels which emphasize age. For example, what should one call the elderly? *Senior citizen* is as condescending as *teenager: elderly* is as pedantic as *adolescent: old folks* is as lacking in conviction as *young person.* A good deal of what Friedenberg calls adult condescension toward adolescence may simply be a function of the fact that when we use the tools of social science to study any age group as an age group we tend to neglect the unique qualities which make the individual living person most appealing. It is a simple fact, for example, that we study objects, not subjects. We tend to study individuals' reactions, not their creative expression. We study patients, not agents. At least this is the situation in our research, if not in our clinical practice.

In any event, Friedenberg perceives a good deal of ambivalence in the response of adults to the termination of their authority over adolescents. Our high schools, he argues, were developed to produce a group of youngsters who could be trusted with the complex machinery of a technological age. This requires a good deal of conformity, which extends not only to one's work life, but also to one's personal and social life. Becoming an American seems often to mean renouncing important differences among individuals, which it would be better to recognize and appreciate.

An important value for the adolescent is his or her self-esteem. In assessing the impact of the school on the self-esteem of adolescents, Friedenberg notes that a main task of the school is that of testing and evaluation. He feels that the self-appraisal of adolescents is too heavily based in the direction of external appraisal and evaluation. Because adolescents are in the process of clarifying their own experience (what Erikson would call identity formation), they are especially vulnerable to external evaluation. The judgments of their immediate environment become more important to them than to younger or older persons. Friedenberg feels that on all sides adolescents are told what is acceptable and what is unacceptable. As we saw in an earlier chapter, the data indicating that conformity increases during adolescence (Costanzo & Shaw, 1966) tend to support this notion. Both the media and the school may teach the adolescent to respond to other persons' expectations, to be a presentable package using the right sort of toothpaste, taking the right sort of courses, and dating the right sort of boy or girl.

With respect to emotional development, Friedenberg cites two sorts of value changes that occur in adolescence. The first is an increased capacity for tenderness. With the development of strong isophilic friendships, a sensitivity develops which stands in contrast with the somewhat unfeeling attitude of the 8- to 10-year-old. The second is a highly increased respect for competence. For example, high school students come to be very critical of their teachers and to know whether or not they are well prepared. In addition, adolescents appear to be highly sensitive to phoniness both in themselves and others. Being unsure of their own identity, they are more sensitive to inconsistency in others.

It is clear that the development of self-esteem, the process of self-clarification, and the development of an increased capacity for tenderness and an increased respect for competence are highly important in the life of the adolescent. Unfortunately, according to Friedenberg, the schools seem to play little part in facilitating these changes. Rather, he sees the contemporary high school as having four roles. First, it is an institution of national socialization; that is, its function is to Americanize the students, to instruct them in the cultural mores which will be required as they take their places in a technological society. A second role is evaluation. The high school has become a major source of certification, and a high school diploma is generally a requirement for entry into other branches of adult society, whether admission to the university or to the world of work. Third, the high school plays its traditional role as transmitter of knowledge and of some intellectual skills and attitudes. Finally, the high school is an administrative and record center. One's medical, social, and intellectual history are recorded, microfilmed, and preserved for the satisfaction of prospective employers, college admissions officers, and others with an adjudged legitimate request for this information.

The high school as an adolescent society

One interesting hypothesis about the role of the high school is that it provides a medium for the development of an adolescent subculture. When American society was largely post-figurative, to use Margaret Mead's term, the main responsibility of the school was to educate the child to confrom to the norms of the adult society and to learn to carry on the tasks dictated by that society. In a co-figurative and even more in a pre-figurative society, however, the school itself becomes a subculture with its own norms. Although these may conflict with the norms of society at large, they are nonetheless highly important in determining the direction of the students' behavior. An excellent study which bears on this point was conducted by James Coleman (1961), who summarized his research in *The Adolescent Society.*

One of Coleman's important conclusions was that the subculture of the adolescent in school is founded on a set of values somewhat at variance with the traditional conception of the school. Coleman examined the values of the students of 10 midwestern high schools of varying size. All but one of the schools were coeducational, and all but one were public schools. Five were located in small towns, three in cities, two in suburbs: one is a working-class suburb and one in an affluent suburb. One question which Coleman asked these students was, "If you could be remembered here at school for one of the three things below, which one would you want it to be? boys: brilliant student, athletic star, most popular; girls: brilliant student, leader in activities, most popular." The results are depicted in Figure 9–2. In this graph, the axis from the upper vertex to the center of the baseline represents scholarship, so that a point at the top of

FIGURE 9-2 How boys and girls would like to be remembered at school, and how their parents would like them to be remembered: the relative importance of scholarship, popularity, and (for boys) athletics or (for girls) activities.

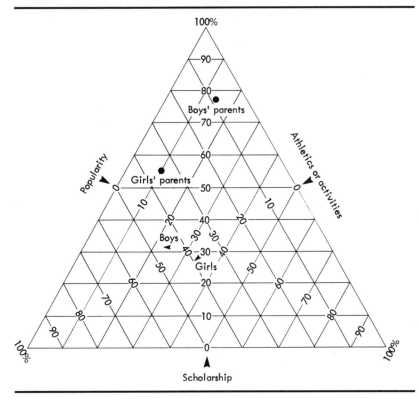

Source: J. Coleman, *Social climates in high schools* (Washington, D.C.: U.S. Government Printing Office, 1961).

the line would represent a school 100 percent of whose students wanted to be remembered as brilliant scholars. The axis extending from the lower-left vertex to the middle of the right side of the triangle represents athletics for boys and activities for girls. Thus, a point at the lower-left vertex would represent a school 100 percent of whose students would like to be remembered as athletic stars or as activity leaders. The axis from the lower right to the middle of the left side represents popularity, so that a point at the lower right would represent a school 100 percent of whose students want to be remembered as most popular. One can see at a glance that athletics are more important to the students than scholarship or popularity and that scholarship really comes out a losing third. The responses to questionnaires that Coleman sent to the parents, however, give a different picture. The parents are more concerned with scholarship, at least so they say, than with the other values represented in the school.

The source of the discrepancy between the values of the parents and the stated values of the students is not clear. Indeed, some of Coleman's data seem to be at odds with this discrepancy. For example, when the boys and girls were asked under what conditions their parents might be proud of them, a larger percentage of the boys reported that their parents would be very proud of them if they made the basketball team than if they became an assistant to the biology instructor. Similarly, a larger percentage of the girls reported that their parents would be very proud of them if they became a cheerleader than if they became an assistant to the biology instructor. These replies do not square with the parents' claim that they want their sons and daughters to be known as brilliant students, rather than as athletes or as the most popular.

Although the reason for the discrepancy is not entirely clear, a number of hypotheses can be presented. One is that the students simply perceive the values of their parents differently than they actually are. A second is that one of the two groups is not being completely honest. Perhaps the parents are distorting their real values and identifying the values which they assume to be "correct." Coleman suggests a third possibility. He believes that the parents undoubtedly do want their children to be scholarly and do place a higher priority on scholarship than on popularity or athletic skill. On the other hand, they may also want whatever is best for their children and may interpret this as being whatever would make the children happy in their own setting or successful in their own subculture. The children, knowing what it takes to be successful in their own subculture, rightly assume that their parents would be proud of them if they were recognized according to its values. Thus, the parents are unwittingly reinforcing values that are generated in the adolescent subculture.

Academic achievement in high school

From the foregoing, it should be clear that academic achievement is only one of the values in the society of high school adolescents. One factor that leads to high achievement relative to ability is the influence of the peer culture. From the research of Coleman and others, it would seem that this is perhaps the most important factor. Among the 10 schools which Coleman examined, the schools with the highest achievement ratings were not necessarily the schools in which the most money was spent on each student. If the per pupil expenditure does not correlate highly with the achievement of individual students, then what is responsible for the differences among the schools? The main factor seems to be the status of academic achievement within the schools themselves. Coleman notes that in a school in which athletics is highly valued, many students will go out for basketball, and those with the most ability will generally make the team. In the same way, in a school in which academic achievement is highly valued, many students will strive for academic rewards, and the students with the greatest ability will achieve significantly. When the social rewards lie elsewhere, students with intellectual ability may neglect scholarship for athletics of some other nonacademic arena. In that case, those who get the highest grades may not have the greatest ability. If fact, they may be a mediocre few who become known as grinds or bookworms.

Another important environmental variable determining academic achieve-

FIGURE 9–3 In a school in which academic achievement is highly valued, many students will strive for academic rewards, and the students with the greatest ability will achieve significantly.

Photograph courtesy of Dan Hughson

ment is the importance that the family attaches to scholarly success. In reviewing the literature on the family relations of intelligent high-achieving and underachieving high school boys, Morrow and Wilson (1961) observed that the high-achieving boy more often came from a home in which he received a good deal of praise and approval, felt a strong sense of belongingness, felt understood by his parents, and identified closely with them. The underachieving boy, on the other hand, more often came from a family in which parents were overly restrictive or in which there was a good deal of parental tension and disagreement. The parents of such boys tended to demand either too much from their youngsters or too little. In their own research, Morrow and Wilson found that a number of variables of family morale were highly important in distinguishing between high-achieving and underachieving high school youngsters. They asked 48 highly intelligent (120 IQ or above) high school boys, half of whom had very high academic averages and the other half of whom had very low averages, to respond to a questionnaire dealing with family morale. In addition to an overall family morale score, there were 16 subscales, each of which comprised six items on their questionnaire. Their results are given in Table 9–2. The authors found that high-achieving boys enjoy family relations in which there is more sharing of recreation, confidence, and ideas and that the parents of high-achieving youngsters are more likely to show both approval and trust to their youngsters. In response, the high achievers tend to show more acceptance of their parents' standards than do the low achievers. Finally, the parents of high-achieving boys tend to show less overrestrictiveness and severity in their discipline.

TABLE 9–2
Family relations scales: Median tests*

Scale title	r†	Highs (N = 48)	Lows (N = 48)	p
Family sharing of recreation	.76	69	44	.02
Family sharing of confidence and ideas	.84	63	35	.01
Family sharing in making decisions	.88	60	44	ns
Parental approval	.56	73	33	.001
Parental affection	.88	60	42	ns
Parental trust	.73	60	25	.001
Parental approval of peer activities	.94	71	42	.01
Student acceptance of parental standards	.69	52	25	.01
Student affection and respect toward parents	.91	58	44	ns
Lack of parental overrestrictiveness	.63	56	29	.01
Lack of parental severity of discipline	.70	69	42	.01
Lack of parental overprotection	.77	52	56	ns
Lack of parental overinsistence on achievement	.75	63	46	ns
Parental encouragement of achievement	.74	60	40	.05
Harmony of parents (N = 40)	.72	63	48	ns
Regularity of home routine	.76	52	46	ns
Overall family morale	.97	67	33	.001

Columns under heading "Percent above median".

* Two-tailed tests.
† Odd-even reliability coefficient, corrected by Spearman-Brown formula.
Source: W. R. Morrow and R. C. Wilson, "Family relations of bright high-achieving and under-achieving high school boys," *Child Development*, 1961, *32*, 501–510. By permission of the author and The Society for Research in Child Development.

The dropout

Another way of demonstrating the importance of family relations for academic achievement is in terms of the family backgrounds of youngsters who drop out of high school. In a study comparing 150 dropouts with a matched group of 150 boys who were successfully completing the last semester of their senior year, Cervantes (1965) demonstrated that the primary relationships within the families of dropouts differed significantly from the primary relationship within the families of high school graduates. The youngster who dropped out of high school was far more likely to come from a home in which there was little understanding and acceptance, and was less likely to receive family encouragement for his educational and occupational plans. There was significantly less communication within the home and significantly less time was spent enjoying leisure activities together. Finally, the dropout reported significantly less happiness within the home.

This is not to gainsay other important factors in a youngster's decision to drop out of school. Lower-class students are significantly more likely to drop out of school (Orskansky, 1967) as are students who lack the social skills required to establish and maintain friendships in the school setting. Students who feel adequate in even one area are more likely to remain in school than are those who see themselves as social and academic misfits.

We have become more and more impressed with the low estimate of self-worth among many students. Books addressed to this topic—for example, I'm OK-You're OK (Harris, 1969); How to Be Your Own Best Friend (Berkowitz & Newman, 1973)—remain on the best-seller lists for months. Suicides among youth continue to climb. From time to time, the whole country seems to convulse with a fit of either expiation or blame, and perhaps the adolescent subculture merely reflects this national attitude. Still, there is a message to the high school teacher and the school counselor in all of this—students cannot practice within their areas of excellence unless they know what these are, and many cannot know that without help. The comparison group need not be one's peers but one's own abilities. In other words, when youngsters want to know what they are best at, they can be helped to assess their strengths and limitations without harsh and competitive comparison with their peers.

VALUES DURING LATE ADOLESCENCE

Some observers of the college scene have held that the values of students have been undergoing a rapid change during the last several years. Since the 1950s, when student values were considered privatistic (Gillespie & Allport, 1955) and conservative, what some have described as a "value revolution" has taken place (Yankelovich, 1972). The values of the students of the 60s were affirmative and public. They centered more on politics and social justice than on individual or private concerns. There was a greater questioning of authority, and at times there was open defiance of the law and order of the establishment.

Although some express concern that the dominant values then became authoritarian and repressive again, the data at least until 1972, did not support that conclusion. One organization which followed the values changes from the mid-60s until 1972 with careful, large-scale sampling techniques, cautioned against the acceptance of a media-generated faddish view of rebellion and decline. Yankelovich (1972) suggested that the task of social scientists was practically the opposite of the approach of the media. While the media might stress the weird and faddish, it is our job to examine the typical. From that point of view, he argued, there was in 1972 a real values revolution occurring on campuses across the country.

According to Yankelovich's data, the new values center on a number of themes, including the following:

Challenge to authority.

The search for substitutes for traditional religious values, particularly those that reflect the Puritan ethic.

A new sexual morality.

A questioning of wars as instruments of policy and of patriotism itself.

A search for cooperant rather than competitive life styles.

Dissatisfaction with marriage in its traditional form of a one-family house and two children.

A shifting from the extrinsic rewards of career (money and status) to its inherent satisfactions.

A change of emphasis from achievement via hard work to living in closer harmony with one's peers and with nature itself. (pp. 25–26)

One aspect of values which seems to be dominant throughout these themes is the notion of commitment. The new values are affirmative statements rather than statements of the thou-shalt-not variety.

The distinction between prescriptive (thou shalt) and proscriptive (thou shalt not) values is a reliable personality dimension (McKinney, 1971) which is related to child-rearing practices. Adolescents whose parents have habitually been more rewarding than punishing tend to have a prescriptive value orientation, whereas adolescents whose parents have disciplined them via punishment tend to be proscriptively oriented.

During the 1960s the values of college students became social as well as affirmative (Wharton, 1969; Keniston, 1968). One study tracing the history of this trend found that the values of college students had been becoming progressively more prescriptive since the 1930s (McKinney, Connolly, & Clark, 1973). This was undoubtedly related to changes in child-rearing practices (Bronfenbrenner, 1958), which gradually became more love-oriented and less discipline-oriented during those years.

During the 1960s large numbers of adolescents and youth participated in radical protest of a political and industrial establishment which they considered corrupt and self-serving. They espoused social values of love and caring to replace those of private gain at the expense of others. Since the 1960s there appears to have been some change from an emphasis on social-moral values to the privatism of personal values, such as achievement and success (McKinney, Hotch & Truhon, 1977). Although the radicalism of the counterculture died down during the 1970s, gradual changes in the values of youth appear not to have undergone a reversal. Only time will tell whether these changes will be permanent. Nor was the decade of the 1960s entirely unique. Social movements among youth have been found throughout history. Table 9–3 taken from Braungart (1975) traces the youth movement of this century.

POLITICAL VALUES AND POLITICAL SOCIALIZATION

One important consequence of recent value changes has been their effect on the legal system and on the political socialization of adolescents. With the age of majority now standing at 18 in the United States, late adolescents are seen as legal adults, with the right to vote and all the other rights of adult members of the community. It has therefore become more important to know what factors influence the political choices of adolescents as well as how the political choices of adolescents differ from those which might be made by children. It has

TABLE 9–3
Temporal location, decisive political events, and youth movements

Temporal location	Decisive political events	Youth movements
1900–1929	Economic growth and cultural liberalism Industrialization, U.S. develops favorable balance of trade and becomes world industrial power World War I Isolationism Prohibition Women's suffrage Roaring Twenties	Youth culture challenges Victorian social and sexual mores
1930–1940	The Great Depression Poverty Election of FDR—New Deal Government economic programs Growth of national socialism in Germany	Youth join antiwar movement Sign Oxford Pledge Campus strikes
1941–1949	World War II Truman administration Atomic bomb Returning GIs Global reconstruction, U.N.	Little youth movement activity
1950–1959	The cold war—Eisenhower years Growth of military-industrial complex Dulles foreign policy Recession McCarthyism 1954 Supreme Court desegregation decision House Un-American Activities Committee	The silent generation
1960–1968	Kennedy-Johnson Years New Frontier Civil rights demonstration Peace Corps, poverty programs Vietnam escalation Assassinations of Kennedy brothers and Martin Luther King, Jr. Great Society programs Ghetto riots and campus disruption	New left New right Civil rights and black power Protest demonstrations, strikes, violence
1969–1973	Nixon-Agnew Years Emphasis on law and order Vietnam war ends, fighting in Southeast Asia continues Inflation, job squeeze Growth of multinational corporations Watergate	Women's rights Ecology movement

Source: Braungart, R. G. Youth and social movements. In S. E. Dragastin, and G. H. Elder, Jr., *Adolesence in the life cycle.* New York: John Wiley & Sons, 1975, p. 260. Reprinted by permission of Hemisphere Publishing Corp.

been demonstrated by Adelson and O'Neil (1966) that political ideas do indeed change with age. These authors found that younger children are more egocentric in their views. Thus, compared to adolescents, young children tend to use more *personalism* in answering questions about government, community, or society. They do not take a sociocentric perspective until sometime around age 11. Children under the age of 13 also tend to have a more negative view of government. For example, they place more emphasis on its coercive functions.

Again, as one might expect from his more egocentric orientation, the young child has a quite different time perspective in the understanding of such concepts as government and community. Adelson and O'Neil found that during adolescence a sense of history becomes prominent. The adolescent is able to understand that the present is influenced by the past and is also able to incorporate a future orientation into thinking about the community. This is not surprising, given the formal operations which become part of the cognitive abilities of the adolescent. The political idealism of the adolescent is part and parcel of such formal operations. Such logical capacities allow the individual to imagine not only what *is,* in a concrete way, but what *might be,* in a more abstract manner. One's political judgment can then be influenced by hypotheses which one can frame for oneself, based on combinations of political events. The young child, on the other hand, is guided simply by the realism of what is. He looks less to the future than to the present.

SUMMARY AND CONCLUSIONS

In this chapter we examined the value structures of adolescents and young adults. We considered three theories which have been addressed to this issue. According to psychoanalytic theory, values develop as the result of identification with the status-bearing parents. Freud's term for this internalized socialization agent was *superego.* The superego, or internalized parental standards, includes both feelings of pride for right-doing, that is, the ego ideal, and feelings of guilt for wrong-doing, that is, conscience. The learning theory interpretation of values is proposed by those who assert that values develop much like any other habit, via positive or negative reinforcement and generalization. A third theory of value development is the perceptual interpretation. According to this view, the activity of the agent is an important element in the acquisition of values. Values, like perceptual schemata, are assumed to develop as a function of reafferent stimulation (feedback) which results from self-initiated behavior.

Ethical or moral values concern right-doing and wrong-doing in interpersonal relations. The cognitive psychology of Piaget, and especially his classic work *The Moral Judgment of the Child* (1965), provides an excellent basis for understanding the development of moral judgment. Piaget contends that the morality of the adolescent is autonomous and is based more on a consideration of the intentions of an act rather than its consequences, whereas the morality of the young child is based on realism and the likelihood of punishment. Kohlberg articulated six stages of moral development which correspond to Piaget's stages of logical thought.

We saw in this chapter that many of the adolescent's values are developed in the school setting, with its emphasis on achievement and preparation for adulthood. Edgar Friedenberg is best known for his analysis of the effect of the high school on adolescent personality development. Other research (Coleman, 1961) has demonstrated that high school students apparently value athletics and popularity more than scholarship and that they perceive their parents as holding similar values, though the parents themselves profess to be more concerned with academic achievement. Possible bases for this discrepancy were discussed.

College students have gradually become more socially oriented (less privatistic) and more affirmative. It is our belief that these value trends have been related to changes in child-rearing practices and that despite the cooling down of the student rebellion of the 1960s there has been no major reversal of these trends.

It has been found that the political values of adolescents develop as they acquire the cognitive capacity to use formal reasoning and to formulate hypotheses based on potential solutions to political problems as well as the capacity to understand the facts of political reality.

SUGGESTED ADDITIONAL READING

Friedenberg, E. Z. *The vanishing adolescent.* New York: Dell, 1959.

McKinney, J. P. The development of values: A perceptual interpretation. *Journal of Personality and Social Psychology,* 1975, 5, 801–807.

Piaget, J. *The moral judgment of the child.* New York: Free Press, 1965.

CHAPTER 10

ADJUSTMENT PROBLEMS OF ADOLESCENCE

I'm nobody! Who are you?
Are you nobody, too?
Then there's a pair of us—don't tell!
They'd banish us, you know.

How dreary to be somebody!
How public, like a frog
To tell your name the livelong day
To an admiring bog!

E. Dickinson

At first sight a chapter on the clinical aspects of adolescence may seem out of place in a text on normal adolescent development. Let us begin therefore by examining some reasons for dealing here with deviant as well as normal behavior.

First of all, normal and abnormal behavior represent a continuum of behavior rather than two dichotomous and mutually exclusive categories. Consequently, it is often difficult if not impossible (and, at any rate, often useless) to decide whether a given behavior is indeed normal under all circumstances.

In a statistical sense, one can define normality as that which occurs frequently in a given population. In that sense what appears normal or appropriate for the adolescent may be aberrant in an adult, and vice versa. This raises the question of whose norms or criteria are being used in defining deviance. For example, boisterous behavior, though disconcerting to parents and teachers, is far more typical of adolescents than of middle-age persons.

Aside from the age-specific aspects of normality, it is important to remember that the circumstances surrounding behavior can also influence our perception of it as appropriate or inappropriate. Sudden crying over the death of one's parent, for example, is quite different from sudden crying in the absence of a relevant stimulus, although on a superficial basis the behavior may appear to be identical in the two instances. Not eating because one is obese and dieting is quite different from the refusal to eat of the emaciated child suffering from anorexia nervosa, a pathological and often life-threatening condition.

Another reason for examining psychopathology in this work is that such an examination can give us a handle on less pathological but still troublesome behavior. It is important to know something about the problems that confront even normal adolescents and about the great variety of their modes of responding. Even under the best of circumstances, some youngsters invariably choose inappropriate response patterns. The parent or teacher who is at least conversant with the clinical aspects of adolescence is in a better position to help such youngsters, if only by being with them in an understanding way when difficulties arise.

After first considering one theoretical position, we will examine in some detail a few areas of psychopathology which occur among adolescents.

A THEORETICAL POSITION

No one theory covers all the varieties of deviant behavior in adolescence. There are a number of theories of delinquency, depression, sexual acting out, and so on. None of these theories, taken by itself, can account for all such inappropriate behavior.

However, it is possible to establish a framework which can help to explain the main goals and developmental tasks of adolescence. In this way a variety of specific psychopathologies can be seen as failures to cope with those goals and tasks.

For this purpose we turn again to the theory of Erik Erikson. It will be recalled that Erikson's main postulate concerning adolescents is that they are coping with the need for personal sameness, that is, for a continuity with their previous experience, and with fantasies about the future. Erikson (1963) explains this phenomenon by reference to an "identity struggle."

The struggle between identity and identity diffusion can reach crisis proportions for adolescents. A number of simultaneously occurring events challenge their previously stable identity. Rapid physical development, disproportionate growth of the sexual organs, the onset of sexual functioning and newly awakened sexual urges, as well as the consequent reshuffling of interpersonal relations and the struggle for independence from their closest associates, namely, their families, all serve to stimulate new questions about themselves and their values. Basically, the question that gets asked is, "Who am I, anyway?" Values that went unquestioned during childhood now come under the closest scrutiny; goals previously unthought of now become real possibilities. Luckily, all this occurs in conjunction with the development of a new cognitive framework. That is, adolescents are simultaneously developing a formal logic, which, as we know, allows for a consideration of the as-if quality of many of these questions.

Adolescents can take on new roles and vary them day by day. They can choose one hairstyle today and another tomorrow. They can change steady girlfriends or boyfriends as often as their parents change clothes. Whereas in adults such inconsistency might be a sign of serious instability, in adolescents it is all a part of trying on a variety of social roles to see which fits best.

Erikson discusses this notion of behavior diversity in a search for fidelity to self in an excellent paper in his volume *The Challenge of Youth* (1965). What Erikson advocates for this age group is a psychosocial moratorium, a time period during which a variety of roles can be tested for their fit and a variety of behaviors can be indulged in without the close attention to consequences which would be demanded of adults. The college years provide a psychosocial moratorium in a professional or occupational life. Students can take a variety of different courses and thus test which of a number of different occupations they would like to make their lifework. This gives them time to examine their own view of their strengths and weaknesses as well as the view which others have of them and to bring these two points of view into balance. In the same way, they can bring their plans for the future into line with their current abilities and their past achievements.

What we have said so far assumes that the adolescent is achieving some sense of stability, of the sameness or continuity which is the hallmark of identity. But how do adolescents handle the threat of identity diffusion? A healthy adolescent does this by defining one's self in the context of a relatively stable social and physical environment. One sees one's own accomplishments as part of a larger social system. It is true that at times he may be overly concerned with the effects of his behavior on others, to the detriment of creative and independent performance. By and large, however, the normal adolescent can maintain a balance between concern for one's subjective experiences and wishes and preoccupation with the environmental reaction to one's behavior.

For disturbed adolescents the task is not so simple. Erikson (1959) has observed a number of unhealthy styles of responding to the problem of identity diffusion. One such style involves the development of a negative identity. To be a nobody, as in the playful verse by Emily Dickinson quoted at the beginning of this chapter, is not really to have no identity. The poet, for example, immediately finds another nobody—the reader—with whom to identify. Together the two can now revel in their nobodiness, looking down on all those who think they are somebody.

One of us recalls a high school classmate whose academic standing in the class was determined almost with certainty by his persistently obtaining the lowest score on a weekly Latin exam. To make matters worse, his seat in the class was similarly determined, as the instructor followed the questionable practice of seating students according to their scores, with poor scorers rating seats at the rear of the room. But that boy had a certain identity, however ignominious, within the class. To have been just about last would, in Erikson's terms, have been more difficult: "At any rate, many a late adolescent, if faced with continuing diffusion, would rather *be nobody or somebody bad, or indeed, dead—and this totally, and by free choice—than be not—quite—somebody*" (Erikson, 1959, p. 132).

Erikson goes on to underline the importance he attaches to the word *totally* in the above quotation. Basically, he means that adolescents very often take extreme positions in an attempt to clarify their own life space. We have seen this view expressed in the theory of Kurt Lewin (1939), who described adolescence in the sociological terms of a marginal man. One characteristic of marginal man is this tendency to take extreme positions or to act totally in an attempt to clarify an otherwise ambiguous area in his life space. Even though adolescents' views on a given subject may change rather frequently, the position they take at any one time tends to be taken with a good deal of passion. This is an example of the kind of totality to which Erikson and Lewin refer. In an attempt to provide at least a semblance of self-certainty, adolescents tend to become dogmatic and to adhere passionately to a point of view.

In the above quotation Erikson suggests that some adolescents cling tenaciously to the catastrophic view that if one is indeed a nobody, then one should behave accordingly and bring one's life to an end. We will deal later with both the fantasy and the actuality of suicide in adolescents. But the reader can already see that Erikson would explain such behavior in terms of negative identity. In his view, some adolescents will seek even a negative identity in the quest for self-clarification. This explains the sudden shift to delinquency in some adolescents who had shown no such tendencies a few years earlier; or the sudden shift to depression and isolation, even to the point of suicide, in other adolescents.

Negative identity is also manifested in some forms of snobbery. Erikson suggests that one can thus deny identity diffusion by identifying with that which one has not earned, be it social position, inherited wealth, foreign birth, and so on. A reverse sort of snobbery can serve the same function. This is seen in Dickinson's poem about being a nobody or in taking a disdainful pride in having come from the wrong side of the tracks and in those who scoff at the material possessions of others.

One aspect of identity diffusion which deserves our attention is the inability to assess one's strengths and weaknesses and to plan accordingly. To a greater or lesser degree a disturbance of time perspective is common to most adolescents, but it reaches pathological proportions in some. Erikson sees the temptation to give up and not to know where to begin or when to quit as serious depression. Carried to their pathological extreme, such sentiments can become suicidal. Associated with such diffusion is the inability to delegate specific time for specific tasks or to concentrate on the task at hand.

SOME SPECIFIC PROBLEMS OF ADOLESCENTS

Having ended the previous section on the rather dismal note of the prevalence of depression in adolescence, perhaps it would be appropriate to begin with that topic as the first of the problems we will deal with.

Depression

Depression is obviously not limited to adolescents alone. However, it takes on a form characteristic of adolescents, as do many of the psychopathologies with which we will be dealing. That is to say, though there are no special pathologies of adolescents as such, there are pathologies which are common and pathologies which are uncommon among adolescents.

During the last few years it has become clear that depression is more preva-

FIGURE 10–1   Adolescence is a time of examining one's strengths and weaknesses as well as the view others have of one and of bringing these two points of view into balance.

Photograph courtesy of J. P. McKinney

lent among adolescents than was once believed. Recent findings also question the assumption that depression rarely occurs in children. In one study of 62 seventh and eighth graders in a parochial school, researchers (Albert & Beck, 1975) concluded that one third of the sample suffered from moderate to severe depression, and that there was an increase in depressive symptomatology from the seventh to the eighth grade. The researchers' definition of depression was based on respondents' answers to the Beck Depression Inventory. The cut-off score defining depression was based on earlier studies in which the test's validity was based on psychiatric evaluation of adults. The procedure is open to question, of course, and the authors are cautious in interpreting their results. Still, it is striking that 35 percent of the sample subscribed to the item "I have thoughts of harming myself but would not carry them out."

Probably the best overall recent reference on depression is a book by Becker (1974), which deals in great detail with the theoretical and clinical aspects of this syndrome. Unfortunately, the picture given is itself depressing. The research has often run into insurmountable problems. Therapeutic techniques have rarely worked across the board, and the prognosis is often not particularly favorable. These findings are no less true for depression in adolescents than for depression in other age groups.

One reason why psychiatrists and psychologists have overlooked the depression of childhood and to some extent of adolescence is that the manifestations of depression vary as a function of age. Thus, one who considers depression to be learned helplessness would naturally not expect to find much depression in children since by virtue of their age they are expected to be helpless. However, the colicky infant may be just as depressed in its own way as the forlorn young lover or the geriatric patient who rocks back and forth crying.

Toolan (1969), a psychoanalyst, suggests that whereas the young baby may manifest its depression in colic, head banging, and crying, the somewhat older child may manifest depression via regression, apathy, or total withdrawal. Toolan further suggests that at a still later age some acting out may be a manifestation of serious depression. A number of other authors have also held that delinquency, and especially sexual and aggressive acting out, are rooted in depression. Indeed, anybody who has taught is familiar with the youngster who, when he or she is not violating the rules of the classroom or demonstrating independence in some obnoxious way, is sad beyond consoling. Again, most teachers have encountered the adolescent who at the end of the term berates the course, the school, the book, the professor, and then begins to berate himself.

Some have argued that depression is really aggression turned inward, and that feelings of guilt are the basis of depression. Others have suggested that depression amounts to a reaction to loss or anticipated loss. These two theoretical positions are clearly reconcilable. Persons who feel guilty for real or imagined transgressions could easily fear the loss of esteem from others or from themselves. The image of oneself as evil could then lead to behaviors tending to support that image, which in turn would lead to further guilt and further depression. Toolan (1962) has found that the firstborn child is more prone to suicide attempts as well as to depression in general. The loss of the parents, which is anticipated in separating from them in adolescence, may be more difficult for the firstborn. In a sense, the relationship of the firstborn to the parents is unique, since, for a time at least, it was unshared with siblings. Alfred Adler, one of Freud's earliest disciples, was among the first to acknowledge the importance of birth order in the development of personality (Adler, 1931; Hall & Lindzey, 1970). The firstborn, according to Adler, was most likely to feel insecure because of the early experience of having his/her privileged position vis-à-vis the parents interrupted by his/her younger siblings. Having been previously given a lot of attention, the firstborn may suddenly feel deprived and blame others for the loss. In this context, one is not surprised by Toolan's findings concerning the higher incidence of depression among firstborn. Toolan notes that the reaction of adolescents to depression is often hostility, especially toward the parents, whom they see as partly responsible. Guilt feelings tend to increase under these circumstances.

As mentioned earlier, the clinical manifestations of depression vary among age groups. Some common reactions of early adolescents which are known as depressive equivalents have been listed by Weiner (1970): boredom and restlessness, fatigue and bodily preoccupation, difficulty in concentration, acting out, and flight to or from people. Weiner holds that each of these equivalents, particularly in an exaggerated state, may be symptomatic of an underlying depression.

The symptomatology of depression during late adolescence is similar to that of depression in adulthood: insomnia, suicidal preoccupation, gloominess, restlessness, inability to concentrate, and so on. Table 10–1, taken from Rosen et al. (1965), indicates the incidence of neurotic-depressive reactions in a group of adolescents who were terminated from outpatient clinics. Of approximately 42,000 boys and girls between the ages of 10 and 19 who received care in outpatient clinics in the United States, percentages given represent those who were diagnosed as neurotically depressive. Note the increase in the incidence of depression with increasing age. Note also the significantly higher proportion of girls with depressive reactions. These are fairly typical findings.

TABLE 10–1
Percent distribution of diagnosed adolescents terminated from outpatient psychiatric clinics with neurotic depressive reaction

	Age					
	10–11	*12–13*	*14–15*	*16–17*	*18–19*	*Total*
Boys	1.3	1.5	1.9	2.1	3.3	1.8
Girls	1.6	1.9	3.3	5.2	9.6	4.3
Total	1.4	1.7	2.5	3.4	6.5	2.7

Source: Adapted from B. M. Rosen et al., "Adolescent patients served in outpatient psychiatric clinics," *American Journal of Public Health,* 1965, 55, p. 1567. By permission of the author and the American Public Health Assn. (Based on approximately 42,000 diagnosed adolescents.) Adapted by Weiner, I. B. *Psychological disturbances in adolescence.* New York: John Wiley & Sons, 1970.

Endocrine disorders are an important correlate of some cases of depression. In some instances, what appears to be genuine depression may simply be an appropriate affective response to illness. In other instances, however, it is clear that depression is induced by endocrinopathies (Sachar, 1975).

One biologically based theory of depression involves monoamines, which serve as transmitters of neural impulses at synapses, or the junctures between neurons. This theory suggests that there is a deficiency of such amines at important neural sites (Baldessarini, 1975). The somatic complaints which often accompany depression are cited in support of the monoamine hypothesis.

A very different interpretation of depression has resulted from research with animals (Seligman and Maier, 1967) which demonstrated that passive acceptance (helplessness) can be a learned phenomenon. Seligman showed that rats could be taught to remain passive in the face of escapable shock by first being exposed to a series of severe, inescapable shocks. Seligman called this learned helplessness and saw in this phenomenon a paradigm for the acquisition of the passive acceptance of the depressed human. In an important series of studies on learned helplessness in children and adolescents, Dweck (1975) and her associates (Dweck & Gilliard, 1975; Dweck & Bush, 1976) found that after they have once failed on a task, children do not attempt to succeed even though they are both motivated and capable. The authors (Dweck & Repucci, 1973) discovered that such children are less likely than most to take personal responsibility for success and failure. When they do acknowledge their role, they are more likely to attribute the success or failure to ability than to effort. Fortunately (Dweck, 1975), it is possible to teach such children that failures can be attributed to their own lack of effort in such a way that they persist and overcome their learned helplessness.

Suicide

The suicide rate has risen alarmingly in the past several years. In the age group between 15 and 24, suicide is one of the major causes of death. In 1957 the rate per 100,000 was 4.0; in 1974 it was 10.9, and in 1975 it climbed to 12.2 (Hart & Keidel, 1979). While some of the increase may be due to a liberalization of reporting practices, it is evident that many suicides still go unreported, and these numbers may represent a conservative estimate. Sometimes physicians are reluctant to report suicides of their young patients. Additionally, one may question the potential for self-destructive motivation in some accident victims; drug overdose, automobile and motorcycle accidents, and accidents with firearms are all prominent in adolescent age groups. For example, automobile accidents, like suicides, are also a major cause of death among teenagers, and many therapists believe that not infrequently the young victim has chosen to be involved or at least has not been as careful as one who valued his life maximally. While more than three times as many boys commit suicide as do girls, the reverse sex ratio is true for suicide attempts (Weiner, 1970). A large number of causes or precipitants have been associated with suicide: distress at home with a concomitant sense of total helplessness, drugs, depression, anxiety, impending mental breakdown, known psychotic condition, discipline at home or school, and failure in a love affair. Perhaps most basic to most of these precipitants is a sense of guilt, worthlessness, helplessness, and rejection. Regardless of the cause or the number of previous suicide attempts, all such gestures are important attempts to communicate and should be taken seriously. Friends, family, and health providers need to assume that the person is serious and offer whatever support is necessary. It is sometimes difficult to offer this genuine concern without reinforcing the suicidal gesture. Such persons obviously need support independently of such emergent cries for help. Secondly, professional assistance should be gotten without delay.

Sally (not her real name) was referred to a psychologist by her pediatrician after she had overdosed on a large bottle of sleeping pills which she had stolen from the local drug store. Sally was 13 years old and in the eighth grade. Her parents had struggled with marital difficulties for the past few years and had fought bitterly in front of Sally and her brother, who was four years younger than Sally. Outsiders considered the younger brother to be brighter and more engaging than Sally, and he was granted favors and doted on by relatives whenever they came to visit. Despite her parents' attempts to equalize this condition and to support Sally, her self-regard continued to decline. She considered herself overweight, yet persisted in snacking copiously between meals. She felt that her breasts were overdeveloped and pendulous, and on the morning of the day she attempted suicide she had conferred with her physician about that. The doctor had rebuffed her and, instead of responding to his patient, had conferred with her parents, hardly speaking to the child. Luckily, Sally's attempt to kill herself was discovered, and she was rushed to the hospital where she was treated and released after a few days and only after she had begun psychotherapy.

However, aside from the ever-present danger of suicide in seriously depressed adolescents, there are other less extreme sequelae of depression. These include inability to concentrate, inability to profit from otherwise beneficial social interaction, and poor school performance. Occasionally, academic failure in otherwise intelligent youngsters can progress to a point at which their future may be unalterably affected.

Schizophrenia

While depression can occur among normal adolescents or as a neurotic or even psychotic condition, schizophrenia is basically a psychosis. That does not mean that the diagnosis is always an easy one to make, since symptoms are often mixed and overlap with other disorders. Schizophrenia, once called dementia praecox (early mental deterioration), has characteristically been found to begin during adolescence and early adulthood. We know that this psychotic condition can occur at any age, but because of the many changes which occur during adolescence, this is still the period of greatest susceptibility.

Schizophrenia refers to a set of disorders characterized by a serious disintegration of ego functioning. Perceptual distortions, such as auditory, tactile, and visual hallucinations, delusions, presumed thought transfer from one individual to another without the benefit of verbal communication, and such verbal irregularities as word salads and neologisms may all characterize the schizophrenic individual. These traits describe an individual who has lost some contact with the reality of his or her environment or whose perception of the environment is at variance with the perception of his or her fellow human beings. In a major study of the symptomatology of adolescent schizophrenia, Spivack, Haimes, and Spotts (1967) identified five major factors which most clearly distinguished the schizophrenic group from other diagnostic categories as well as from normals:

1. Bizarre cognition: thought transfer, hallucinations, disconnected or incoherent speech.
2. Bizarre action: unusual postures, facial expressions, putting inedible objects in one's mouth.
3. Schizoid withdrawal: an inability or unwillingness to enter into meaningful communication or social contact; rather the patient lives in his or her own world, staring into space.

4. Emotional detachment: the classic "split" between affect and cognition (the word *schizophrenia* comes from Greek words meaning split mind).
5. Poor emotional control: emotional overreaction to events; anger especially, tends to be uncontrolled.

While hospitalization is sometimes necessary in the treatment of an acute schizophrenic episode, often such youngsters can be helped with intensive psychotherapy as outpatients. The two primary ingredients in their treatment are the establishment of a trusting relationship between therapist and client and the provision of help to correct distorted perceptions of reality (Weiner, 1970).

Alex (not his real name) was referred to one of us when he was 17 and a senior in high school. He believed that he was cursed with an evil side which would someday do great harm to someone. At times he imagined hearing voices telling him what to do. For example, he felt he could not walk to the bus stop without first walking halfway back and then beginning again. Such compulsive behavior is not uncommon among young schizophrenics. He was obsessed with thoughts about Hitler and thought his own evil side was Hitler-like. Since Alex's contact with reality, while fragile, never got so loose that he was a danger to himself or others, he could be helped by intensive psychotherapy as an outpatient.

Anorexia nervosa

A somewhat rare, yet none the less very important, psychological disturbance that occurs almost exclusively during adolescence and early adulthood is the eating disorder known as anorexia nervosa. Patients with this disorder refuse to eat, and quite naturally, their weight drops precipitously and in some cases fatally. Surprisingly, patients suffering from anorexia nervosa do not believe they are getting thin. Quite the reverse, they often complain about being too heavy and insist on losing more and more weight. To this end many anorexics not only refuse food, but also exercise vigorously and maintain a distorted body image which allows them to believe they must continue to lose weight so as not to get fat.

Anorexia nervosa affects young women far more frequently than it does men. An important feature of the disorder in women is amenorrhea, or sudden cessation of the menses. Most of those affected come from upper and upper-middle class families, where they were well cared for and where they have learned to be compliant, and obedient. Some have argued, however, (Bruch, 1966) that very often these children have grown up in atmospheres that have prevented the free expression of their feelings and their autonomy. One characteristic frequently commented upon is the issue of parental control and the adolescent's ambivalence about emancipation, which may be complicated with guilt, hostility, and a sense of obligation. Other authors have commented on the sexual components in the etiology of anorexia nervosa, emphasizing the struggle some adolescents have accepting their sexual identity (Guiora, 1967). For women anorexia nervosa may represent a denial of femininity as well as a rejection of the responsibilities of adulthood.

Just as there are a variety of interpretations concerning the origins of anorexia nervosa, so is there a difference of opinion about the therapy of choice. Suggested treatment procedures include psychoanalytic psychotherapy (Margolis & Jernberg, 1960), desensitization (Hallsten, 1965), positive reinforcement (Leitenberg, Agras & Thomson, 1968), as well as various drug therapies (Crisp, 1965; Ushakov, 1971).

The student interested in further reading on anorexia nervosa will find an excellent account in Bruch's (1973) *Eating Disorders,* and in a more popularized account, *The Golden Cage* (Bruch, 1978).

Agnes (a pseudonym) was admitted to the hospital after she had lost 40 pounds in two months, going from 121 to 81. Concurrent with her weight loss was the disruption of her menstrual cycle. During the time prior to admission, Agnes' diet consisted of a half glass of milk per day.

Agnes' mother was a 50-year-old divorced woman who weighed 280 pounds. Mrs. G. had been in several weight reduction programs without success. Recently she had been dieting, and her weight loss appeared to be correlated with her daughter's symptoms. The relationship between Agnes and her mother appeared to be symbiotic. Mrs. G. assumed full responsibility for the emotional support of her family. She made the task easier by denying or inhibiting the expression of feeling in her family. By setting herself up as a censor of emotion in this way, Mrs. G. assumed a powerful controlling position.

Because of her sudden and potentially life-threatening weight loss, Agnes required hospitalization. Treatment consisted of a combined behavior modification program aimed at getting Agnes to begin eating and family psychotherapy designed to help her family resolve the fusion of roles and the control issues which had plagued them.

Delinquency

During recent years it has become clear that one of the main social problems in the United States is the crime committed by young offenders. Juvenile delinquency refers to the illegal acts committed by minors. As such, it is a legal or sociological variable rather than a psychological variable. In a sense it is a dependent rather than an independent variable. That is, it refers to behavior resulting from other psychological or sociological conditions.

It is difficult to estimate the incidence of delinquency. Horrocks (1969) estimates that 3 percent of youth between the ages of 10 and 17 are seen in the courts each year because of illegal activities. He estimates further that somewhere between 10 percent and 15 percent of adolescents become involved in crime or delinquency, much of which goes unreported. Data on the incidence of delinquency, however, is often misleading because of the varying reporting practices from community to community. In addition, one has to take into consideration the number of adolescents who commit delinquencies without ever getting caught and the number who, having been caught, are merely reprimanded. In some instances only the parents are notified, while in others the police are informed but the cases are not brought to court. Finally, there are the delinquents about whom the statistics are clear—who do, indeed, appear in the courts.

In addition to the varying reporting practices of different communities, there are differences in reporting as a function of sex, social class, type of delinquency, and so on. Social class differences and racial differences in delinquency may reflect such differences in reporting and sentencing. It is much easier, for example, to report a delinquency to parents in an intact family where the parents are at home a good deal of the time than to parents who are rarely, if ever, at home or who are so busy trying to provide for the family financially that they cannot take care of its psychological needs.

Various theories of the etiology of delinquency have been advanced. Some have argued that delinquency is largely the result of family variables. The following factors have been cited as causal in a number of studies: discord between parents, the prolonged absence of a parent, inconsistency of discipline within the home, parental rejection, lack of masculine identification in boys, and low socioeconomic status of the family.

Others have argued that the gang is mainly responsible for delinquent behavior. They hold that individuals learn maladaptive or illegal behavior by imitating the behavior of their peers. Still others (for example, Stanfield, 1966) have tested the hypothesis of an interaction among family and gang variables. Stanfield found that delinquency was significantly related to the father's occupational status, to the father's discipline, and to the involvement of the individual with peer activity. Each of these variables predicted to a significant extent the likelihood that a boy might become delinquent. Fathers of low occupational status were more likely to have delinquent boys than were fathers of high occupational status; fathers whose discipline was lax or erratic were far more likely to have delinquent boys than were fathers whose discipline was consistent; and boys who were frequently involved in gang activities were more likely to become delinquent than were boys who only occasionally participated in gang activities.

More interesting, howver, Stanfield found an interaction among these variables. He noted, for example, that the factor of discipline was much more important in low-status families than in high-status families. That is, in high-status families the sort of discipline exercised by the father had less effect on the likelihood of the child's becoming delinquent than it did in low-status families. One explanation of that finding may be that in communities of low socioeconomic status alternative behavior patterns exist outside the home. A child who has an unpleasant family situation can therefore turn to peers who are involved in delinquency and develop such a lifestyle himself. If a child comes from a community of high socioeconomic status, however, even though the family experiences may be unpleasant, the child is less likely to violate the law (see Table 10–2).

Another example of such an interaction is presented in Table 10–3. Stanfield found that in families of high socioeconomic status the amount of peer activity engaged in by youngsters tends to affect their entry into delinquency. This is not as true in families of low socioeconomic status. In communities of high socioeconomic status it takes far more contact with the street culture for the boy to enter delinquency than would be true in communities of low socioeconomic status.

TABLE 10–2
Delinquency, socioeconomic status, and discipline: Percentage with convictions for delinquency

	Father's occupation	
	Low-status	High-status
Father's discipline		
Erratic or lax	39% (n = 77)	21% (n = 43)
Consistent	17% (n = 46)	13% (n = 40)
	Diff. = 22%	Diff. = 20%
	$\chi^2 = 5.31$	$\chi^2 = 0.54$
	P < .05	p > .60

Source: R. E. Stanfield, "The interaction of family variables and gang variables in the etiology of delinquency." *Social Problems*, 1966, *13*, 411–17. By permission of the author and the Society for the Study of Social Problems.

TABLE 10–3
Delinquency, socioeconomic status, and peer involvement: Percentage with convictions for delinquency

	Father's occupation	
	Low-status	High-status
Peer activity		
Frequent	31% (n = 83)	28% (n = 47)
Occasional	27% (n = 67)	8% (n = 51)
	Diff. = 4%	Diff. = 20%
	$\chi^2 = 0.17$	$\chi^2 = 5.39$
	p > .60	p < .05

Source: R. E. Stanfield, "The interaction of family variables and gang variables in the etiology of delinquency," *Social Problems*, 1966, *13*, 411–17. By permission of the author and the Society for the Study of Social Problems.

Still another example of an interaction between two sociological variables is presented in Table 10–4. These data demonstrate the interaction between the father's discipline and the amount of peer activity. If fathers are relatively consistent in their discipline, the amount of peer activity has little effect on the likelihood that their sons will become delinquent. On the other hand, if fathers are erratic or lax in their discipline, their sons are more likely to be influenced by the amount of peer activity that they engage in. The street culture has a greater influence on boys who come from families that are inconsistent in their discipline.

These results show that no single factor explains the etiology of delinquency. Indeed, it is probable that no set of factors taken in aggregate accounts for delinquency. Rather, a number of psychological and sociological variables interact with one another in the production of delinquent behavior.

It is also important to remember that delinquency is not a unitary dimension. A variety of possible adolescents' behaviors will get them into trouble with the law. Thus, Weiner (1970) distinguishes between adaptive and maladaptive de-

TABLE 10–4
Delinquency, discipline, and peer involvement: Percentage with convictions for delinquency

	Father's discipline	
	Erratic or lax	*Consistent*
Peer activity		
Frequent	43% (n = 60)	16% (n = 44)
Occasional	23% (n = 57)	14% (n = 42)
	Diff. = 20%	Diff. = 2%
	$\chi^2 = 4.66$	$\chi^2 = 0.01$
	p < .05	p > .80

Source: R. E. Stanfield, "The interaction of family variables and gang variables in the etiology of delinquency," *Social Problems*, 1966, *13*, 411–17. By permission of the author and the Society for the Study of Social Problems.

linquency. Following Jenkins (1955, 1957), he considers adaptive delinquency to be goal-directed behavior which involves learning from experience. On the other hand, maladaptive delinquency refers to more rigid behaviors which result from frustration and are not easily changed by punishment. The main distinction here seems to be that adaptive delinquency can be explained in terms of some relatively rational motivation. The adaptive delinquent may be motivated by a need for status in the peer group, by a strong desire for material objects which are easily stolen, and so on. On the other hand, unsocialized aggressive delinquency, which would be classified as maladaptive, is characterized by brutality, defiance, and irrationality.

Other distinctions can be made. For example, some have distinguished between social and solitary delinquency. According to Weiner, this closely parallels the adaptive-maladaptive distinction. Finally, some psychiatrists have distinguished between delinquency as a neurotic symptom and delinquency as a characterological orientation. Neurotic delinquency might be associated with such things as compulsions, depression, and a need to be recognized. Erikson would interpret the seeming need to be punished in some adolescents as a reflection of a negative identity. As someone once said, "It's better to be wanted for murder than not to be wanted at all." On the characterological side, the classification of a sociopathic, or antisocial, personality, though of questionable diagnostic significance, still occurs in the literature. Often the term *sociopathic* refers to an inability to separate the desire to do something from impulsive acting out. It is difficult to differentiate this from obsessional thought and compulsive behavior. Weiner (1970) distinguishes characterological from symptomatic delinquency.

He argues that the two are best differentiated in terms of the individual's basic personality style, and that this can be inferred from psychological testing and interviews. The following are prominent features in the characterological, or psychopathic delinquent: lack of remorse and personal loyalty, impulsive action, shallow interpersonal relations, a low need for affection, low tolerance for anxiety and frustration, and inability to delay gratification. When a delinquent person cannot be characterized by these traits, Weiner suggests that the delinquency is more likely symptomatic, especially if other neurotic tendencies are prominent.

Child-rearing practices figure prominently among the various etiological interpretations of delinquency. Some have argued that parents sometimes subtly reinforce antisocial behavior. They may vent their own frustrations, for example, through vicarious satisfaction in seeing their youngsters act out. In other circumstances, delinquent adolescents may be used as scapegoats in already disrupted families. It may be easier to reinforce subtly the delinquent activity of the adolescent as a major concern in the family than to face the deep-seated conflict between the parents. Occasionally a youngster from a supposedly intact family will suddenly come into conflict with the law in such a way that he or she seems to want to get caught. Such youngsters are often referred for psychological counseling. In treating such youngsters, one of us has found that their behavior may suddenly improve when the whole family is brought into counseling, and they become aware that their parents are willing to seek help in communicating with each other and with their children. At times it has almost seemed that these youngsters had used their delinquency as a way of sending up a signal for help not only for themselves but for their families.

It is important that teachers and counselors learn to see delinquency not as the inexplicable behavior of incorrigible youngsters but rather as learned and motivated behavior. If we accept the premise that maladaptive behaviors are learned in the same way that appropriate behaviors are learned, then it becomes possible to understand how children have acquired maladaptive responses and it becomes easier to teach them new and more appropriate responses. Moreover, if the motivational system which maintains delinquent behavior is understood, it becomes far easier to provide help to those who might otherwise think of themselves as simply unworthy persons. Such a self-defeating attitude can only perpetuate delinquency which thus becomes a self-fulfilling prophecy.

Violence

Perhaps one of the most disconcerting aspects of the whole troublesome area of juvenile delinquency is the large number of adolescents who are involved in violent criminal acts. Violence here refers to willful physical injury of another person or to the damage or destruction of property. The extent of youthful involvement in crimes of violence can be seen in Table 10–5, which was compiled from the *Uniform Crime Reports* for 1979.

Why has violence become a way of life for many youth, and why is violence on the rise in the United States? The position taken here is that, for the most part, violence is learned. It is learned in the same way as nonviolent behavior is learned, namely, through reinforcement and modeling. The social learning of aggression in children has been studied and demonstrated by Bandura and Walters (1963) and Bandura, Ross, and Ross (1961).

When one asks why youth are heavily involved in violence, a number of issues become apparent. One is that youth attempt to establish their identity through their behavior rather than their possessions. Lacking the power to

TABLE 10–5
Total arrest trends, 1970–1979

Offense charged	Number of persons arrested								
	Total all ages			Under 18 years of age			18 years of age and over		
	1970	1979	Percent change	1970	1979	Percent change	1970	1979	Percent change
Total	5,184,125	5,513,617	+6.4	1,313,902	1,357,668	+3.3	3,870,223	4,155,949	+7.4
Murder and nonnegligent manslaughter	9,771	11,027	+12.9	1,100	1,039	−5.5	8,671	9,988	+15.2
Forcible rape	11,757	18,040	+53.4	2,473	2,849	+15.2	9,284	15,191	+63.6
Robbery	60,231	83,273	+38.3	19,272	25,571	+32.7	40,959	57,702	+40.9
Aggravated assault	94,127	148,433	+57.7	15,294	24,431	+59.7	78,833	124,002	+57.3
Burglary	222,982	285,656	+28.1	117,859	142,877	+21.2	105,123	142,779	+35.8
Larceny–theft	489,818	718,521	+46.7	247,587	295,760	+19.5	242,231	422,761	+74.5
Motor vehicle theft	100,613	88,376	−12.2	57,104	45,562	−20.2	43,509	42,814	−1.6
Arson	7,065	10,723	+51.8	4,273	5,697	+33.3	2,792	5,026	+80.0
Violent crime	175,886	260,773	+48.3	38,139	53,890	+41.3	137,747	206,883	+50.2
Property crime	820,478	1,103,276	+34.5	426,823	489,896	+14.8	393,655	613,380	+55.8
Crime Index total	996,364	1,364,049	+36.9	464,962	543,786	+17.0	531,402	820,263	+54.4

Note: data from 3,943 agencies; 1979 estimated population 114,952,000.
Source: U.S. Department of Justice. F.B.I. uniform crime reports: Crimes in the United States 1979. Washington, D.C., U.S. Government Printing Office, 1980.

change the social structure in which they live and lacking much of the legal leverage necessary to defend themselves against exploitation, they often rely on protest to express their frustrations. In the recent past such protests have frequently led to violence. In addition, there is often a conflict between the legal obligations of adolescents and the privileges that are accorded them. Before a recent Supreme Court ruling changed the age of majority from 21 to 18, many adolescents were subject to the same legal obligations and penalties as adults while being denied the privileges of adulthood, including adequate legal defense.

Moreover, some adolescents find it difficult to adapt to an adult culture which is undergoing rapid change. In our culture, the changes taking place in adolescents are complicated by rapid social changes. Values learned at one age become outmoded at another. As a result, one can observe widely differing lifestyles among youth from one short span of years to the next. The youth of the 1950s, for example, were primarily passive and privatistic (Keniston, 1960; Gillespie & Allport, 1955). The alienated youth of that decade were followed by the strikingly different activists of the 1960s (Keniston, 1968). Unfortunately, during the 1960s the peaceful student protests of social injustices, such as violations of civil rights, usurpations of political power by persons in high office, and illegal war, gave way to student violence.

In considering the roots of violence among the young, it is important to remember that all cultures have legitimated certain forms of violence and that the United States has been no exception to this rule. Some forms of violence have even been institutionalized. The most obvious example is war. Less obvious examples include certain contact sports, such as boxing, wrestling, and to some extent, football. Institutionally sanctioned violence also includes the punishment meted out to children for misbehavior. When such punishment is extreme, it would be considered child abuse and subject to legal penalties, but less extreme forms have been used by parents and school authorities with inpunity and have even been encouraged in some quarters. Although the spanking of children is a dwindling practice in the public schools, the practice has certainly not disappeared completely. In addition, many parents feel quite justified is using physical force to correct the behavior of their children. Although this may seem a far cry from the violence of youth, a growing number of social scientists believe that such early modeling is an important antecedent to later violence. This is especially true when the early models of physical force are persons whose power is envied by those for whom they care. Under such circumstances, children are known to identify with those in authority and to imitate their behavior. A young child often finds it difficult to discriminate between violence that is institutionalized and legitimate and violence that is not. The parent who strikes a child while telling him not to hit his brother is providing the child with a confusing double message.

Another example of the modeling of aggression is provided by the violence depicted in the media. A study by Eron et al. (1972) has demonstrated rather convincingly that watching a heavy dose of violence on television when one is in the early grades of elementary school is related to acts of violence committed in later adolescence. By means of a statistical technique known as cross-lag panel analysis, Eron et al. were able to demonstrate that there is a significant correlation between early violent television watching and later aggressive behavior but that the converse is not true. That is, early aggression *is not* related to later watching of violent television shows, but early exposure to violence on television *is* related to later aggressive behavior. As with all correlational approaches, however, there is always the possibility that an extraneous variable may be influencing the relationship. That is, it is possible that some unknown factor influences both the early viewing of violence on television and later aggressive behavior. Still, the fact that the correlation between early viewing of TV violence and later aggression is significantly higher than the correlation between early aggression and later viewing of TV violence strongly suggests the direction of the causal chain. Whether a decrease in exposure to TV violence would *alone* reduce later violence is still an empirical question which needs to be answered with experimental approaches. The laboratory work of Bandura and Walters (1963) suggests that such an effect does occur. Although this makes intuitive sense, it is important to have the kind of data provided by Eron in order to make the case conclusive.

Wolfgang (1970) also gives examples of the modeling of aggression via advertising which associates a product with violent behavior. One well-known example is automobile advertising. Wolfgang cites the following examples taken from such advertising:

> Glamour and thrill in the cars are meant to be associated with speed and power through such verbs as "runs away", "roars", "growls"; adjectives like "dynamic", "powerful", "exciting", "wild", "ferocious", "swinging"; nouns like "missile", "rocket", "tiger", "stinger". Phrases of advertising include "just pull the trigger", "start billing yourself as the human cannon ball", "want action?", "fire the second stage", "aim it at the road". Longer excerpts make clear the intended associations:
>
> (a) "For stab-and-steer men, there is a new 3-speed automatic you can lock in any gear. . . . make small noises in your throat. Atta boy, tiger."
>
> (b) "This year let yourself go for power."
>
> (c) "All new! All muscle! . . . with Advanced Thrust engineering . . . and an almost neurotic urge to get going. Drive it like you hate it—it's cheaper than psychiatry."
>
> (d) "Nobody said a nice car can't play mean now and then." (p. 16)

Such isolated examples may not appear to be relevant until one considers the incidence of traffic accidents among the young. Wolfgang cites data which indicate that "of all youth 13 to 25 years of age who died in a recent 10-year span, 42 percent died as a result of traffic accidents" (p. 16). The experimental proof of the association between such automobile advertising and traffic deaths still remains to be seen, however. One experiment would be to eliminate violent advertising of this sort in a given locality and to check the effects on the incidence of traffic accidents among the young. The causal link between such machismo and accidents, however, is probably more complex and undoubtedly involves a wide variety of antecedents.

Runaways

Some youth violently aggress against institutions which they find confining, restricting, punitive, or discriminatory, whereas other youth run away from such institutions. In an earlier chapter we discussed the antecedents and consequences of dropping out of school. An even more vital institution from which some drop out is the family. Our purpose here is to discuss briefly the reasons for running away and to examine what life is like for runaways in the United States. By runaways we are referring to persons under the age of 18 who leave home without permission and stay away overnight or longer. This is a social issue of some magnitude. In 1969, for example, over 500,000 adolescents under the age of 17 were reported as runaways. At that time the age of majority was still 21, and youngsters could technically be classified as runaways if they had left home without permission even up to that age. However, it has always been difficult to get statistics on runaways who are 18 or older since many such cases go unreported. The major concern, however, is with the younger child, and indeed, for several years the average age of runaways has been 15. The reasons that are given for running away include the following: broken homes, extreme poverty, cruelty and abuse, school failure, separation of the parents, desertion of the children, and alcoholism within the home.

In describing the runaway episode, some (for example, Ambrosino, 1971) have maintained that it occurs most often in the summer or in the month of December. However, a study of over 700 runaways (Shellow et al., 1967) failed to reveal any seasonal variations. There was, however, a significant tendency for youngsters, particularly girls, to run away on Fridays and Saturdays more often than on other days of the week. This, coupled with the hours at which girls were more likely to leave (between 6:00 P.M. and midnight), suggests that the dating situation was used as a screen for leaving home.

Shellow et al. found a number of significant differences between runaways and a normal control group. There was less stability in the families of the runaways. For example, the addresses of these families changed significantly more often over a five-year period. However, there was little difference in the education of the parents in the two groups or in their occupational standing. Although a large percentage of the runaways reported difficulties and conflict at home, their parents did not admit to conflict significantly more often than did the parents of the nonrunaways.

The school experiences of the runaways and the control subjects also differed significantly. The runaways tended to have significantly lower grade-point averages, to be absent more often, and to transfer from one school to another more frequently at the junior high school level. A rather interesting negative finding was that the runaways did not show a greater propensity for dropping out of school before the runaway episode. Shellow et al. speculate that dropping out and running away are two different means for coping with the stresses of the school situation. Although most runaways return within a week, some stay away indefinitely. Indeed, in some instances the parents refuse to let them return.

What becomes of runaways? Many turn to friends and relatives for a short time, for food and a place to stay. This, however, has certain built-in disadvantages since such friends and relatives may sympathize with the parents and report the youngster's presence to them. At any rate, such an arrangement is only temporary at best. By and large, runaways tend to find themselves in the sections of large cities which are most likely to provide them with shelter and food. Unfortunately, there is often a high price to pay. Runaways are often unable to cope with their financial difficulties and become all-too-easy prey for drug peddlers, pimps, and persons engaged in a variety of other illegal activities. The legal aspects of the runaways' situation are beyond the scope of this presentation, though it should be apparent to the reader that the psychological and sociological problem of running away is complicated by the fact that it is also illegal.

One might well ask how runaways can survive at all under these circumstances. One of the ways in which they survive is by joining communities of others in a like situation. By working together and sharing their resources, such runaways can provide themselves with the essential requirements for daily living. In addition, halfway houses, drop-in centers, huckleberry houses, and the like, whose purpose is to provide shelter for runaways, have sprung up recently in a number of cities. In many instances these have been legally sanctioned, at least as temporary residences, especially if the runaways allow their parents to be informed of their whereabouts. The runaways can then often get professional and semiprofessional help and can sometimes begin the task of reconciliation with their parents. There are also underground and not-so-underground communications systems, including a variety of telephone hot lines and emergency counseling centers. These are often staffed largely by the runaways themselves, but they often have professional advisers to whom they can turn. In any event, these communication systems provide lonely and destitute runaways with a listening ear and often with information about where they can get food, shelter, and further help.[1]

Drug use

It is well known that both adults and youth inappropriately ingest, smoke, sniff, and otherwise abuse a large number of chemical substances. However, it is difficult to arrive at accurate estimates of the incidence of such abuse. It is also often difficult to judge the effects of such abuse on the users and the best way of controlling such behavior. Some would even question whether the aim of controlling so-called drug abuse is a valid goal in itself.

One of the main difficulties in studying the drug taking of adolescents is the lack of clarity in the definitions used. The term *drug* itself is used vaguely and in a variety of ways. When one speaks about the drug problem, what is generally meant is the use of street drugs and not the therapeutic use of drugs prescribed

---

[1] A list of such hot lines as well as a list of services in large cities have been provided as appendices to Ambrosino's (1971) book *Runaways*. In large cities, more recent lists are undoubtedly available from Travelers Aid, Child and Family Services, and so on.

by a physician. Alcohol is also generally not considered to be part of the drug problem.

For our purposes, *drug* will be defined in the same way that it was defined by the National Commission on Marijuana and Drug Abuse: "any substance other than food which by its chemical nature affects the structure or function of the living organism." Though the term *drug* may have many social and scientific meanings to the layman, this definition clearly includes such things as tobacco, alcohol, and aspirin as well as street drugs and marijuana. Some of these chemical substances are therapeutic, and some are not; some are legal, and some are not. All of them however, have effective doses, toxic doses, and lethal doses. Our approach, then, will be to refrain from dichotomizing between the consumption of illegal drugs, or drugs which are considered socially harmful or bad, and the consumption of drugs which are supposedly good, safe, therapeutic, or at least not illegal.

The term *narcotic* is even more misused. Originally it was used to mean anything that could induce stupefaction and sleep (narcosis), which would include alcohol. Now it is generally used to mean any drug on the street which has been classified as illegal. We will try to stick with the more operational term *psychoactive substances,* which the National Commission on Marijuana and Drug Abuse has defined as "those which have the capacity to influence behavior by altering feeling, mood, perception or other mental state."

A list of the most commonly abused substances is given in Table 10–6. The reader who is interested in a more detailed description of the effects of these drugs and their addictive properties will find an excellent, unbiased account in the book, *Recreational Drugs,* by Lawrence Young and his coauthors (1977). Although there has been a recent rise in the abuse of these substances, particularly among middle and upper-class youth, it is well known that the problem is not something new. It existed, for example, in the military during the Civil War, when opium and morphine were used medicinally and were easily available over the counter. According to the National Commission on Marijuana and Drug Abuse, in the early years of this century pharmaceutical companies used heroin in cough suppressants, which were readily available in medical practice. Not until 1910 did the country become worried about heroin and the opiates and their capacity to induce dependency.

There is a difference, however, between this early sort of drug problem and the problem encountered head on in the 1960s. In the late 1800s and early 1900s, the habitual use of opium, morphine, or heroin began with what seemed to be an appropriate therapeutic dose. In contrast, the drug problem of the 1960s concerned street use by middle- and upper-class youngsters. In the recent rash of illegal drug use large numbers of youth were involved for the first time, and their use of drugs was in large part associated with a more general protest against the prevailing political, educational, and social standards. This defiance of institutional standards and adult values led to a variety of unorthodox lifestyles. There is far too little information, however, to infer antecedent-consequent relationships between the use of drugs and these lifestyles. What is important is that a variety of social conditions which youth viewed as intolera-

TABLE 10–6
A classification of the most common street drugs

Drugs	Addictive properties
1. *Opiates:* This is the group most people refer to as narcotics. Used medically as pain killers.	
Opium—white powder from the unripe seed of a poppy plant. Can be taken orally, or smoked through a pipe.	
Morphine—an opium extract, it is one of the most powerful medically used pain killers.	Strongly addictive.
Heroin—prepared from morphine, this drug is outlawed even from medical use. Can be sniffed, injected under the skin or into a vein. "Smack," "scag," "H," "junk."	Strongly addictive.
2. *Stimulants* ("uppers"): These drugs stimulate the nervous system, i.e., make their user more lively or "up."	Not physically addictive like the opiates, but the stimulants can create a psychological craving.
Amphetamines—taken as a tablet or capsule, or injected into the blood stream. These produce a decreased sense of fatigue, an increase in self-confidence, talkativeness, restlessness, and an increased sense of alertness. As dosage increases, amphetamines can produce irritability, distrust of people, hallucinations, and amphetamine psychosis, or loss of contact with reality. Examples: Dexedrine—"dex" or "dexies," Benzedrine—"bennies," Methedrine—"speed" or "crystal meth," Biphetamine—"footballs."	
Cocaine—a white powder derived from cocoa leaves, can be sniffed or liquefied and injected into a vein. Creates a fast and powerful "high."	Can produce a strong craving; not physically addictive.
3. *Psychedelics:* Mind altering substances, which can change a person's perception of his or her surroundings. Some ("hallucinogens") cause hallucinations.	
LSD—a very powerful psychedelic, LSD is often "dropped" (i.e., taken orally—for example, on a sugar cube), but can be injected. Can create a euphoria, a sense of beauty in common objects. However, reactions are extremely diverse and unpredictable. Can also produce fear, panic, and psychotic-like reactions. "Acid."	
DMT—a fast-acting psychedelic, not as powerful as LSD. An ingredient of many plants found in the tropics, DMT can also be produced synthetically, often mixed with marijuana and smoked, it can also be sniffed, eaten, or injected.	Addiction is unknown.
Psilocybin—a psychoactive ingredient of a number of mushrooms. Not as strong as LSD, reactions are also diverse, unpredictable, and often determined by set.	Nonaddictive.
Peyote—derived from a cactus. This drug can produce dramatic visual effects, probably the result of the ingredient mescaline.	Nonaddictive, although tolerance develops.

TABLE 10–6 (continued)

Drugs	Addictive properties
Mescaline—the hallucination ingredient of peyote, mescaline can be taken as a capsule, tablet, or liquid.	Nonaddictive, although tolerance develops rapidly.
Marijuana—leaves of the hemp plant. Smoked for its effect of mild euphoria. Can cause changes in perception, mood, feeling of well being and sometimes fear. "Pot," "Grass."	
Hashish—the most potent ingredient of marijunana	No evidence that it is addictive.
THC—again, a derivative of the hemp plant. THC is the purified extract of the resin. The psychoactive ingredient of marijuana and hashish.	Not addictive.
4. *Depressants* ("downers"):	
Alcohol—slows the functions of the brain responsible for thinking and coordination.	Highly addictive.
Barbiturates—sedatives, some of which are used medically as sleep inducers. Examples: Seconal—"red devils," Nembutal—"yellow jackets," Amytal—"blue heavens", blue devils," Luminal—"purple hearts," Tuinal—"rainbows", "double trouble."	Can cause physical dependence and addiction.
Tobacco—dried leaves of the nicotine plant, tobacco is smoked in cigarettes, cigars, pipes, can be sniffed or chewed, can cause lung cancer, emphysema, and a variety of related ills.	Highly addictive.
Tranquilizers—used medically to alleviate tension and anxiety. Do not induce sleep except in heavy doses. Examples: Miltown, Equanil, Librium, Valium.	Addiction can occur with prolonged and heavy use.

ble, given their general moral upbringing, were being perpetuated by the adult culture. A war of questionable legality in the Far East, the failure to implement civil rights legislation, corruption in politics, and what appeared to be an outdated and hypocritical sexual ethic were among the well-known targets of this general protest.

When marijuana use began to increase among white middle-class adolescents in the 1960s, it began to be misclassed as a narcotic, largely because it was illegal. At that time the drug policies in the United States began to lose face validity. The pervasive view among nonusers that drugs in general were dangerous led to panic, which in turn led to overgeneralization and, at times, to indefensible drug policies. Heavy penalties for the possession of marijuana, including fines and jail sentences, were later seen as nondeterrent and unnecessary. By the end of the 1960s the term *narcotic* was being replaced with the term *dangerous drugs,* and later the policies shifted to general drug abuse. There was a growing tendency to distinguish between soft drugs and hard drugs, which really meant to distinguish marijuana from all the others. Though this terminology conveniently distinguishes between marijuana and such hard drugs as cocaine and heroin, it does not say what other drugs should be classed as hard. The current tendency is to class drugs according to their habit-inducing qualities.

Some of the earlier inconsistencies in drug policies became relatively apparent when the surgeon general's office finally established that the use to tobacco could be harmful to health. Before that time, and even afterward, the public policies and discussion surrounding the elimination of nonmedical drug use did not address themselves to tobacco and alcohol, except to declare that these were not drugs. It is important to remember however, that there were vested interests with lobbies in the state and national legislatures in both the alcohol and tobacco industries. One stated reason for the concern about the use of street drugs was their risk to health. Then why not also tobacco? Why had the issue of risk to health never been raised with such panic in connection with alcohol abuse, which was known to be one of the country's major health problems? Also, one might question the sincerity of a professed concern for health in a country which had let its delivery of health care in other areas slip well below that of far poorer countries. There was no public outcry when the use of street drugs had been confined to the lower classes. The health issue was never raised as feverishly in connection with the food and medical care shortages of impoverished Americans. For such reasons, public policies based on concern about the risk of health carried little weight among users of street drugs.

The argument that psychoactive substances were harmful because they altered moods was also dismissed, again largely because no objections were raised to alcohol. In addition, there were medically approved mood-altering drugs. At least 15 percent of the adult population used psychoactive drugs for medicinal purposes.

In short, education aimed at explaining the risk involved does not seem to help reduce the use of street drugs. The consumption of tobacco is perhaps the most potent example. Even coercion cannot eradicate their use, certainly not among those who are already dependent upon such drugs. The Commission on Marijuana and Drug Abuse has argued that not until the patterns of drug-taking behavior are considered will the problem of drug abuse among youth be tackled adequately. Although it is important to have strong public policies on illegal drug use, what is needed first is greater coherence and greater flexibility in the laws which now exist.

In an article in the *Saturday Review,* Richard DeLone (1972) commented on the widespread belief that little is known about youth who are involved in drug abuse. His own research flies in the face of this belief: "There is considerable consistency to these findings—a consistency that cuts across all socioeconomic levels and that has led some researchers to believe that drug abuse can be accurately predicted" (p. 30). DeLone mentions five characteristics of drug abusers which studies reveal consistently:

1. A large number of young drug abusers come from broken families or from families in which a good deal of pessimism, helplessness, and frustration is

expressed by the parents. DeLone argues that there is little cohesion in the family life of the large majority of young drug abusers.

2. The frustration of young drug abusers and their cynicism about their families in many instances tends to be generalized to an alienation from the society of their peers.

3. DeLone cites the lack of consistent guidelines, self-direction, and self-confidence.

4. Studies have revealed that "drug abusers as a whole tend to form only superficial friendships (in which the ritual of drug use may provide the effect of gregariousness)" (p. 30).

5. Finally, DeLone cites the well-known phenomena that abusers of illegal substances are in academic difficulties and lack motivation.

Although this capsule description of the young drug abuser is by no means intended as a definitive statement of a syndrome, the consistency with which these observations appear in the research should provide direction for further research (Braucht et al., 1973).

Recent research evidence confirms the clinical hunch that therapists have had for a long time that there is a connection between drug use and depression. In a cautious and well-designed study of 80 10th and 11th graders, the researchers (Kaplan, et al., 1980) found a significant correlation between marijuana use and scores on a measure of depressive symptomatology. Earlier research (Paton et al., 1977) had found a similar correlation among users of illegal drugs other than marijuana. As yet we have very little basis for making cause-effect inferences, since most of the research done in this area has been of a correlational nature. However, there is a certain logic to the argument that the poor health habits of depressed adolescents are related to their low self-esteem and that drug abuse may, in effect, be a form of self-medication. As with other behavioral phenomena, drug use may not be a single psychological entity but the outcome of a number of different circumstances. The meaning of drug use may therefore vary along a number of psychological and social dimensions.

SUMMARY AND CONCLUSIONS

In this chapter we have used the theory of Erikson, especially his concept of identity versus identity diffusion, to provide an understanding of adolescent psychopathology. A number of changes occurring at puberty and afterward create a discontinuity with previous experience which is disruptive for adolescents. These include rapid physical growth, the beginning of sexual development, intense sexual feelings, and rearrangements of interpersonal alliances. Erikson suggests that adolescents begin to ask "Who am I?" because of the changes taking place in the present and their hopes for the future.

In the face of the threat of identity diffusion adolescents may vary their choices from week to week in a way which would seem to be a mark of serious instability if it occurred in an adult. Erikson argues, however, for a psychosocial moratorium during adolescence, a period in which to try on a variety of social roles before making more permanent choices of vocation, occupation, partner, life-style, and so on.

Adolescents who can define themselves against a relatively stable and enduring social background (that is, when their choices result in relatively consistent environmental changes), can achieve a mature identity. When they fail to achieve such an identity and identity diffusion occurs, the result is often some form of psychopathology.

We have dealt with some forms of adolescent deviant behavior. Our selection was dictated by our observations of the incidence of each problem and associated difficulties in otherwise normal adolescents.

We now know that depression can occur at any age but that it has different behavioral expressions in each age group. In adolescence, depression is often related to problems associated with the loosening of ties to parents and becoming independent. A frequent adolescent reaction to depression is hostility and delinquent acting out.

One behavior associated with depression which has increased alarmingly in the past few years is suicide and suicide attempts. Such attempts always need to be taken seriously and require professional help.

A psychotic disorder which can occur during adolescence is schizophrenia, characterized by serious disintegration of ego functioning. Again requiring professional help, some schizophrenics, but not all, require hospitalization.

Anorexia nervosa represents a rare, yet potentially life-threatening eating disorder, usually associated with adolescence. More common among the middle and upper social classes and more common among females, anorexia nervosa may be related to an unwillingness to assume an adult sexual role.

It has been found difficult to judge the incidence of delinquency because of the differential reporting for different groups (for example, by age, sex, socioeconomic class, and so on). However, most observers agree that juvenile delinquency has increased during the recent past. Family and gang variables, and more important, their interaction, are known to be associated with delinquent behavior.

A form of delinquency that is on the increase is juvenile violence. Violence in adolescence is a learned phenomenon. Although frustration with seemingly uncaring parents, or with an unresponsive political system, may be antecedent to juvenile violence, the acquisition of the behavior itself follows the same rules of learning as the acquisition of any other form of behavior.

Whereas some adolescents respond to the threat of identity diffusion by hostility and violence, others respond by retreating. Running away from home, like dropping out of school, is an adolescent problem of some magnitude.

Finally, we have dealt briefly with the issue of "drug abuse" among adolescents. Again, a main problem is the lack of clear definitions for many of the terms used to describe abused substances and the behavior associated with their abuse. Whereas the terms *narcotic* and *drug* have both been misused, the term *psychoactive substance* seems more operationally clear. Inconsistencies in U.S. drug policies have been cited. A profile of the consistent user has been given with the precaution that it not be considered a "syndrome" but rather the product of some consistent findings relevant to substance abuse.

SUGGESTED ADDITIONAL READING

Blos, P. *The young adolescent: Clinical studies.* New York: Free Press, 1970.

Braucht, G. N., et al. Deviant drug use in adolescence: A review of psychosocial correlates. *Psychological Bulletin,* 1973, *79,* 92–106.

Meeks, J. E. *The Fragile Alliance.* Baltimore: Williams & Wilkins, 1971.

GLOSSARY

Abstinence   The attitude toward sexual behavior which considers premarital intercourse wrong under any circumstances.

Accommodation   Alteration of behavior to meet the demands of the environmental situation.

Accommodators, transcenders, social activists, apartheids, black worlders   The five orientations cited by Lewis Jones as roles of black youth today.

ACTH   A hormone secreted by the pituitary gland which stimulates the adrenal cortex. This secretion is responsible for the onset of the growth spurt and is thus called the growth hormone.

Adaptive delinquency   Goal-directed lawbreaking (for example, lawbreaking to achieve status or to obtain material goods).

Adolescence   The period of human development extending roughly from the beginning of puberty to the attainment of maturity.

Androgen   The male sex hormone responsible for the development of masculine sex characteristics and functions.

Assimilation   The transformation of newly acquired material into already existing cognitive structures.

Authoritarianism   A value system characterized by rigidity, a lack of warmth, less use of rational control, and more use of coercion.

Autonomy   The ability to respond independently.

Axillary hair   Underarm hair.

Bar mitzvah   The Jewish religious ceremony of initiation into adult responsibility. Bar Mitzvah (or bat mitzvah, for girls) occurs when the initiate is 13 years old.

Clique   The mutual peer choices of a small cluster of people.

Co-figurative culture   Margaret Mead's term for a cultural style in which the children learn from their peers as well as in the home.

Cognition   The psychology of knowing or thinking.

Cognitive dissonance   The state occurring in an individual whose behaviors are not in agreement with his or her beliefs or attitudes.

Cohort   Age mates; a group of subjects who were born during the same period.

Coitus   Sexual intercourse.

Commitment   In Erikson's theory, a definite emotional assent or agreement to a particular decision; e.g., religious, occupational or political choice.

Conjunctive   In Sullivan's theory, a type of dynamism that leads to overcoming separateness.

Conscience   The punitive component of the superego in Freudian theory.

Control group   A group of subjects in an experimental design who do not receive the experimental treatment.

Correlation   The relationship of dependence between two variables such that change in one is accompanied by change in the other.

Crisis   In Erikson's theory, a period of time during which one is choosing among alternatives; e.g., occupational or religious affiliation choices.

Cross-lag panel analysis   A statistical technique which involves the calculation of correlations between the same measures taken at two different times.

Cross-sectional approach   A method in which subjects of different ages are studied simultaneously to ascertain age differences.

Cultural continuities   Uniformities in what is expected of persons as children and as adults. For example, children are conditioned to eat three meals a day and do so throughout adult life.

Cultural discontinuities   Changes in the expectations placed on persons as adults from what was expected of them as children. For example, children are expected to be submissive, whereas adults are expected to be dominant.

Cultural relativism   The view that psychological principles derived from research in one culture cannot be directly applied to other cultures.

Decentration   The ability to abstract from the objective characteristics of a situation and to deal with their mental representation.

Depression   A psychiatric condition marked by such symptoms as melancholy, restlessness, insomnia, crying, and fatigue.

Despair   Erikson's term for the loss or lack of ego integrity. A state in which life is not accepted and time is perceived as running short. Characteristics of this state are disgust, misanthropy, and contempt for others.

Deviant sample   A group of subjects drawn from a population which differs in one or more ways from the general population.

Disintegration   Sullivan's term for the state of personality upheaval and difficulty in functioning.

Disjunctive   In Sullivan's theory, a type of dynamism that leads to psychosocial disintegration and separateness.

Dispersal   The leaving of animals from their home of infancy when they reach maturity.

Double standard   The attitude which considers premarital sexual intercourse to be acceptabie for males but not for females.

Drug   Any substance other than food which affects the structure or function of an organism.

Dynamism   Sullivan's term for the relatively stable pattern of energy transformations which characterizes interpersonal relations.

Ego   Freud's term for the aspect of the personality which mediates between the id impulses and the demands of the external environment.

Ego ideal   A psychoanalytic term for the representation in the personality of what the ego strives to be.

Ego integrity   The culmination of Erikson's eight stages of development. This state is marked by acceptance of one's self, acceptance of others, and acceptance of the fact that one's life is one's own responsibility.

Egocentrism   The inability to differentiate between subject and object.

Estrogen   The female sex hormone responsible for the development of feminine sex characteristics and functions.

Ethology   The study of behavior across several species of animals.

Factor analysis   A statistical technique for reducing correlations among a large number of variables to a smaller number of meaningful factors.

Foreclosure   In Erikson's theory, an identity status characterized by an early commitment without the benefit of the consideration of alternatives (i.e., crisis).

Formal operational reasoning   The final cognitive level in Piaget's theory, generally not reached until adolescence. This stage of reasoning is characterized by an ability to deal with problem in a formal (not concrete) manner.

Generativity   The term by which Erikson characterizes the middle adulthood stage of development when this is marked by creativity, productivity, and a concern for the next generation.

Gonadotropic hormones   Hormones produced by the pituitary which stimulate activity of the gonads.

Gonads   The testes or ovaries.

Growth spurt   An acceleration in the growth rate, especially in height, that occurs shortly before or in the early years of adolescence.

Heterophilic love   A love relationship with a member of the opposite sex.

Homophilic love   See Isophilic love.

Human dilemma   For Rollo May, the problem of being both subject and object, of acting and being acted upon, at the same time.

Hybrid vigor hypothesis   A suggested explanation for the secular trend (q.v.).

Due to genetic factors the mean height of the offspring of two parents will be slightly closer to the height of the taller parent, and this is known as hybrid vigor.

Id A term in Freudian theory for the component of the personality which is the center of drives and impulses.

Identification Freud's term for the child's emotional tie with its parents. Also used in the sense of imitation or behavioral similarity.

Identity An individual's style and beliefs, especially as they relate to his or her meaning to other people.

Identity diffusion Erikson's term for an individual style which is not unified.

Identity formation The recognition by an individual of a certain unity of his or her personality over time.

Idiographic approach A research method in which one particular individual is studied.

Imaginary audience The adolescent's feeling that he or she is the center of others' attention.

Independent variable The factor in an experimental design whose effects on the dependent variable are to be studied.

Intimacy The antithesis of isolation (Erikson). The psychosocial stage of late adolescence following identity versus identity diffusion. An emotional commitment involving a mutual sharing based on trust.

Isolate An individual not chosen by the other individuals depicted in a sociogram.

Isolation The lack of intimacy (q.v.). The absence of a resolution of the psychosocial task of late adolescence (Erikson).

Isophilic love A love relationship with a member of the same sex as oneself.

Laissez-faire The practice of noninterference.

Latency period The period from about 5 to 12 years of age when aggressive and sexual impulses are kept in check.

Leader The member of a group who carries out administrative and executive functions.

Libido General psychic energy in Freud's psychosexual theory.

Locus of control The individual's view of self as being either primarily influenced by or primarily influencing the environment.

Longitudinal approach A research method in which changes in the same person are studied over a considerable period of time.

Maladaptive delinquency A rigid antisocial behavior pattern which is not easily changed by punishment (for example, brutality, defiance).

Marginal man A person who is not a fully participating member of a group, especially one who stands on the boundary between two groups, uncertain of his or her group membership.

Menarche The first occurrence of menstruation.

Modeling Acting is such a way as to facilitate another's imitation of the behavior.

Moratorium In Erikson's theory, an identity status characterized by an ongoing crisis without a firm commitment, as yet.

Narcotic Originally used to mean a sleep-inducing drug; now used to mean any illegal drug.

Negative identity A socially undesirable definition of the self.

Nomothetic approach Research procedures which are designed to study several individuals and to discover general laws.

Normative approach A research method which attempts to set up statistical norms.

Onanism of necessity Compulsive masturbation.

Operant conditioning The use of reinforcement to elicit a behavior within the control of the organism.

Permissiveness with affection The attitude which accepts premarital intercourse if love or strong affection is present.

Permissiveness without affection The attitude which accepts premarital intercourse whether or not affection is present.

Personalism Taking an egocentric rather than a sociocentric view.

Pituitary gland An endocrine gland whose secretions control the other endocrine glands and influence growth, metabolism, and maturation. Also called hypophysis.

Post-figurative Margaret Mead's term for a cultural style in which the children learn from their parents.

Pre-figurative Margaret Mead's term for a cultural style in which the parents learn from their children.

Preoperational stage In Piagetian theory, the second stage of cognitive development, from approximately two to seven years of age, during which the child has developed language but cannot yet perform concrete operations.

Prescriptive values Values which reflect a "thou shalt" orientation.

Primal horde A hypothesized prehistoric "family" group, which consisted of one dominant male, his females, and a number of subordinate younger males.

Proscriptive values Values which reflect a "thou shalt not" orientation.

Psychoactive drug A substance which has the capacity to influence a person's behavior by altering his or her mental state.

Psychosocial moratorium A period during which an adolescent may experiment with a variety of roles in order to help form his or her identity.

Puberty rite A ceremony initiating a young person into the adult life of a community.

Reafferent stimulation Changes contingent on one's own behavior; feedback.

Recapitulation The doctrine that in his or her personal development the individual passes through a series of stages that represent stages in the evolutionary development of the species.

Reinforcement   Any action by the experimenter that will elicit a desired behavior from the subject.

Rites of passage   Ceremonies held in some societies in which an individual participates in order to be officially considered an adult.

Schema   The term in Piagetian theory for the most basic element in the psychology of thinking. A pattern or basis for the interpretation or representation of environmental stimulation.

Schemata   Patterns or bases for the interpretation or representation of environmental stimulation. The plural form of schema.

Second period of negativism   A period in adolescence, similar to one that occurs in early childhood, during which an individual attempts to assert his or her independence.

Secular trend   The direction of change taking place over successive generations. Exemplified in the tendency of children to reach full adult stature at an earlier age than was true of children 50 or 100 years ago.

Sensori motor stage   In Piagetian theory, the first stage of cognitive development, from birth to approximately two years of age, when the child is acquiring skills and directly adapting to the environment.

Sociocenter   The member of a group who reduces tensions initiated by its leadership.

Socioeconomic status   The position of an individual in a population, as determined by such factors as level of income, level of education, type of occupation, and so on.

Sociogram   A pictorial representation of associations within a group.

Stage of concrete operations   In Piagetian theory, the third stage of cognitive development, from approximately 7 to 12 years of age, when conservation problems can be solved and reasoning is limited to the content of an argument.

Stage of formal operations   In Piagetian theory, the fourth and final stage of cognitive development. Occurs during adolescence when the individual learns to formulate hypotheses and engage in deductive reasoning, causal thinking, and scientific explanation.

Stagnation   Erikson's term for the failure of generativity to develop during middle adulthood. Characterized by boredom and interpersonal impoverishment.

Stimulus generalization   The tendency of the individual to behave similarly in similar situations.

Sturm und Drang (storm and stress)   Emotional turmoil in adolescence. Once believed to be a necessary accompaniment of growth, it is now recognized as a result of certain cultural influences.

Superego   In Freudian theory, the component of the personality which keeps gratification of the id impulses within the bounds acceptable to society. Develops as the result of identification with the parents and acts as an internal rewarder and punisher.

Telenomic trends   Values perceived as characteristic of happiness or unhappiness.

Validity   The degree to which a test actually measures what it is supposed to measure.

Vicarious   Realized through imagined or sympathetic participation in the experience of another.

Vicarious reinforcement   The notion that an individual can be reinforced indirectly by observing another person receive reinforcement for a given behavior.

Youth   This term has several definitions. It is used by Keniston to refer to a postadolescent period of mainly college youth that lasts until approximately age 25.

REFERENCES

Adelson, J. (ed.). *Handbook of adolescent psychology.* New York: John Wiley & Sons, 1980.

Adelson, J., & O'Neil, R. P. Growth of political ideas in adolescence: The sense of community. *Journal of Personality and Social Psychology,* 1966, *4,* 295–306.

Adler, A. *What life should mean to you.* Boston: Little, Brown, 1931.

Akiwenzie, I. Personal communication, 1980.

Albert, N., & Beck, A. T. Incidence of depression in early adolescence: A preliminary study. *Journal of Youth and Adolescence,* 1975, *4,* 301–307.

Allport, G. W. The use of personal documents in psychological science. Social Science Research Council, Bulletin 49, 1942.

Ambrosino, L. *Runaways.* Boston: Beacon Press, 1971.

American Psychological Association. Ethical standards for research with human subjects. *APA Monitor,* 1972, *3* (5, supplement, 19 pages).

American Psychological Association. Revised ethical principles adopted. *APA Monitor,* 1973, *4* (1, 2).

Anastasi, A. Heredity, environment, and the question, "How?" *Psychological Review,* 1958, *65,* 197–208.

Anastasi, A. *Psychological testing.* 3d ed. New York: Macmillan, 1968.

Anthony, E. J. Children at risk from divorce: A review. In E. J. Anthony and C. Koupernik (Eds.), *The child in his family: Children at psychiatric risk* (Vol. 3). New York: John Wiley & Sons, 1974, pp. 461–477.

Anthony, J. The reactions of adults to adolescents and their behavior. In G. Caplan & S. Lebovici (Eds.), *Adolescence: Psychosocial perspectives.* New York: Basic Books, 1969.

Aries, P. [*Centuries of childhood: A social history of family life*] (Robert Baldick, Trans.). New York: Vintage Books, 1962.

Aristotle, *Rhetorica.* In R. McKeon (Ed.). [*The basic works of Aristotle.*] (W. R. Roberts, Trans.). New York: Random House, 1941.

Asch, S. E. Effects of group pressure on the modification and distortion of judgments. In E. E. Maccoby, T. M. Newcomb, & E. L. Hartley (Eds.), *Readings in social psychology.* New York: Holt, Rhinehart & Winston, 1958.

Baldessarini, R. J. Biogenic amine hypothesis in affective disorders. In F. F. Flack and S. C. Draghi (Eds.), *The nature and treatment of depression.* New York: John Wiley & Sons, 1975.

Baldwin, J. *Go tell it on the mountain.* New York: Signet Books, 1953.

Bandura, A. *Adolescent aggression.* New York: Ronald Press, 1959.

Bandura, A., The stormy decade: Fact or fiction? *Psychology in the Schools,* 1964, *1,* 224–231.

Bandura, A.; Ross, D.; & Ross, S. A. Transmission of aggression through imitation of aggressive models. *Journal of Abnormal and Social Psychology,* 1961, *63,* 575–582.

Bandura, A., & Walters, R. *Social learning and personality development.* New York: Holt, Rinehart & Winston, 1963.

Baumrind, D. Child care practices anteceding three patterns of preschool behavior. *Genetic Psychology Monographs,* 1967, *75,* 43–88.

Becker, J. *Depression: Theory and research.* New York: John Wiley & Sons, 1974.

Bell, R. R. *Premarital sex in a changing society.* Englewood Cliffs, N.J.: Prentice-Hall, 1966.

Benedict, R. Continuities and discontinuities in cultural conditioning. *Psychiatry,* 1938, *1,* 161–167.

Berenda, R. W. *The influence of the group on the judgments of children.* New York: Kings Crown Press, 1950.

Berkowitz, B., & Newman, M. *How to be your own best friend.* New York: Random House, 1971.

Bettelheim, B. *Symbolic wounds.* Glencoe, Ill.: Free Press, 1954.

Bloch, D. Sex education practices of mothers. *Journal of Sex Education and Therapy.* 1972, *7,* 7–12.

Boring, E. G. *A history of experimental psychology.* 2d ed. New York: Appleton-Century-Crofts, 1950.

Braucht, G. N., Brakarsh, D., Follingstad, D., & Berry, K. L. Deviant drug use in adolescence: A review of psychosocial correlates. *Psychological Bulletin,* 1973, *79,* 92–106.

Braungart, R. G. Youth and social movements. In S. Dragastin and G. Elder, Jr. (Eds.), *Adolescence in the life cycle.* New York: John Wiley & Sons, 1975.

Brill, A. A., (Ed.). *The basic writings of Sigmund Freud.* New York: Random House, 1938.

Brittain, C. V. Adolescent choices and parent-peer cross-pressures. *American Sociological Review,* 1963, *23,* 385–391.

Broderick, C. B. Sexual behavior among preadolescents. *Journal of Social Issues,* 1966, *22,* 6–21.

Broman, B. G., Dahlberg, G., & Lichtenstein, A. Height and weight during growth. *Acta Paediatrica,* 1942, *30,* 1–66.

Bronfenbrenner, U. *Two worlds of childhood: U.S. and U.S.S.R.* New York: Russell Sage Foundation, 1970.

Brown, J. K. Adolescent initiation rites among preliterate peoples. In R. E. Grinder (Ed.), *Studies in adolescence.* New York: Macmillan, 1963.

Brown, J. K. Female initiation rites: A review of the current literature. In D. Rogers (Ed.), *Issues in adolescent psychology.* New York: Appleton-Century-Crofts, 1969.

Bruch, H. Anorexia nervosa and its differential diagnosis. *Journal of Nervous and Mental Disease,* 1966, *141,* 555–556.

Bruch, H. *Eating disorders.* New York: Basic Books, 1973.

Bruch, H. *The golden cage.* Cambridge, Mass.: Harvard University Press, 1978.

Bruner, J. S., & Goodman, C. C. Value and need as organizing factors in perception. *Journal of Abnormal and Social Psychology,* 1947, *42,* 33–44.

Buber, M. *I and thou.* 2d ed. New York: Charles Scribner's Sons, 1958.

Burns, R. B. Age and mental ability: Re-testing with thirty-three years' interval. *British Journal of Educational Psychology,* 1966, *36,* 116.

Cattell, R. B. Fluid and crystallized intelligence. In I. J. Jenkins & D. G. Paterson (Eds.), *Studies in individual differences.* New York: Appleton-Century-Crofts, 1961.

Cervantes, L. F. *The dropout: Causes and cures.* Ann Arbor: University of Michigan Press, 1965.

Chilman, C. S. *Adolescent sexuality in a changing American society: Social psychological perspectives.* DHEW Publication No. (NIH) 79–1426, 1978.

Clarke, A. E., & Ruble, D. N. Young adolescents' beliefs concerning menstruation. *Child Development,* 1978, *49,* 231–234.

Cloutier, R., & Goldschmid, M. L. Individual differences in the development of formal reasoning. *Child Development,* 1976, *47,* 1097–1102.

Cobliner, W. G. Pregnancy in the single adolescent girl: The role of cognitive functions. *Journal of Youth and Adolescence,* 1974, *3,* 17–29.

Cohen, Y. A. *Social structure and personality.* New York: Holt, Rinehart & Winston, 1961.

Cohen, Y. A. *The transition from childhood to adolescence.* Chicago: Aldine Publishing, 1964.

Cole, L., & Hall, I. N. *Psychology of adolescence.* 7th ed. New York: Holt, Rinehart & Winston, 1970.

Coleman, J. *Social climates in high schools.* Washington, D.C.: U.S. Government Printing Office, 1961.

Coles, R. *Erik H. Erikson: The growth of his work.* Boston: Little, Brown, 1970.

Coles, R., & Brenner, J. American youth in a social struggle: The Appalachian volunteers. *American Journal of Orthopsychiatry,* 1968, *38,* 31–46.

Collins, J. K. Adolescent dating intimacy: Norms and peer expectations. *Journal of Youth and Adolescence,* 1974, *3,* 317–328.

Committee on Adolescence, Group for the Advancement of Psychiatry. *Normal adolescence.* New York: Charles Scribner's Sons, 1968.

Conger, J. J. *Adolescence and youth: Psychological development in a changing world.* New York: Harper & Row, 1973.

Costanzo, P. R., & Shaw, M. E. Conformity as a function of age level. *Child Development,* 1966, *37,* 967–975.

Crandall, V. C. *Expecting sex differences and sex differences in expectancies: A developmental analysis.* Paper presented at 86th Annual Convention of the APA, Toronto, August 1978.

Crisp, A. H. Clinical and therapeutic aspects of anorexia nervosa. A study of 30 cases. *Journal of Psychosomatic Research,* 1965, *9,* 67–78.

Cronbach, L. J. *Essentials of psychological testing.* 3d ed. New York: Harper & Row, 1960.

Curtis, R. L. Adolescent orientations toward parents and peers: Variations by sex, age, and socioeconomic status. *Adolescence,* 1975, *10,* 483–494.

Danner, F. W., & Day, M. C. Eliciting formal operations. *Child Development,* 1977, *48,* 1600–1606.

Davitz, J. R. Social perception and sociometric choice in children. *Journal of Abnormal and Social Psychology,* 1955, *50,* 173–176.

DeLone, R. H. The ups and downs of drug abuse education. *Saturday Review,* 1972, *55,* 46, 27–32.

Despert, J. L. *Children of divorce.* Garden City: Doubleday, 1953.

DeVries, R. The two intelligences of bright, average, and retarded children. Paper presented at the biennial meeting of the Society for Research in Child Development, Philadelphia, March 29, 1973.

DeVries, R. Relationships among Piagetian, I.Q., and achievement assessments. *Child Development,* 1974, *45,* 746–756.

Dickinson, E. *The complete poems of Emily Dickinson.* Boston: Little, Brown, 1924.

Douvan, E., & Adelson, J. *The adolescent experience.* New York: John Wiley & Sons, 1966.

Dreyer, P. H. Sex, sex roles, and marriage among youth in the 1970s. In R. J. Havighurst and P. H. Dreyer (Eds.). *Youth: The seventy-fourth yearbook of the National Society for the Study of Education.* Chicago: University of Chicago Press, 1975.

Dunphy, D. C. The social structure of urban adolescent peer groups. *Sociometry,* 1963, *26,* 230–246.

Dweck, C. S. The role of expectations and attributions in the alleviation of learned helplessness. *Journal of Personality and Social Psychology,* 1975, *31,* 674–685.

Dweck, C. S., & Gilliard, D. Expectancy statements as determinants of reactions to failure: Sex differences in persistance and expectancy change. *Journal of Personality and Social Psychology,* 1975, *32,* 1077–1084.

Dweck, C. S., & Repucci, N. D. Learned helplessness and reinforcement responsibility in children. *Journal of Personality and Social Psychology,* 1973, *25,* 109–116.

Dweck, C. S., & Bush, E. S. Sex differences in learned helplessness: I. Differential debilitation with peer and adult evaluators. *Developmental Psychology,* 1976, *12,* 147–156.

Dye, N. W., & Very, P. S. Developmental changes in adolescent mental structure. *Genetic Psychology Monographs,* 1968, *78,* 55–88.

Elder, G. H., Jr. Parental power legitimation and its effect on the adolescent. *Sociometry,* 1963, *26,* 50–65.

Elkind, D. Conceptual orientation shifts in children and adolescents. *Child Development,* 1966, *37,* 493–498.

Elkind, D. Egocentrism in adolescence. *Child Development,* 1967, *38,* 1025–1034.

Elkind, D. *Child sense and child development research.* Paper presented at APA Convention, New York, September 1979.

Ellis, A. The sex revolution, *Sexology,* 1966, *32,* 660–664.

Emmerich, H. J. The influence of parents and peers on choices made by adolescents. *Journal of Youth and Adolescence,* 1978, *7,* 175–180.

Erikson, E. H. *Childhood and society.* New York: W. W. Norton, 1950.

Erikson, E. H. *Young man Luther: A study in psychoanalysis and history.* New York: W. W. Norton, 1958.

Erikson, E. H. Identity and the life cycle. *Psychological Issues.* New York: International Universities Press, 1959, *1* (whole no. 1).

Erikson, E. H. *Childhood and Society.* 2d ed. New York: W. W. Norton, 1963.

Erikson, E. H. *Insight and responsibility.* New York: W. W. Norton, 1964. (a)

Erikson, E. H. A memorandum on identity and Negro youth. *Journal of Social Issues,* 1964, *20,* 29–42. (b)

Erikson, E. H. *The Challenge of Youth.* New York: Doubleday, 1965.

Erikson, E. H. *Identity: Youth and crisis.* New York: W. W. Norton, 1968.

Erikson, E. H. *Gandhi's truth: On the origins of militant nonviolence.* New York: W. W. Norton, 1969.

Eron, L. D., Huesmann, L. R., Lefkowitz, M. M., & Walder, L. O. Does television violence cause aggression? *American Psychologist,* 1972, *27,* 253–263.

Faust, M. S. Developmental maturity as a determinant in prestige of adolescent girls. *Child Development,* 1960, *31,* 173–184.

Feltz, D. Athletics in the status system of female adolescents. *Review of Sport and Leisure,* 1978, *3,* 98–108.

Finney, J. C. Some maternal influences on children's personality and character. *Genetic Psychology Monographs,* 1961, *63,* 199–278.

Flavell, J. H., & Wohlwill, J. F. Formal and functional aspects of cognitive development. In D. Elkind & J. H. Flavell (Eds.). *Studies in cognitive development: Essays in honor of Jean Piaget.* New York: Oxford University Press, 1969.

Floyd, H. H., & South, D. R. Dilemma of youth: The choice of parents or peers as a frame of reference for behavior. *Journal of Marriage and the Family,* 1972, *34,* 627–634.

Ford, C. S., & Beach, F. A. *Patterns of sexual behavior.* New York: Harper & Row, 1951.

Fox, G. L. *The family's role in adolescent sexual behavior.* 1979. Available from: Publications Coordinator, IEL, 1001 Connecticut Avenue, no 732, Washington, D. C. 20036.

Frazier, A., & Lisonbee, L. K. Adolescent concerns with physique. *School Review,* 1960, *58,* 397–405.

Freedman, M. B. The sexual behavior of American college women: An empirical study and an historical survey. *Merrill-Palmer Quarterly,* 1965, *11,* 33–48.

Freud, A. [*The ego and the mechanisms of defense.*] (C. Baines, Trans.). New York: International Universities Press, 1948.

Freud, A. Psychoanalytic study of the child. *Adolescence,* 1958, *13,* 255–278. (a)

Freud, A. Adolescence. In R. S. Eissler, et al., (Eds.) *Psychoanalytic study of the child* (Vol. 13). New York: International Universities Press, 1958. (b)

Freud, A. *The writings of Anna Freud: The ego and the mechanisms of defense.* Rev. ed. New York: International Universities Press, 1966.

Freud, S. Three contributions to the sexual theory. *Nervous and Mental Disorder Monograph Series,* 1925, No. 7.

Freud, S. [*A general introduction to psychoanalysis.*] (J. Riviere, Trans.). New York: Permabooks, 1953.

Freud, S. [*The ego and the id*] (J. Riviere, Trans.; J. Strachey, Ed.). New York: W. W. Norton, 1960.

Friedenberg, E. Z. *The vanishing adolescent.* New York: Dell, 1959.

Friedenberg, E. Z. *Coming of Age in America.* New York: Random House, 1965. (a)

Friedenberg, E. Z. *The dignity of youth and other atavisms.* Boston: Beacon Press, 1965. (b)

Frieze, I. H. Women's expectations for and causal attributions of success and failure. In M. Mednick, S. Tangre, & L. Hoffman (Eds.), *Women and Achievement.* Washington, D.C.: Hemisphere Publishing, 1975.

Galton, F. *Hereditary genius: An inquiry into its laws and consequences.* New York: Appleton-Century-Crofts, 1870.

Gardner, E. F., & Thompson, G. G. *The Syracuse scales of social relations.* New York: Harcourt Brace Jovanovich, 1958.

Gardner, E. F., & Thompson, G. G. Investigation and measurement of the social values governing interpersonal relations among adolescent youth and their teachers. Cooperative Research Project No. 259A (8418) SU and 2598 (8418) OSU, Cooperative Research Program of the Office of Education, United States Department of Health, Education, and Welfare, 1963.

Garrett, H. The equalitarian dogmatism. *Perspectives in Biology and Medicine,* 1961–62 *4,* 480–484.

Garrison, K. C. *Psychology of adolescence.* (6th ed.). Englewood Cliffs, N.J.: Prentice-Hall, 1965.

Gates, G. S. An experimental study of the growth of social perception. *Journal of Educational Psychology,* 1923, *14,* 449–462.

Gesell, A.; Ilg, F. L.; & Ames, L. B. *Youth: The years from ten to sixteen.* New York: Harper & Row, 1956.

Getzels, J. W., & Jackson, P. W. The highly intelligent and highly creative adolescent: A summary of some research findings. In C. W. Taylor & F. Barron (Eds.), *Scientific creativity: Its recognition and development.* New York: John Wiley & Sons, 1963.

Gillespie, J., & Allport, G. *Youth's outlook on the future.* New York: Random House, 1955.

Ginott, H. *Between parent and teenager.* New York: Macmillan, 1969.

Glueck, S., & Glueck, E. *Unraveling juvenile delinquency.* New York: Commonwealth Fund, 1950.

Goethals, G. W., & Klos, D. *Experiencing youth: First-person accounts.* Boston: Little, Brown, 1970.

Golburgh, S. (Ed.). *The experience of adolescence.* Cambridge, Mass.: Schenkman, 1965.

Goodman, P. *Growing up absurd.* New York: Vintage Books, 1956.

Goudsblom, J. *Dutch society.* New York: Random House, 1967.

Greulich, W. W. Physical changes in adolescence. In N. E. Henry (Ed.). *Adolescence:*

The forty-third yearbook of the National Society for the Study of Education. Chicago: University of Chicago Press, 1944.

Grinder, R. E., & Spector, J. C. Sex differences in adolescents' perceptions of parental resource control. *Journal of Genetic Psychology,* 1965, *106,* 337–344.

Grinnell, G. B. *The Cheyenne Indians: Their history and ways of life.* New Haven: Yale University Press, 1923.

Group for the Advancement of Psychiatry, Committee on Adolescence. *Normal adolescence.* New York: Charles Scribner's Sons, 1968.

Grummon, D. L., & Barclay, A. M. *Sexuality: A search for perspective.* New York: Van Nostrand Reinhold, 1971.

Guilford, J. P. Three faces of intellect. *American Psychologist,* 1959, *14,* 469–479.

Guilford, J. P. *The nature of human intelligence.* New York: McGraw-Hill, 1967.

Guiora, A. Z. Dysorexia: A psychopathological study of anorexia nervosa and bulimia. *American Journal of Psychiatry,* 1967, *124,* 3–8.

Gustin, J. C. The revolt of youth. *Psychoanalysis and the Psychoanalytic Review,* 1961, *98,* 78–90.

Hall, G. S. *Adolescence.* 2 vols. New York: Appleton-Century-Crofts, 1904.

Hall, C. S. *A primer of Freudian psychology.* New York: World, 1954.

Hall, C. S., & Lindzey, G. *Theories of personality.* New York: John Wiley & Sons, 1957.

Hall, C. S., & Lindzey, G. *Theories of personality.* (2d ed.). New York: John Wiley & Sons, 1970.

Hall, C. S., & Lindzey, G. *Theories of Personality* (3d ed.). New York: John Wiley & Sons, 1978.

Hallsten, E. A., Jr. Adolescent anorexia nervosa treated by disensitization. *Behavior Research and Therapy,* 1965, *3,* 87–91.

Harper, L. V. Ontogenetic and phylogenetic functions of the parent-offspring relationship in mammals. In D. S. Lehrman, R. A. Hinde, & E. Shaw (Eds.), *Advances in the study of behavior.* New York: Academic Press, 1970.

Harris, D., & Tseng, S. C. Children's attitudes toward peers and parents as revealed by sentence completions. *Child Development,* 1957, *28,* 401–411.

244

Harris, L. J. Sex-related variations in spatial skills. *Spatial representation and behavior across the life span: Theory and applications.* New York: Academic Press, to be published.

Harris, T. A. *I'm O.K.—You're O.K.: A practical guide to transactional analysis.* New York: Harper & Row, 1969.

Hart, N. A., & Keidel, G. C. The suicidal adolescent. *American Journal of Nursing.* 1979, 79, 80–84.

Hartup, W. Peer interaction and social organization. In P. H. Mussen (Ed.), *Carmichael's manual of child psychology.* (3d ed.). New York: John Wiley & Sons, 1970.

Hatcher, S. L. M. The adolescent experience of pregnancy and abortion: A developmental analysis. *Journal of Youth and Adolescence,* 1973, 2, 53–102.

Havighurst, R. J. *Developmental tasks and education.* New York: Longmans Green, 1953.

Havighurst, R. J. (Ed.). *Youth: The seventy-fourth yearbook of the National Society for the Study of Education.* Chicago: University of Chicago Press, 1975.

Head, H: *Studies in neurology.* (Vol. 2.). London: Hodder & Stoerghton and Oxford University Press, 1920.

Hebb, D. O. *The organization of behavior.* New York: John Wiley & Sons, 1949.

Held, R., & Bossom, J. Neonatal deprivation and adult rearrangement: Complementary techniques for analyzing plastic sensory-motor coordinations. *Journal of Comparative and Physiological Psychology,* 1961, 54, 33–37.

Hess, R. D., & Goldblatt, I. The status of adolescents in American society: A problem in social identity. *Child Development,* 1957, 28, 459–468.

Hilkevitch, R. R. Social interaction processes: A quantitative study. *Psychological Reports,* 1960, 7, 192–201.

Hill, W. F. Learning theory and the acquisition of values. *Psychological Review,* 1960, 67, 317–331.

Himes, J. H. Secular changes in body proportions and composition. *Monographs of The Society for Research in Child Development,* 1979, 44, 28–58.

Hoffman, M. L. Moral development in adolescence. In J. Adelson (Ed.), *Handbook of adolescent psychology.* New York: John Wiley & Sons, 1980.

Horrocks, J. E. *The psychology of adolescence.* (3d ed.). Boston: Houghton Mifflin, 1969.

Horrocks, J. E., & Buker, M. E. A study of friendship fluctuations of preadolescents. *Journal of Genetic Psychology,* 1951, 78, 131–144.

Horrocks, J. E., & Thompson, G. G. A study of friendship fluctuations of rural boys and girls. *Journal of Genetic Psychology,* 1946, 69, 189–198.

Huizinga, J. *Homo ludens.* Boston: Beacon Press, 1950.

Hunt, J. McV. *Intelligence and experience.* New York: Ronald Press, 1961.

Iacovetta, R. G. Adolescent-adult interaction and peer group involvement. *Adolescence,* 1975, 10, 327–336.

Inhelder, B., & Piaget, J. [*The growth of logical thinking.*] (A. Parsons & S. Milgram, Trans.). New York: Basic Books, 1958.

Ishwaran, K. *Family life in the Netherlands.* The Hague: Uitgeverij Van Keulen, 1959.

Izard, C. E. Personality similarity and friendship. *Journal of Abnormal and Social Psychology,* 1960, 61, 47–51.

Jenkins, R. L. Adaptive and maladaptive delinquency. *Nervous Child,* 1955, 11, 9–11.

Jenkins, R. L. Motivation and frustration in delinquency. *American Journal of Orthopsychiatry,* 1957, 27, 528–537.

Jensen, A. R. Reducing the heredity-environment uncertainty. In *Environment, heredity, and intelligence.* Reprint Series No. 2. Compiled from *Harvard Educational Review,* 1969, 209–243.

Jessor, S. L., & Jessor, R. Transition from virginity to nonvirginity among youth: A social-psychological study over time. *Developmental Psychology,* 1975, 11, 483–484.

Johnson, O. G., & Bommarito, J. W. *Tests and measurements in child development.* San Francisco: Jossey-Bass, 1971.

Johnston, B. *Ojibway heritage.* Toronto: McClelland & Stewart, 1976.

Jones, E. (Ed.). *Collected papers of Sigmund Freud.* New York: Basic Books, 1959.

Jones, H. E. Adolescence in our society. In *The family in a democratic society* ("Anniversary papers of the Community Service Society of New York"). New York: Columbia University Press, 1949. Reprinted in J. Seidman (Ed.), *The adolescent: A book of readings.*

(Rev. ed.) New York: Holt, Rinehart, & Winston, 1960.

Jones, H. E., & Conrad, H. S. The growth and decline of intelligence. *Genetic Psychology Monographs*, 1933, *13*, 223–298.

Jones, L. The new world view of Negro youth. In M. Sherif and C. W. Sherif (Eds.), *Problems of youth*. Chicago: Aldine Publishing, 1965.

Jones, M. C. The later careers of boys who were early- or late-maturing. *Child Development*, 1957, *28*, 113–128.

Jones, M. C., & Bayley, N. Physical maturing among boys as related to behavior. *Journal of Educational Psychology*, 1950, *41*, 129–148.

Jones, M. C., & Mussen, P. H. Self-conceptions, motivations, and interpersonal attitudes of early- and late-maturing girls. *Child Development*, 1958, *29*, 491–501.

Kacerguis, M. A., & Adams, G. R. Erikson state resolution: The relationship between identity and intimacy. *Journal of Youth and Adolescence*. 1980, *9*, 117–126.

Kallen, D. J. Les adolescents decident de leur sexuality. In *Collection Bioethique*, Les Cahiers du Centre de Bioethique, Institut de Recherches Cliniques de Montreal, *3*, & *Medicine et Adolescents*, Le Presses de L'Universite Lavel, Quebec, Automme, 1980.

Kanin, E. J. An examination of sexual aggression as a response to sexual frustration. *Journal of Marriage and the Family*, 1967, *29*, 428–433.

Kaplan, S. A., Nussbaum, M., Skomorowsky, P., Shenker, I. R., & Ramsey, P. Health habits and depression in adolescence. *Journal of Youth and Adolescence*, 1980, *9*, 299–304.

Katchadourian, H. *The biology of adolescence*. San Francisco: W. H. Freeman, 1977.

Kay, C. L., & McKinney, J. P. Friendship fluctuation in normal and retarded children. *Journal of Genetic Psychology*, 1967, *110*, 223–241.

Keating, D. P. Precocious cognitive development at the level of formal operations. *Child Development*, 1975, *46*, 276–280.

Keating, D. P., & Schaefer, R. A. Ability and sex differences in the acquisition of formal operations. *Developmental Psychology*, 1975. *11*, 531–532.

Keniston, K. *The uncommitted: Alienated youth in American society*. New York: Dell, 1960.

Keniston, K. *Young radicals: Notes on committed youth*. New York: Harcourt Brace Jovanovich, 1968.

Kiell, N. *The adolescent through fiction: A psychological approach*. New York: International Universities Press, 1959.

Kiell, N. *The universal experience of adolescence*. Boston: Beacon Press, 1964.

Kinsey, A. C.; Pomeroy, W. B.; & Martin, C. E. *Sexual behavior in the human male*. Philadelphia: Saunders, 1948.

Kinsey, A. C.; Pomeroy, W. B.; Martin, C. E.; & Gebhard, P. H. *Sexual behavior in the human female*. Philadelphia: Saunders, 1953.

Kluckhohn, C. Values and value orientations in the theory of action. In T. Parsons & E. A. Shils (Eds.), *Toward a general theory of action*. Cambridge, Mass.: Harvard University Press, 1951.

Koenig, F., & Falkenstein, H. Female undergraduate attitudes toward distribution of the birth control pill on the campus. *Journal of Youth and Adolescence*, 1972, *1*, 197–201.

Koff, E., Rierdan, J., & Jacobson, S. The personal and interpersonal significance of menarche. *Journal of the American Academy of Child Psychiatry*, 1981, *5*, 148–158.

Koff, E., Rierdan, J., & Silverstone, E. Changes in representation of body image as a function of menarcheal status. *Developmental Psychology*, 1978, *14*, 635–641.

Kohlberg, L. The development of modes of moral thinking and choice in the years 10 to 16. Unpublished doctoral dissertation, University of Chicago, 1958.

Kohlberg, L. The development of children's orientations toward a moral order: 1. Sequence in the development of moral thought. *Vita Humana*, 1963 (a), *6*, 11–33.

Kohlberg, L. Moral development and identification. In H. A. Stevenson (Ed.), *Child psychology: The sixty-second yearbook of the National Society for the Study of Education*. Chicago: University of Chicago Press, 1963 (b).

Kohlberg, L. Moral education in the schools: A developmental view. *School Review*, 1966, *74*, 1–29.

Köhler, W. *The place of value in a world of facts*. New York: Meridian Books, 1959.

Kohn, A. R., & Fiedler, F. E. Age and sex

differences in the perception of persons. *Sociometry*, 1961, *24*, 157–164.

Kohn, M. Social class and parental values. *American Journal of Sociology*, 1959, *64*, 337–351.

Kohn, M. Social class and parent-child relationships: An interpretation. *American Journal of Sociology*, 1963, *68*, 471–480.

Kuhlen, R. G., & Houlihan, N. B. Adolescent heterosexual interest in 1942 and 1963. *Child Development*, 1965, *36*, 1049–1052.

Kuhn, D.; Ho, V.; & Adams, C. Formal reasoning among pre-' and late adolescents. *Child Development*, 1979, *50*, 1128–1135.

Kurtines, W., & Grief, E. The development of moral thought: Review and evaluation of Kohlberg's approach. *Psychological Bulletin*, 1974, *81*, 453–470.

L'Abate, L. The status of adolescent psychology. *Developmental Psychology*, 1971, *4*, 201–205.

Lawson, A. E. Relationships among performances on three formal operations tasks. *The Journal of Psychology*, 1977, *96*, 235–241.

Lefcourt, H. M. Internal versus external control of reinforcement: A review. *Psychological Bulletin*, 1966, *65*, 206–220.

Leitenberg, H.; Agras, W. S.; & Thompson, L. E. A sequential analysis of the effect of selective positive reinforcement in modifying anorexia nervosa. *Behavior Research and Therapy*, 1968, *6*, 211–218.

Lerner, R. M., & Karabenick, S. A. Physical attractiveness, body attitudes, and self-concept in late adolescents. *Journal of Youth and Adolescence*, 1974, *3*, 307–316.

Lerner, R. M.; Karson, M.; Meisels, M.; & Knapp, J. R. Actual and perceived attitudes of late adolescents and their parents: The phenomenon of the generation gaps. *Journal of Genetic Psychology*, 1975, *126*, 195–207.

Lewin, K. Field theory and experiment in social psychology: Concepts and methods. *American Journal of Sociology*, 1939, *44*, 868–897.

Lewin, K., Lippitt, R., & White, R. K. Patterns of aggressive behavior in experimentally created "social climates." *Journal of Social Psychology*, 1939, *10*, 271–299.

Lifton, R. J. Youth and history: Individual change in postwar Japan. In E. H. Erikson (Ed.), *The challenge of youth*. Garden City, N.Y.: Anchor Books, 1965.

Light, C.; Zax, M.; & Gardiner, D. Relationship of age, sex, and intelligence level to extreme response style. *Journal of Personality and Social Psychology*, 1965, *2*, 907–909.

Linn, M. C. Influence of cognitive style and training on tasks requiring the separation of variable schema. *Child Development*, 1978, *49*, 874–877.

Liverant, S. Intelligence: A concept in need of re-examination. *Journal of Consulting Psychology*, 1960, *24*, 101–110.

Luckey, E. B., & Nass, G. D. A comparison of sexual attitudes and behavior in an international sample. *Journal of Marriage and the Family*, 1969, *31*, 364–379.

Maccoby, E. E., & Jacklin, C. N. *The psychology of sex differences*. Stanford: Stanford University Press, 1974.

MacFarlane, J. W. Studies in child guidance: 1. Methodology of data collection and organization. *Monographs of the Society for Research in Child Development*, 1938, *3*, Serial No. 6.

Magill, R. A.; Ash, M. J.; and Smoll, F. L. (Eds.). Children in sports: a contemporary anthology. Champaign, Ill.: Human Kinetics Publishers, 1978.

Malina, R. M. Secular changes in size and maturity: Causes and effects. *Monographs of the Society for Research in Child Development*, 1979, *44*, 59–102.

Manning, P. Rural "WASP" youth: Structure and sentiments. In *Youth: The seventy-fourth yearbook of the National Society for the Study of Education*. Chicago: University of Chicago Press, 1975, 306–339.

Marcel, G. *The mystery of being. Vol. 1: Reflection and mystery*. Chicago: Regnery/Gateway, 1960.

Marcia, J. E. Development and validation of ego identity status. *Journal of Personality and Social Psychology*, 1966, *3*, 551–558.

Marcia, J. E. Ego identity status: Relationship to change in self-esteem, "general maladjustment," and authoritarianism. *Journal of Personality*, 1967, *35*, 118–133.

Marcia, J. E. Identity six years after: A follow up study. *Journal of Youth and Adolescence*, 1976, *5*, 145–160.

Marcia, J. E., & Friedman, M. L. Ego identity status in college women. *Journal of Personality*, 1970, *38*, 249–263.

Margolis, P. M., & Jernberg, A. Anaclitic therapy

in a case of extreme anorexia. *British Journal of Medical Psychology,* 1960, *33,* 291–300.

Martens, R., and Seefeldt, V. *Guidelines for children's sports.* Washington, D.C.: National Association for Sports and Physical Education, 1979.

Martorano, S. C. A developmental analysis of performance on Piaget's formal operations task. *Developmental Psychology,* 1977, *13,* 666–672.

Maxwell, P. H.; Connor, R; & Walters, J. Family member perceptions of parent role performance. *Merrill-Palmer Quarterly,* 1961, *7,* 31–37.

May, R. *Psychology and the human dilemma.* Princeton, N.J.: D. Van Nostrand, 1967.

McCary, J. L. *Human sexuality.* Princeton, N.J.: D. Van Nostrand, 1967.

McCord, J., & Howard, A. Familial correlates of aggression in non-delinquent male children. *Journal of Abnormal and Social Psychology,* 1961, *62,* 79–93.

McDaniel, C. O., Jr. Dating roles and reasons for dating. *Journal of Marriage and the Family,* 1969, *31,* 91–107.

McKinney, J. P. A multidimensional study of the behavior of severely retarded boys. *Child Development,* 1962, *33,* 923–938.

McKinney, J. P. The development of choice stability in children and adolescents. *Journal of Genetic Psychology,* 1968, *113,* 79–83.

McKinney, J. P. Educational and vocational decision making of Dutch adolescents. *Pedagogische Studien,* 1970, *47,* 389–397.

McKinney, J. P. The development of values: Prescriptive or proscriptive? *Human Development,* 1971, *14,* 71–80.

McKinney, J. P. Review of P. H. Mussen (Ed.), *Carmichael's manual of child psychology* (3d ed.), Vol. 2. *American Journal of Educational Research,* 1972, *9,* 621–625.

McKinney, J. P. The structure of behavioral values of college students. *Journal of Psychology,* 1973, *85,* 235–244.

McKinney, J. P. The development of values: A perceptual interpretation. *Journal of Personality and Social Psychology,* 1975, *5,* 801–807.

McKinney, J. P.; Connolly, M.; & Clark, J. Development of a prescriptive morality: An historical observation. *Journal of Genetic Psychology,* 1973, *122,* 105–110.

McKinney, J. P., Hotch, D. F., & Truhon, S. The

organization of behavioral values during late adolescence: Change and stability across two eras. *Developmental Psychology,* 1977, *13,* 83–84.

Mead, M. *Sex and temperament in three primitive societies.* New York: Mentor Books, 1935.

Mead, M., *Coming of age in Samoa.* New York: Mentor Books, 1949.

Mead, M. *Growing up in New Guinea.* New York: Mentor Books, 1953.

Mead, M. *Culture and commitment: A study of the generation gap.* Garden City, N.Y.: Doubleday, 1970.

Meeks, J. E. *The fragile alliance.* Baltimore: Williams & Wilkins, 1971.

Meissner, W. W. Parental interaction of the adolescent boy. *Journal of Genetic Psychology,* 1965, *107,* 225–233.

Meredith, H. V. Change in the stature and body weight of North American boys during the last 80 years. In L. P. Lipsitt & C. C. Spiker (Eds.), *Advances in child development and behavior.* Vol. 1. New York: Academic Press, 1963.

Michener, J. A. What's good about today's youth. *U.S. News & World Report,* December 10, 1973, 48–55.

Milgram, N. A., & Milgram, R. M. Group versus individual administration in the measurement of creative thinking in gifted and non-gifted children. *Child Development,* 1976, *47,* 563–565.

Milgram, R. M.; Milgram, N. A.; Rosenbloom, G.; & Rabkin, L. Quantity and quality of creative thinking in children and adolescents. *Child Development,* 1978, *49,* 385–388.

Milne, A. A. Halfway down. In A. A. Milne, *When we were very young.* London: Methuen, 1924.

Montemayor, R. Children's performance in a game and their attraction to it as a function of sex-typed labels. *Child Development,* 1974, *45,* 152–156.

Moreno, J. L. *Sociometry, experimental method, and the science of society.* Beacon, N.Y.: Beacon House, 1951.

Morrow, W. R., & Wilson, R. C. Family relations of bright high-achieving and underachieving high school boys. *Child development,* 1961, *32,* 501–510.

Moshman, D. Consolidation and stage formation

in the emergence of formal operations. *Developmental Psychology*, 1977, *13*, 95–100.

Moshman, D. Development of formal hypothesis testing ability. *Developmental Psychology*, 1979, *15*, 104–112.

Mountain Visitor, The. Even cubs can't skip that difficult age. *Gatlinburg Press*, *7*, 18, 1971.

Muller, P. *The tasks of childhood*. New York: McGraw-Hill, 1969.

Mussen, P. H., & Jones, M. C. Self-conceptions, motivations, and interpersonal attitudes of late- and early-maturing boys. *Child Development*, 1957, *28*, 243–256.

Mussen, P. H., & Jones, M. C. The behavior-inferred motivations of late- and early-maturing boys. *Child Development*, 1958, *29*, 61–67.

Muuss, R. E. *Theories of adolescence*. (2d ed.) New York: Random House, 1968.

Muuss, R. E. Adolescent development and the secular trend. *Adolescence*, 1970 (a), *5*, 267–284.

Muuss, R. E. Puberty rites in primitve and modern societies. *Adolescence*, 1970 (b), *5*, 109–128.

Nesselroade, J. R., & Baltes, P. B. Adolescent personality development and historical change: 1970–1972. *Monographs of The society for Research in Child Development*, 1974, *39*, 1–79.

Newman, B. M., & Newman, P. R. Development through life: A psychosocial approach. Homewood, Ill.: Dorsey Press, 1975.

Niemark, E. D. Longitudinal development of formal operations thought. *Genetic Psychology Monographs*, 1975, *91*, 171–225.

Offer, D. Normal adolescents: Interview strategy and selected results. *Archives of General Psychiatry*, 1967, *17*, 285–290.

Offer, D. Attitudes toward sexuality in a group of 1500 middle-class teen-agers. *Journal of Youth and Adolescence*, 1972, *1*, 81–90.

Offer, D., & Offer, J. *From teenage to young manhood*. New York: Basic Books, 1975.

Offer, D.; Sabshin, M.; & Marcus, I. Clinical evaluation of normal adolescents. *American Journal of Psychiatry*, 1965, *121*, 864–872.

Ontario Ministry of Culture and Recreation. *You and your child in hockey*. Toronto, 1975. With permission.

Orshansky, M. Children of the poor. In D. Schreiber (Ed.), *Profile of the school dropout*. New York: Vintage Books, 1967.

Palmquist, W. J. Formal operational reasoning and the primacy effect in impression formation. *Developmental Psychology*, 1979, *15*, 185–189.

Pannor, R.; Massarik, F.; & Evans, B. *The unmarried father*. New York: Springer, 1971.

Pasquali, L., & Callegari, A. I. Working mothers and daughters' sex-role identification in Brazil. *Child Development*, 1978, *49*, 902–905.

Patel, A. A., & Gordon, J. E. Some personal and situational determinants of yielding to influence. *Journal of Abnormal and Social Psychology*, 1960, *61*, 411–418.

Paton, S., Kessler, R., & Kandel, D. Depressive mood and adolescent illicit drug use: a longitudinal analysis. *Journal of Genetic Psychology*, 1977, *131*, 267–289.

Peevers, B. H., & Secord, P. F. Developmental changes in attribution of descriptive concepts to persons. *Journal of Personality and Social Psychology*, 1973, *27*, 120–128.

Peterson, A. C. Physical androgyny and cognitive functioning in adolescence. *Developmental Psychology*, 1976, *12*, 524–533.

Peterson, A. C., & Wittig, M. A. Differential cognitive development in adolescent girls. In *Female adolescent development*, New York: Brunner/Mazel, Inc., 1979, 47–59.

Piaget, J. [*The construction of reality in the child.*] (M. Cook, Trans.) New York: Basic Books, 1954.

Piaget, J. *The origins of intelligence in children*. New York: W. W. Norton, 1963.

Piaget, J. *The moral judgment of the child*. New York: Free Press, 1965.

Piaget, J. *Six psychological studies*. (D. Elkind, Ed.) New York: Random House, 1967.

Plato, Laws. [In *The dialogue of Plato.*] (B. Jowett, Trans.). Vol. 4. (4th ed.) Oxford: Clarendon Press, 1953.

Podd, M. H. Ego identity status and morality: The relationship between two developmental constructs. *Developmental Psychology*, 1972, *6*, 497–507.

Ponsioen, J. A. De jeugd als nieuwe leeftijdsgroep in ontwikkelingslanden. *Mens en Maatschappij*, 1963, *38*, 134–145.

Radke-Yarrow, M. The measurement of children's attitudes and values. In P. H. Mussen (Ed.), *Handbook of research methods in child development*. New York: John Wiley & Sons, 1960.

Ratner, S. C., & Denny, M. R. *Comparative psychology: Research in animal behavior.* Homewood, Ill.: Dorsey Press, 1964.

Reiss, I. L. *Premarital sexual standards in America.* New York: Free Press, 1960.

Reiss, I. L. The sexual renaissance in America. *Journal of Social Issues,* 1966, *22,* 123–137.

Rest, J. New approaches in the assessment of moral judgment. In T. Likona (Ed.), *Moral development and behavior.* New York: Holt, Rinehart & Winston, 1976.

Rest, J., Davison, M., & Robbins, S. Age trends in judging moral issues: A review of cross-sectional, longitudinal, and sequential studies of the defining issues test. *Child Development,* 1978, *49,* 263–279.

Reynolds, E. L., & Wines, J. V. Individual differences in physical changes associated with adolescence in girls. *American Journal of Diseases in Children,* 1948, *75,* 329–350.

Reynolds, E. L., & Wines, J. V. Physical changes associated with adolescence in boys. *American Journal of Diseases in Children,* 1951, *82,* 529–547.

Roback, A. A. *A history of American psychology.* New York: Library Publishers, 1952.

Roberge, J. J. Developmental analysis of two formal operational structures: Combinatorial thinking and conditional reasoning. *Developmental Psychology,* 1976, *12,* 563–564.

Roche, A. F. Secular trends in stature, weight, and maturation. *Monographs of the Society for Research in Child Development.* 1979, *44,* 3–27.

Rokeach, M. *Beliefs, attitudes, and values.* San Francisco: Jossey-Bass, 1968.

Rokeach, M. *The nature of human values.* New York: Free Press, 1973.

Rosen, B. M., Bahn, A. K., Shellow, R., & Bower, G. M. Adolescent patients served in outpatient psychiatric clinics. *American Journal of Public Health,* 1965, *55,* 1563–1577.

Rosenbach, D.; Crockett, W. H.; & Wapner, S. Developmental level, emotional involvement, and the resolution of inconsistency in impression formation, *Developmental Psychology,* 1973, *8,* 120–130.

Rosenberg, M. Parental interest and children's self-conceptions. *Sociometry,* 1963, *26,* 35–49.

Rosenberg, M. *Society and the adolescent self-image.* Princeton, N.J.: Princeton University Press, 1965.

Ross, R. J. The development of formal thinking and creativity in adolescence. *Adolescence,* 1976, *11,* 609–617.

Rotter, J. B. Generalized expectancies for internal vs. external control of reinforcement. *Psychological Monographs,* 1966, *80* (1, whole No. 609)

Rowe, I., & Marcia, J. E. Ego identity status, formal operations, and moral development. *Journal of Youth and Adolescence,* 1980, *9,* 87–99.

Rubin, I. Is there a sex revolution? *Sexology,* 1965, *32,* 220–222.

Rue, L. L., III. *Cottontail.* New York: Thomas Y. Crowell, 1965.

Sachar, E. J. Endocrine factors in depressive illness. In F. F. Flack and S. C. Draghi (Eds.), *The nature and treatment of depression.* New York: John Wiley & Sons, 1975.

St. Clair, S., & Day., H. D. Ego identity status and values among high school females. *Journal of Youth and Adolescence,* 1979, *8,* 317–326.

Scanlan, T. K., and Passer, M. W. Anxiety-inducing factors in competitive youth sports. In F. L. Smoll and R. E. Smith (Eds.), *Psychological perspectives in youth sports.* New York: John Wiley & Sons, 1978.

Scarr-Salapatek, S. Race, social class, and IQ. *Science,* 1971, *174,* 1285–1295.

Schaie, K. W. Methodological problems in descriptive developmental research on adulthood and aging. In J. R. Nesselroade & H. W. Reese (Eds.), *Life span developmental psychology: Methodological issues.* New York: Academic Press, 1973.

Schenkel, S., & Marcia, J. E. Attitudes toward premarital intercourse in determining ego identity status in college women. *Journal of Personality,* 1972, *40,* 472–482.

Schilder, P. *The image and appearance of the human body.* New York: International Universities Press, 1950.

Seligman, M. E. P. and Maier, S. F. Failure to escape traumatic shock, *Journal of Experimental Psychology,* 1967, *74,* 1–9.

Shellow, R., Schamp, J. R., Liebow, E., and Unger, E. Suburban runaways of the 1960's. *Monographs of the Society for Research in Child Development,* 1967, *32,* Serial No. 111.

Sherman, G. Soviet youth: Myth and reality. In E. H. Erikson (Ed.), *The challenge of youth*. Garden City, N.Y.: Anchor Books, 1965.

Sherman, J., & Fennema, E. The study of mathematics by high school girls and boys: Related variables. *American Educational Research Journal, 1977, 14*, 159–168.

Shipman, W. C. Age of menarche and adult personality. *Archives of General Psychiatry, 1964, 10*, 155–159.

Shock, N. W. Some physiological aspects of adolescence. *Texas Reports on Biology and Medicine, 1946, 4*, 289–310.

Shorten, M. *Squirrels*. London: Collins Press, 1954.

Siegel, I. E. How intelligence tests limit understanding of intelligence. *Merrill-Palmer Quarterly, 1963, 9*, 39–56.

Signell, E. Cognitive complexity in person perception and nation perception: A developmental approach. *Journal of Personality, 1966, 34*, 517–537.

Simon, W.; Berger, A. S.; & Gagnon, J. H. Beyond anxiety and fantasy: The coital experiences of college youth. *Journal of Youth and Adolescence, 1972, 1*, 203–222.

Simpson, E. Moral development research: A case study of scientific cultural bias. *Human Development, 1974, 17*, 81–106.

Skorepa, C. A.; Horrocks, J. E.; & Thompson, G. G. A study of friendship fluctuations of college students. *Journal of Genetic Psychology, 1963, 102*, 151–157.

Smith, M. J. Social learning of violence in minor hockey. In F. L. Smoll and R. E. Smith (Eds.), *Psychological perspectives in youth sports*. New York: John Wiley & Sons, 1978.

Smoll, F. L., and Smith, R. E. (Eds.). *Psychological perspectives in youth sports*. New York: John Wiley & Sons, 1978.

Sorenson, R. C. *Adolescent sexuality in contemporary America*. New York: World, 1973.

Sorosky, A. D. The psychological effects of divorce on adolescents. *Adolescence, 1977, 12*, 123–136.

Spearman, C. General intelligence objectively determined and measured. *American Journal of Psychology, 1904, 15*, 201–293.

Spiker, C. C., & McCandless, B. R. The concept of intelligence and the philosophy of science. *Psychological Review, 1954, 61*, 255–266.

Spivack, G., Haimes, P. E., & Spotts, J. Adolescent symptomatology and its measurement. *American Journal of Mental Deficiency, 1967, 72*, 74–95.

Stanfield, R. E. The interaction of family variables and gang variables in the etiology of delinquency. *Social Problems, 1966, 13*, 411–417.

Stierlin, H. *Separating parents and adolescents*. New York: New York Times Book Co., 1974.

Stone, C. A., & Day, M. C. Levels of availability of a formal operational strategy. *Child Development, 1978, 49*, 1054–1065.

Sullivan, H. S. *The interpersonal theory of psychiatry*. New York: W. W. Norton, 1953.

Sykes, G. *The society of captives*. Princeton, N.J.: Princeton University Press, 1958.

Tanner, J. M. *Growth at adolescence*. Oxford: Blackwell Scientific Publications Ltd., 1962.

Tanner, J. M. Earlier maturation in man. *Scientific American*, January 1968, *218*, 21–27.

Terman, L. M. *Psychological factors in marital happiness*. New York: McGraw-Hill, 1938.

Thomas, J. (Ed.). *Youth sports guide for coaches and parents*. Washington, D.C.: Manufacturers' Life Insurance Co. and The National Association for Sports and Physical Education, 1977.

Thompson, G. G. Children's groups. In P. H. Mussen (Ed.), *Handbook of research methods in child development*. New York: John Wiley & Sons, 1960.

Thompson, G. G., & Gardner, E. F. Adolescents' perceptions of happy-successful living. *Journal of Genetic Psychology, 1969, 115*, 107–120.

Thompson, G. G., & Horrocks, J. E. A study of friendship fluctuations of urban boys and girls. *Journal of Genetic Psychology, 1947, 70*, 53–63.

Thompson, L. *Culture in crisis*. New York: Harper & Row, 1950.

Thorndike, E. L. *Educational psychology*. New York: Lemcke & Buechner, 1903.

Thurstone, L. L. Primary mental abilities. *Psychometric Monographs*, No. 1. Chicago: University of Chicago Press, 1938.

Toder, N. L., & Marcia, J. E. Ego identity status and response to conformity pressure in college women. *Journal of Personality and Social Psychology, 1974, 26*, 287–294.

Toolan, J. M. Depression in children and adolescents. *American Journal of Orthopsychiatry, 1962, 32*, 404–415.

Toolan, J. M. Depression in children and adolescents. In G. Caplan and S. Lebovici (Eds.), *Adolescence: Psychosocial perspectives.* New York: Basic Books, 1969.

Torrance, E. P., and Dauw, D. C. Attitude patterns of creatively gifted high school seniors. *Gifted Child Quarterly,* Summer 1966, 53–57.

Tuma, E., & Livson, N. Family socioeconomic status and adolescent attitudes to authority. *Child Development,* 1960, *31,* 387–399.

Udall, L. *Me and mine: The life story of Helen Sekaquaptewa.* Tucson: The University of Arizona Press, 1977.

United Nations Educational, Scientific, and Cultural Organization. Declaration of the rights of the child. *UNESCO Courier,* 1960, *11,* 15–21.

Urberg, K. A. Sex role conceptualizations in adolescents and adults. *Developmental Psychology,* 1979, *15,* 90–92.

Ushakov, G. K. Anorexia nervosa in modern perspectives. In J. G. Howells (Ed.), *Adolescent psychiatry.* Edinburgh: Oliver and Boyd, 1971.

Van Gennep, A. *[The rites of passage.]* (M. Vizedom & G. L. Caffee, Trans.) Chicago: University of Chicago Press, 1960.

Vincent, C. E. Teenage unwed mothers in American society. *Journal of Social Issues,* 1966, *22,* 22–23.

Waber, D. P. Sex differences in cognition: A function of maturation rate? *Science,* 1976, *192,* 572–574.

Waber, D. P. Sex differences in mental abilities, hemispheric lateralization, and rate of physical growth at adolescence. *Developmental Psychology,* 1977, *13,* 29–38.

Waber, D. P. Cognitive abilities and sex-related variations in the maturation of cortical functions. In *Sex-related differences in cognitive functioning.* New York: Academic Press, 1979, 161–186.

Waldhorn, A., & Waldhorn, H. (Eds.). *The rite of becoming: Stories and studies of adolescence.* Cleveland: World, 1966.

Wallach, M. A., & Kogan, N. *Modes of thinking in young children.* New York: Holt, Rinehart & Winston, 1965.

Waterman, A. S., Geary, P. S., & Waterman, C. K. Relationship between freshman ego identity status and subsequent academic behavior: A test of the predictive validity of Marcia's categorization system for identity status. *Developmental Psychology,* 1972, *6,* 179.

Waterman, A. S.; Geary, P. S.; & Waterman, C. K. Longitudinal study of changes in ego identity status from the freshman to the senior year at college. *Developmental Psychology,* 1974, *10,* 387–392.

Waterman, A. S., & Waterman, C. K. Ego identity status and decision styles. *Journal of Youth and Adolescence,* 1974, *3,* 1–6.

Weiner, I. B. *Psychological disturbances in adolescence.* New York: John Wiley & Sons, 1970.

Wesman, A. G. Intelligence testing. *American Psychologist,* 1968, *23,* 267–274.

Westman, J. C. Effect of divorce on a child's personality development. *Medical Aspects of Human Sexuality,* 1972, *6,* 40–55.

Wharton, J. R. Toward an affirmative morality. *Saturday Review,* July 12, 1969.

Whitebourne, S. K., & Weinstock, C. S. Adult development: *The differentiation of experience.* New York: Holt, Rinehart & Winston, 1979.

Whiting, J. W. M.; Kluckhohn, R.; & Anthony, A. The function of male initiation ceremonies at puberty. In E. E. Maccoby, T. M. Newcomb, & E. L. Hartley (Eds.), *Readings in social psychology.* (3d ed.) New York: Holt, Rinehart & Winston. 1958.

Whyte, W. F. A slum sex code. *American Journal of Sociology,* 1943, *49,* 24–31.

Wilkinson, D. Black youth. In *Youth: The seventy-fourth yearbook of the National Society for the Study of Education.* Chicago: University of Chicago Press, 1975, 285–305.

Wolfgang, M. E. The culture of youth. In *Task Force Report on Juvenile Delinquency and Youth Crime.* Washington, D.C.: U.S. Government Printing Office. 1967.

Wolfgang, M. E. *Youth and violence.* Washington, D.C.: U.S. Government Printing Office, 1970.

Woodworth, R. S. Racial differences in mental traits. *Science.* 1910, *31,* 171–180.

Wylie, L. Youth in France and the United States. In E. H. Erikson (Ed.), *The challenge of youth.* Garden City, N.Y.: Anchor Books, 1965.

Wynne-Edwards, V. C. *Animal dispersion in relation to social behavior.* Edinburgh: Oliver & Boyd, 1962.

Yankelovich, D., Inc. *The changing values on campus: Political and personal attitudes of today's college students.* New York: Washington Square Press, 1973.

Yarrow, M. R., & Campbell, J. D. Person perception in children. *Merrill-Palmer Quarterly,* 1963, *9,* 57–72.

Young, F. W. The function of male initiation ceremonies: A cross-cultural test of an alternate hypothesis. *American Journal of Sociology,* 1962, *67,* 379–396.

Young, L. A., Young, L. G., Klein, M. M., Klein, D. M., Beyer, D. *Recreational drugs.* New York: Macmillan, 1977.

Zelnik, M. Sex education and knowledge of pregnancy risk among U.S. teenage women. *Family Planning Perspectives,* 1979, *11,* 355–357.

Zelnik, M., & Kantner, J. F. Sexual and contraceptive experience of young unmarried women in the United States, 1976 and 1971. *Family Planning Perspectives,* 1977, *9,* 55–71.

AUTHOR INDEX

SUBJECT INDEX

*This book has been set VIP, in 9 and 8 point Optima,
leaded 3 and 2 points respectively. Chapter numbers
are 16 point Optima Medium and chapter titles are 20
point Optima Medium. The overall type area is 30 by
47½ picas.*